Approaches to Media Discourse

Advance Praise for *Approaches to Media Discourse*

'An editor's introduction and eight excellent papers, by acknowledged experts, present current approaches to media discourse. Critical discourse analysis, cultural studies, conversation analysis, the analysis of page layout, reception of news broadcasts, are applied to newspapers, television and radio. A state-of-the-art presentation, invaluable for students and researchers in the growing field of media discourse.' *Roger Fowler, University of East Anglia*

'This admirable collection of papers by some of the most eminent scholars in the field of media studies combines breadth of coverage with depth of analysis, and programmatic methodological statements with detailed empirical studies. It will be an indispensable text in its field for many years to come.' *Andreas H. Jucker, Professor of English Linguistics, Justus Liebig University, Giessen*

'A useful entry point for anyone seeking to understand the diverse approaches found under the umbrella label of "media discourse".' *Jean Aitchison, Professor of Language and Communication, University of Oxford*

'*Approaches to Media Discourse* provides a sharp collection of critical essays, mainly on the news media. Leading writers on media discourse introduce their theoretical methods and make them work on specific instances from the press, radio and television, as well as texts produced by selected audiences. Readers can test and compare the applicability and relevance of various approaches and adapt them to their own examination of the media.' *Ulrike H. Meinhof, University of Bradford*

Approaches to Media Discourse

Edited by Allan Bell and Peter Garrett

First published 1998

2 4 6 8 10 9 7 5 3 1

Blackwell Publishers Ltd
108 Cowley Road
Oxford OX4 1JF
UK

Blackwell Publishers Inc.
350 Main Street
Malden, Massachusetts 02148
USA

British Library Cataloguing in Publication Data

A CIP catalogue record for this book is available from the British Library.

Library of Congress Cataloging-in-Publication Data

Approaches to media discourse / edited by Allan Bell and Peter Garrett.
    p. cm.
    Includes bibliographical references and index.
    ISBN 0-631-19887-3 (alk. paper). – ISBN 0-631-19888-1 (pbk. : alk. paper)
    1. Mass media and language. 2. Discourse analysis. 3. Conversation analysis. I. Bell, Allan. II. Garrett, Peter, 1950– .
    P96.L34A66   1997
    302.23′01′4—dc21

                                               97-5253
                                                 CIP

Typeset in 10½ on 13 pt Palatino
by Best-set Typesetter Ltd., Hong Kong
Printed and bound in Great Britain by MPG Books Ltd, Bodmin, Cornwall

This book is printed on acid-free paper

Contents

Preface

This book began life at a Victorian country mansion in Wales in the hot July of 1995. Two dozen specialists gathered for three days at Dyffryn House for the Cardiff Round Table on Media Discourse. The core papers presented on that occasion were intended for this collection on approaches to media discourse, making the event the conference of these proceedings rather than vice versa. Scholars who had developed the main frameworks for analysing media discourse presented and exemplified their approaches, each with a respondent and discussion from the rest of those present.

Numbers invited to the Round Table were limited to ensure a size conducive to fruitful discussion. In addition, some of those invited were unable to be present. This inevitably restricted the number of approaches that could be represented. Those who came, however, were particularly attracted by the chance to gather with a small number of like-interested scholars for an intensive time concentrating on one area. The format worked well, and the next in the annual Cardiff Round Table series – on another topic in language and communication – will have taken place before this volume of papers from the first of these events is published.

As convenors of that meeting and editors of this collection, we are happy to acknowledge the contribution of all participants to a very valuable meeting and to the quality of the book which has grown from it: Jean Aitchison, Stuart Allan, Allan Bell, Nikolas Coupland, Howard Davis, Tatiana Dobrosklonskaya, Peter Garrett, Sharon Goodman, David Graddol, David Greatbatch, Sandra Harris, Andreas Jucker, Stephanie Marriott, Philip Mitchell, Kay Richardson, Itzhak Roeh, Srikant Sarangi, Paddy Scannell, Wenche Vagle, Teun van Dijk and Theo van Leeuwen. As well as the papers published in this book, other presentations at the Round Table covered a wide range of work: changes in media discourse in the former Soviet bloc (Davis, Dobrosklonskaya), the discourse of peace and war in Israeli media (Roeh), dialect and social stereotyping in television sitcoms (Marriott), the development of dialogue formats on Norwegian radio (Vagle), British headlines about crime (Aitchison), the use of non-standard English in British newspapers (Goodman), and social work in the media (Sarangi). The participants included mostly linguists and discourse analysts who study media texts, but there were also some media sociologists present. As well as from the UK, we came from the Netherlands, Norway, Germany, Israel, Russia and New Zealand.

We gladly acknowledge the support of the Centre for Language and Communication Research at the University of Wales Cardiff, and in particular of the Centre's Director, Nikolas Coupland. Blackwell Publishers sponsored the meeting as well as publishing this volume, and we are grateful for some travel support from the British Academy. Allan Bell's involvement in the enterprise as a whole is due in part to support from the British Council, New Zealand Public Good Science Fund, the Department of Linguistics at Victoria University of Wellington, and the Centre for Language and Communication Research of the University of Wales Cardiff.

At Blackwell's, we thank Philip Carpenter and Steve Smith for their guidance throughout the production of the book.

Peter Garrett, Cardiff
Allan Bell, Auckland

Notes on Contributors

Stuart Allan is Lecturer in Media and Cultural Studies at the University of Glamorgan. His publications have been primarily concerned with cultural theory, media sociology and nuclear issues, and include a co-edited volume (with Barbara Adam), *Theorizing Culture: An Interdisciplinary Critique After Postmodernism* (UCL Press/NYU Press: 1995). He is currently writing a book entitled *News Culture* (Open University Press), as well as co-editing one entitled *News, Gender and Power* (Routledge). He is also the deputy editor of *Time and Society* (Sage Journals).

Allan Bell has been both making and studying media language and discourse for many years, combining work as an independent researcher in mass communication and sociolinguistics with freelance journalism and media consultancy. He has worked as journalist and editor in the daily and weekly press. He has researched media language in several countries, especially New Zealand and the United Kingdom. He is affiliated as a Senior Research Fellow to the Linguistics Programme, Department of English, University of Auckland. In 1994 he held a fellowship at the Centre for Language and Communication Research, University of Wales Cardiff. His publications include 'Language style and audience design' (*Language in Society*: 1984), *The Language of News Media* (Blackwell: 1991) and 'Language and the media' (*Annual Review of Applied Linguistics*: 1995). He is (with Nikolas Coupland) co-founder and editor of the *Journal of Sociolinguistics* (Blackwell).

Norman Fairclough is Professor of Language in Social Life in the Department of Linguistics and Modern English Language, Lancaster University. He has published *Language and Power* (Longman: 1989), *Discourse and Social Change* (Polity Press: 1992), *Media Discourse* (Edward Arnold: 1995) and *Critical Discourse Analysis* (Longman: 1995).

Peter Garrett is Senior Lecturer in Language and Communication at the Centre for Language and Communication Research, University of Wales Cardiff. His research and publications are primarily in the areas of language attitudes and language awareness. He co-edited (with Carl James) *Language Awareness in the Classroom* (Longman: 1991), and is currently editor of the journal *Language Awareness* (Multilingual Matters). He has published articles in many journals, including *Language in Society, Language and Communication, Multilingua, Journal of Multilingual and Multicultural Development, Language and Education,* and *Language Culture and Curriculum.*

David Greatbatch is University Research Fellow in the School of Social Studies, University of Nottingham. He has written extensively on conversation analysis, media discourse and professional/client interaction. His publications include articles in the *American Journal of Sociology, American Sociological Review, Language in Society,* and *Law and Society Review.* He is currently completing a book on news interviewing, entitled *The Political News Interview: The History and Dynamics of a Social Form,* with John Heritage and Steven Clayman.

Gunther Kress is Professor of Education/English at the Institute of Education, University of London. He is interested in the complex interrelations of social and cultural matters and their representations in the form of signs. He has published in the areas of critical discourse analysis and social semiotics: (with Robert Hodge) *Language as Ideology* (Routledge: 2nd edn, 1993) and *Social Semiotics* (Polity Press: 1989); *Learning to Write* (Routledge: 1993); (with Theo van Leeuwen) *Reading Images: The Grammar of Visual Design* (Routledge: 1996). He has also published *Linguistic Processes in Sociocultural Practice* (Oxford University Press: 1989); *Writing the Future: English and the Making of a Culture of Innovation* (Sheffield, National Association of Teachers of English: 1995); *Before Writing: Rethinking the Paths to Literacy* (Routledge: 1996). He has taught at universities in Australia and the UK.

Kay Richardson is Senior Lecturer in Communication Studies at the University of Liverpool. Her published research is partly in media studies and partly in applied linguistics. She is co-author (with John Corner and Natalie Fenton) of a book on audience interpretations of TV documentaries about the nuclear power industry, *Nuclear Reactions* (John Libbey Publishers: 1990), and co-editor (with Ulrike Meinhof) of *Text, Discourse and Context: Representations of Poverty in Britain* (Longman: 1994). She has also published in the journals *Language and Communication, Text* and *Social Semiotics*.

Paddy Scannell is Reader in Media Studies at the Centre for Communication and Information Studies at the University of Westminster, where he has taught since 1967. He is a founding editor of the journal *Media, Culture and Society*. He has published widely on many aspects of broadcasting. His books include: *A Social History of British Broadcasting, 1923–1939* (with David Cardiff; Blackwell: 1991); an edited collection on *Broadcast Talk* (Sage: 1991) and, most recently, *Radio, Television and Modern Life* (Blackwell: 1996). His current research interests include the phenomenology of media, and communication and culture in Africa.

Teun A. van Dijk is Professor of Discourse Studies at the University of Amsterdam. After earlier work in literary studies, text grammar and the psychology of text comprehension, his research in the 1980s focused on the study of news in the press and the reproduction of racism through various types of discourse. In each of these domains, he published several books. His current research in 'critical' discourse studies focuses on the relations between power, discourse and ideology. He is founder-editor of the international journals *Text* and *Discourse and Society*, and editor of the four-volume *Handbook of Discourse Analysis* (1985) and the two-volume *Discourse Studies: A Multidisciplinary Introduction* (Sage: 1996). He has lectured widely in Europe and the Americas, and has been visiting professor at several universities in Latin America.

Theo van Leeuwen is Professor of Communication at the School of Media of the London College of Printing. He studied screenwriting and direction at the Netherlands Film Academy in Amsterdam, and linguistics at Macquarie University and the University of Sydney. After working as a film and television producer in his native Holland and in Australia, he lectured in Media and Communication at Macquarie University. He is co-author (with Gunther Kress) of *Reading Images: The Grammar of Visual Design* (Deakin University Press: 1990), and (with Philip Bell) of *The Media Interview: Confession, Contest, Conversation* (1994).

Acknowledgements

The authors and publishers gratefully acknowledge the following for permission to reproduce copyright material: the *Daily Mirror*, the *Sun*, the *Guardian*, *the Observer*, *Washington Post*, Reuters, *Neue Kronenzeitung*, *Täglich Alles*, *Sydney Morning Herald*, BBC, and ITN. Every effort has been made to obtain permission to reproduce copyright material. The publishers apologize for any errors or omissions in the above list and would be grateful to be notified of any corrections that should be incorporated in the next edition or reprint of this book.

Chapter 1

Media and Discourse: A Critical Overview

Peter Garrett and Allan Bell

Approaches to Media Discourse presents for scholars and students some of the main ways in which media discourse has been studied. It is intended both to introduce students to the available frameworks, and, for scholars, to mark the state of the art in media discourse studies. Our brief for contributors to the volume was to outline their own approach or analytical framework for media discourse; to illustrate it in depth by close analysis of example media texts, including their production and reception, and sociopolitical dimensions; and to offer practical guidelines on applying their approach.

Most of the contributions were originally presented at the Cardiff Round Table on Media Discourse which we convened in 1995 at the University of Wales Cardiff. The Round Table brought together a selected group of the leading specialists in media discourse. It offered them the chance to present their approaches and to receive feedback from colleagues in the field. But this book is not a conference proceedings. Rather the reverse: the Round Table meeting was in large part planned as a dress rehearsal for the book.

Media and Discourse

So what is media discourse and why the interest in it? The first of these questions immediately runs into the problem of terminological clarity. There is a conspicuous lack of agreement on definitions of both *discourse* and *text* (see for example Widdowson, 1995). It is clearly not our intention in this brief introduction to attempt to establish clarity in such a complex field. But it is an issue: if we are studying media discourse, what is discourse? Media studies is very much a multidisciplinary area, and different disciplines are working with their own notions of what these terms mean. For example, in the more sociologically oriented areas, discourse is considered primarily in relation to social contexts of language use. In linguistics, discourse tends to focus more on language and its use. Recent years have seen steps towards a constructive fusion of these two traditions (Boyd-Barrett, 1994: 23). This volume is very much a product of such mutual interest, and we hope an encouragement to further co-operative development.

Language in the modern media cannot realistically be seen in terms of the traditional linguistic distinction between the terms *discourse* and *text*, as spoken and written language respectively. Spoken language traditionally entailed a co-present listener who was able to affect the speaker's flow of discourse, but usually spoken language in the media does not allow that (cf. Bell, 1991). And if written texts traditionally implied a remote reader unable to influence the flow of discourse, then spoken language in the media shares such properties. Another cause of this blurring of distinctions has been the change in perspectives on where the meanings of texts reside. '... Text-as-meaning is produced at the moment of reading, not at the moment of writing ... [this] takes away from that text the status of being the originator of that meaning' (Fiske, 1987: 305; see also Meinhof, 1994: 212f). Since meanings are now seen to be more a product of negotiation between readers and texts, text takes on more of the interactive qualities of discourse.

Such developments in part account for the failure to distinguish sharply between discourse and text in some literature today, and for the statements that the difference is negligible (see Widdowson, 1995: 161f). However, for many, as will be seen in this volume, a new distinction has emerged. *Text* tends to be used to refer to the outward manifestation of a communication event, whereas use of the term *discourse* may be exemplified through a statement by Cook (1992: 1) about discourse analysis:

> [I]t is not concerned with language alone. It also examines the context of communication: who is communicating with whom and why; in what kind of society and situation, through what medium; how different types of communication evolved, and their relationship to each other.

For discourse analysis to achieve this in media contexts, definitions of media texts have moved far away from the traditional view of text as words printed in ink on pieces of paper to take on a far broader definition to include speech, music and sound effects, image, and so on.

Graddol (1994b: 41) maintains that most texts can be regarded as communicative artifacts, and that, as such, they are a product of a technology. Media texts, then, reflect the technology that is available for producing them. The music and sound effects of modern media can act in similar ways to prosodic features in spoken texts – grouping items, marking boundaries, indicating historical periods or distant locations, and so on. Against this technological background, Kress and van Leeuwen are able to refer to the layout of newspaper pages as 'text' in their chapter in this volume. And knowing that any artifact has a history and has been crafted into a final form gives a context for Bell's insights into how the final shape of a news story is affected by the process of selection and editing.

Why then the interest in media discourse? The media have long been a focus amongst those working with language and communication, as well as others working within the broader field of media studies. Bell (1995a: 23) gives four main reasons for this. Firstly, media are a rich source of readily accessible data for research and teaching. Secondly, media usage influences and represents people's use of and attitudes towards language in a speech community. Thirdly (and related), media use can tell us a great deal about social meanings and stereotypes projected through language and communication: for example in the use of foreign languages in advertisements (Haarmann, 1984; Cheshire and Moser, 1994), in radio disc jockey style-shifting (N. Coupland, 1985), and in the television portrayal of the elderly (Robinson and Skill, 1995). Fourthly (and again relatedly), the media reflect and influence the formation and expression of culture, politics and social life.

Coverage

This book includes a wide range of frameworks and approaches to media discourse: Conversation Analysis (Greatbatch); Critical Discourse Analysis from both sociocognitive (van Dijk) and discourse-practice (Fairclough) perspectives; Cultural Studies (Allan); a structural discourse analysis (Bell); reception analysis (Richardson); and a 'grammar' of visual design (Kress and van Leeuwen). All of these attend closely to the form of media texts, but are also informed to varying degrees by social and political analysis. Van Dijk, Bell, Greatbatch, and Kress and van Leeuwen expound detailed analytical frameworks and apply them closely to their various example media texts. The chapters by Fairclough, van Dijk and Allan range widely over sociopolitical as well as discoursal concerns, in keeping with the 'critical' stance of their authors.

However, the range of the media genres the book discusses is comparatively narrow. All are in the 'factual' rather than 'fictional' realm, and all but one cover news (van Dijk's focus is opinion pieces such as editorials). Other media genres have been researched, of course: for example, see Cook (1992) on advertising discourse; Talbot's (1992) analysis of a teenage magazine; and J. Coupland (1996) on dating advertisements. But most of the work in media discourse has been on the 'factual' genres, and particularly news. (So, let it be said, has most of the sociological analysis of mass communications – it is only in the more recent schools of cultural, critical and literary studies that a focus on other genres predominates.) This emphasis reflects the status of the news as the most prestigious of daily media genres, and its role at the centre of the exercise of power in modern societies. Within the focus on the news, however, coverage is diverse – analysis of hard news discourse (Bell, Fairclough), visual design (Kress and van Leeuwen), interviews (Greatbatch, Fairclough), television news openings (Allan), and television news stories and their reception (Richardson). Geographically, some of the data are drawn mainly from the USA, New Zealand and Austria, but most come from the United Kingdom, which is where a high proportion of media discourse work is carried out and where most of the contributors are currently based. The contributions are evenly divided in their focus on broadcast versus print media. Bell, van Dijk, and Kress and van Leeuwen deal with the daily press; Allan, Greatbatch and Richardson with television; and Fairclough with radio.

One of the most instructive ways to approach this book is to compare how different contributors have dealt with similar kinds of data or research questions. For example, both Greatbatch and Fairclough analyse antagonistic news interviews, from Conversation Analysis and Critical Discourse Analysis viewpoints respectively. This enables us to see how their different approaches work in practice, what they entail, what they offer, what kind and quality of findings they yield. Similarly, Bell, Richardson and Allan all analyse the texts of news stories, and their approaches can also be compared. Both Allan and van Dijk deal with texts about two of the villains of Western international relations – Gadhafi of Libya and Saddam Hussein of Iraq. Both analysts characterize how 'Us' versus 'Them' stereotyping functions in coverage of these nations. Greatbatch also analyses an earlier news interview (*circa* 1980) in which the Soviet Union was the targeted 'Them'.

Critical Approaches

In the past few years, the study of media language and discourse has gained a coherence and focus it previously lacked. Pioneering analyses of media discourse conducted in the 'Critical Linguistics' framework (e.g. Fowler et al., 1979; Kress and Hodge, 1979) had been stimulating but less than satisfactory.

The approach called 'Critical Discourse Analysis' (CDA) represents an outgrowth of the work of the British and Australian pioneers of Critical Linguistics, particularly Fowler and Kress, in convergence with the approaches of the British discourse analyst Fairclough and Dutch text linguist van Dijk. CDA has produced the majority of the research into media discourse during the 1980s and 1990s, and has arguably become the standard framework for studying media texts within European linguistics and discourse studies. Thus, several of the contributors to this book work out of a CDA approach. They are also the leading contributors to the theoretical section of a CDA reader (Caldas-Coulthard and Coulthard, 1996). Conversely, a high proportion of CDA work has focused on the media. Some 40 percent of the papers published in the CDA journal *Discourse and Society* deal with media data, as do half the chapters in Caldas-Coulthard and Coulthard (1996).

Neither of these facts is surprising. CDA has an explicit sociopolitical agenda, a concern to discover and bear witness to unequal relations of power which underlie ways of talking in a society, and in particular to reveal the role of discourse in reproducing or challenging sociopolitical dominance. The media are a particular subject of CDA analysis because of their manifestly pivotal role as discourse-bearing institutions.

CDA also offers the potential for applying theoretically sophisticated frameworks to important issues, so is a natural tool for those who wish to make their research socially activist. But CDA is best viewed as a shared perspective encompassing a range of approaches rather than as just one school, as we shall see in the different frameworks of contributors to this volume. CDA is criticized (see Hammersley, 1996; Widdowson, 1995, 1996; Fairclough, 1996), but it nevertheless holds a hegemonic position in the field of media discourse, such that other approaches tend to have to position and define themselves in relation to CDA.

The Contributions

Van Dijk

Teun van Dijk has long been a leading theorist and advocate of discourse analysis as an interdisciplinary approach to the analysis of texts in social context. His framework aims to integrate the production and interpretation of discourse as well as its textual analysis. In the 1980s he began to apply his theory and methodology of discourse analysis to media texts. He published two pioneering companion volumes on his 'new, interdisciplinary theory of news in the press' (1988b: vii). *News as Discourse* (1988b) appeared as a primary theoretical contribution to the analysis of news stories. It was supplemented by a volume of case studies, *News Analysis* (1988a), drawn mainly from large-scale studies of international news reporting and of racism in the European press. Van Dijk's is the most comprehensive work on media discourse to date, and he has continued to extend the range of his work on to themes such as racism in the media, and other genres such as opinion texts and editorials – his topic in his contribution to this book.

Van Dijk's approach falls under the rubric of Critical Discourse Analysis (he is founder and editor of the journal *Discourse and Society*). In his chapter, he looks at the nature of opinions and how they are expressed in editorials in the press. To do so, he works within the framework of a larger project on discourse and ideology, and employs a multidisciplinary theory of ideology.

A fundamental question that van Dijk's theory addresses is: how are societal structures related to discourse structures? Van Dijk argues that they cannot be related directly. If they were, then there would be no need for ideology, and moreover, all actors in a social group would do and say the same thing. He posits a framework in which societal structures can only be related to discourse structures through social actors and their minds: mental models mediate between ideology and discourse. Hence his theory has three main components: social functions, cognitive structures, and discursive expression and reproduction. These bridge the gap between macro and micro levels of analysis.

Discourse structures which may contain underlying ideological positions range from microstructures such as lexical items and grammatical structures to macrostructures such as topics or themes expressed indirectly in larger stretches of text or whole discourses. These macrostructures are organized hierarchically: macrorules define the most important information in a text. These are evident, for example, when we give a summary of a text. Such macrorules draw upon the reader's world knowledge. At the macrolevel, then, this is a point at which meanings are assigned by readers.

But readers do not 'impose' coherence only at the global level; they do this at the local level too. A sequence of sentences, for example, may have coherence read into it through the reader's mental model. This is an important implication of van Dijk's model. Not only is a text just a fraction of a model, but people understand much more than a text actually expresses.

There are two points to be made here in relation to other chapters in this volume. First of all, one of the underpinnings of Bell's chapter is that knowing what a text says is usually not straightforward. We need to look carefully at what texts actually say and what they do not say, to identify the points where there is vagueness, ambiguity, lack of obvious coherence, etc. Carrying out such analysis gives a firmer basis for considering ideological issues.

The second point relates to the readers. One of the most potent forces at work in van Dijk's discourse is the 'ideological square'. This functions to polarize in and out groups in order to present the 'We' group in a favourable light and the 'They' group unfavourably. With a close analysis of editorials and opinion pieces, van Dijk shows how the American prestige press presents national leaders such as Gadhafi and Saddam Hussein as 'Them' in contrast with nations such as Israel which are regarded as 'Us'.

How do the readers respond to this when they are from different groups? The media are not directed at a homogeneous society, untouched by divisions of power and interests, as van Dijk himself says. It is often pointed out amongst media discourse researchers how relatively little study has been made of how readers respond. It is clearly not within the scope of van Dijk's chapter to do so, though his chapter sets out a theoretical basis from which to approach it. Richardson's paper in this volume is one of the comparatively rare examples of studies that combine analysis of media discourse with analysis of reception of that discourse.

Bell

Allan Bell has researched in the area of media language since the 1970s, primarily in New Zealand and the UK. He worked initially on microlinguistic features of news language in a variationist framework (a disciplinary background still seen in his co-founding and editing of the *Journal of Sociolinguistics*). More recently he turned to the macrolinguistic level of discourse in the media, developing an analytical framework in his book *The Language of News Media* (1991), which is one of the three principal texts in the field (together with Fowler, 1991 and Fairclough, 1995a).

Bell's chapter sets out and applies a framework for examining the structure of news stories. His 1991 book had three main themes to it – the processes which produce media language, the notion of the news story and the role of media audiences. The chapter in this volume emphasizes in particular the first two of these themes.

Bell's work is characterized by an unusual mix of careers as both journalist/editor and academic. This has enabled him to draw on 'observant participation' in journalism – an inside knowledge of journalistic practices. His analysis of news stories in this book is informed by what the surface of news texts can tell us about the origins and inputs of stories. As Bell shows in his chapter, it is important to understand how these production processes work if one is to understand the eventual form and content of the news text. But Bell's prime focus in this volume is the discourse structure of news stories. He shows how news stories differ from other kinds of narrative.

The approach to discourse analysis that Bell sets out in this volume enables us to interrogate the story to try to reveal its event structure, to address the question: what does the story say actually happened? By this means, we are better able to uncover gaps or unclarities, to see what the text does not say. At that point, we are better prepared to engage in what he refers to as the 'ideological detective work' of more critical discourse approaches.

He analyses examples of one-sentence stories published in British newspapers, showing that even a single sentence can involve a high level of discourse complexity as journalists try to pack in as much information as possible. He offers detailed guidelines for analysing the event structure and discourse structures of news stories, and applies them to a *Daily Mirror* story about the arrest of IRA suspects. The analysis of the events, actors, times and places in a story shows up inconsistencies, incoherence, gaps and ambiguities within the story, conflicting forces during the story's production by journalist and copy-editor, and implications for readers' comprehension.

Bell also focuses on time as one of the crucial dimensions of news stories and news work. There is rarely chronological order in a news story. Temporal sequence is subordinated to news values such as the negativity value of the component events. This can lead to considerable difficulty for readers in identifying precisely (even in a single-sentence story) who did what, where and when. Stories are given in instalments. There are undoubtedly advantages in this for newsrooms at work: stories can be quickly cut down, perhaps to the lead paragraph or sentence, and stories can soon have more sentences or paragraphs 'bolted on'.

Allan

Cultural Studies is the context for Stuart Allan's contribution to this volume. His approach has more recently been informed by critical, postmodern approaches to media and society. This shows up in his interest in time in the media, and his deputy editorship of the journal *Time and Society*.

Allan's chapter provides an evaluative assessment of Cultural Studies as an approach to media discourse, in particular to televisual news discourse. He highlights news discourse as a research problematic within Cultural Studies and briefly sketches the history of work on news in that tradition. He identifies the issue of 'hegemony' as the key point of departure from earlier (positivistic) approaches, and considers the problem of how news naturalizes dominant forms of 'common sense' – the 'NowHere' of the news – along with the implications for the ideological reproduction of social divisions and hierarchies.

After assessing the place of contributors such as Gramsci and Williams to the cultural studies tradition, Allan proceeds to outline the main features of Hall's (1980) influential 'encoding/decoding' model (which also figures importantly in the chapters by Richardson and Scannell). He focuses on three 'moments' of media communication outlined in this model: the moment of production (encoding); the moment of the text; and the moment of meaning negotiation (decoding) by the audience. The encoding/decoding model goes beyond the standard three-stage model of communication – sender–message–receiver – to take seriously the intermeshing of the three moments. Each of the moments is examined with an eye to its importance for investigating how televisual news discourse serves hegemony through its self-presentation as natural common sense. Allan analyses the opening sequences of televised news programmes to see how they frame the material they are presenting, and how they key viewers in to the lead stories which follow.

Allan concludes by suggesting that there is a need to reverse the direction of the enquiries into televisual news discourse in order to discern the slippages, fissures and silences which always threaten to compromise its discursive authority.

Fairclough

Norman Fairclough has developed his approach to media discourse over a decade or more through his concern with language, discourse and power in society. His early books (1989, 1992) focused on the place of language and discourse in sociopolitical power and processes of social change, often using media texts as examples. His more recent book on *Media Discourse* (1995a) focuses his work on media texts and contexts. As with other critical discourse analysts, Fairclough's approach draws on Halliday's functional framework. To this, though, he adds a knowledge of more recent social theory, drawing particularly on the French theorist Foucault. He has developed his approach independent of the media focus we see in his chapter here, and his work covers a broader range of media texts than that of, say, van Dijk and Bell.

Like van Dijk's, Fairclough's framework has three components (but, as we will show later, one of these is crucially different). The first dimension is text or discourse analysis, which includes micro levels (e.g. vocabulary, syntax) and macro levels of text structure, as well as interpersonal elements in a text. The second is analysis of discourse practices. This looks at how a text is constructed and interpreted, and also how it is distributed. The media, of course, distribute to receivers a considerable number of texts from other sources. Analysis of discourse also considers the discourse practices of different social domains (such as political discourse). Fairclough calls these *orders of discourse* (a term adapted from Foucault). The third dimension is analysis of social practices, focusing in particular on the relation of discourse to power and ideology. Although Fairclough's and van Dijk's versions of CDA both have three components, they differ on the nature of the central, mediating dimension. Where van Dijk sees 'sociocognition' – cognitive structures and mental models – as mediating between discourse and society, Fairclough sees this central role as occupied by the discourse practices through which texts are produced and received. However, Fairclough makes the point himself that the analysis of discourse practice has sociocognitive aspects (which is the focus of van Dijk's chapter) and intertextual aspects. His own focus is on the latter.

In the analysis of discourse practice, Fairclough is particularly concerned with two trends: *marketization* (or *commodification*) of discourse, and *conversationalization* of discourse (which may or may not serve the *democratization* of discourse). These are both instances of *intertextuality*, where there is an admixture of different language styles or genres within a text. Marketization relates to a process that began in many areas in Western democracies in the 1980s, where many aspects of life and institutions were increasingly viewed in terms of commercial models. Hence, for example, the promotional language of advertising encroached more and more into other domains (e.g. universities), in a sense colonizing other areas of discourse in society (Fairclough, 1993). The evaluative stance taken towards these constructs tends to be generally negative (though J. Coupland (1996) has pointed to their potential for empowerment).

Democratization is seen as a shift towards increased informality in language in areas such as the news, which are more traditionally associated with a voice of authority. Fairclough points to the ambiguities here: there appears to be a move towards democratization, but this democratization is nevertheless restricted to an institutional representation of the voices of ordinary people. Similarly, the more general tendency towards conversationalization, in which, say, panel interviews may be conducted in ways that are strikingly similar to TV chat shows, cannot simply be interpreted as a sign that previously closed domains are opening up. There is also the possibility that this is merely pseudo-conversation, acting as a more effective mask for the exercise of power. Fairclough's chapter analyses radio coverage of an incident in Northern Ireland. He notes the basically monologic nature of news bulletins, as compared with the dialogic character of the rest of the news programme. Interestingly, Schlesinger (1987: 249) noticed the beginnings of 'conversationalization' in his study of production practices in the 1970s BBC. At the time, news bulletins were produced by the News Department and the surrounding news programmes by the separate Current Affairs Department. Whether this bifurcation of production still operates and influences news presentation styles in the 1990s is a question that could usefully be researched.

Greatbatch

The application of Conversation Analysis (CA) to broadcast news interviews has been pioneered by three colleagues – Heritage and Clayman in the USA, and Greatbatch in the UK. Their collective findings are to appear in a long-awaited book (Heritage et al., forthcoming). David Greatbatch's close analyses of interviews broadcast on British television over more than a decade have provided significant insights into how this genre of media talk operates for its participants. His contribution to this volume distils a CA approach to news interviews together with key examples and findings.

Broadcasting offers opportunities to analyse a range of spoken genres, such as interviews, telephone conversations, and various kinds of monologues. For the most part, such analysis has been conducted using the methods of CA, which sets out to describe how conversations are structured, for example in their openings, closings and turn-takings. Much of this research has focused on radio and TV interviews, in particular because of their sociopolitical emphasis. Broadcast technology has taken a relatively private speech event and transformed it into one that is for public consumption, and which has developed its own norms. CA researchers such as Greatbatch, looking at how news interviews are structured around questions and answers, have found differences from the features of ordinary conversations.

Interviews operate under various institutional constraints. One of these is that interviewers ask questions and interviewees answer them, but such constraints are not always adhered to. So interviewees may start to ask questions. In such instances, the interviewer will generally sanction the digression and eventually retrieve the interview so that it once more operates within the constraint. Greatbatch's chapter looks at the constraint that interviewers should take a neutralistic stance. Analysing excerpts from several news interviews on British television, he shows how news interviews operate within this constraint. Interviewers elicit the views of others without expressing opinions of their own. If the interviewer posits a contentious proposition, it will often be attributed to absent third parties. The maintenance of such a neutralistic stance requires the co-operation of the interviewees, of course, and usually this is forthcoming. On the occasions when there may be challenges to the interviewer's neutralism, these are usually quickly repaired and the constraints restored.

CA pays meticulous attention to the details of conversations, and Greatbatch's analysis shows how much we can learn through just such a close reading of news interviews.

Kress and van Leeuwen

Theo van Leeuwen and Gunther Kress are pioneers in analysis of the visual dimension of printed texts. Kress was one of the founders of Critical Linguistics (e.g. Kress and Hodge, 1979), and has been publishing on media discourse since the 1970s. Van Leeuwen has worked hands-on in film and television scripting and directing as well as in research and teaching. Kress and van Leeuwen have researched the analysis of visual design in Australia and the UK, and have published successive textbooks on this neglected area (1990, 1996). Their *Reading Images: The Grammar of Visual Design* is the first advanced textbook on the topic.

Kress and van Leeuwen consider texts from a multimodal perspective, to include semiotic modes that accompany language or through which language is realized. They argue that with the increase in the use of the visual mode with texts, it is essential that scholars now focus on and clarify the interplay between the verbal and the visual. Their chapter in this book sets out ideas which are a step towards developing such a descriptive framework.

In this chapter, the object of their analysis is the layout of front pages of newspapers. They examine how headlines, blocks of text and photographs are set out on the front page into coherent and meaningful structures, which differ interestingly across different newspapers. The underlying function of layout is textual, affording order and coherence. Kress and van Leeuwen's framework attributes meanings to these features of layout according to whether they appear on the left or the right of the page, or towards the top or the bottom, or towards the centre as opposed to at the margins.

Kress and van Leeuwen suggest that the left and right sides of newspaper front pages represent the Given and New respectively, with Given referring to something the reader already knows, or a departure point for the message, and New to things not yet known to which the reader must pay close attention. Visual cues (e.g. size, colour, tonal contrasts) can create hierarchies of importance by giving different degrees of salience to items. And framing (lines, spaces) can suggest connections and separateness amongst the items.

The authors do not claim that newspapers always adhere to the same layout conventions. But it is suggested that there are regularities that would stand up to quantitative analysis of large samples, and conventions that are regular enough for change over time to be identifiable.

Kress and van Leeuwen state that their chapter is intended in part to assemble items for a new research agenda, and it does indeed raise important research issues. It would be interesting to investigate whether media designers verify the values associated here with left and right, centre and margins etc., whether readers 'understand' these layouts, and indeed, whether any such understandings operate at a level of consciousness that allows readers to articulate them. Cross-cultural studies are needed to investigate whether the semiotics of layout are different (and in what ways) in cultures with writing systems that go from right to left, or top to bottom on the page.

Richardson

Kay Richardson has specialized in research on the reception of media texts, particularly in co-operative work. With Corner and Fenton, she undertook and authored a study of how British audiences interpret television documentaries about the nuclear power industry (Corner et al., 1990). While other contributors to this volume touch on how audiences receive media texts (e.g. Bell, Allan), reception is the focus of Richardson's chapter, specifically of news about the economy. She analyses a BBC news broadcast on the British economy, focusing on elements of economic understanding and areas of ambiguity and indeterminacy. This analysis then provides a basis for exploring the responses of the audience to the news item, concentrating on what they recall from the screening, how their comprehension of new information in the text is influenced by textual form, and the effects of their background understanding of the economy and economic reasoning.

The audience comprises members of six groups: Conservative and Labour Party members, science students, university security staff, local government officers, and unemployed. One would expect, then, different mental models, frameworks of personal and social knowledge and understanding to be operating on the text, resulting in interpretative variation. Alternatively, audience groups may share the interpretation of the text, but not give it the same value: hence a Labour Party audience hearing a Conservative Party text will not attempt to impose Labour values upon it. They will make sense of it as a Conservative text to which they are opposed.

It is very much a characteristic of this type of study that there are in fact two sets of texts for analysis. Firstly there is the news text itself (the primary text), and secondly – indeed, equally – the recorded discussions of the respondents are also texts for analysis.

Scannell

Paddy Scannell is a media researcher with an abiding interest in how language operates in broadcast media. He is one of the founding editors of the journal *Media, Culture and Society*, and has focused on the history of British broadcasting. He has edited a wide-ranging collection of essays on *Broadcast Talk* (1991), and brings a non-linguist's eye to the study of media discourse. His chapter in this volume has a different brief from the others. It is not to set out and demonstrate a particular approach to media discourse, but rather to comment on the part played by discourse analytical approaches in the whole research area of mass communication. Scannell begins by asking what 'media language' is addressing, and then sets out two main approaches to media and language. These two approaches, which he labels the ideological and the pragmatic, differ in that the latter takes reality (at least initially) at its face value, and the former does not. The former is a hermeneutics of suspicion ('being in the head') and the latter a hermeneutics of trust ('being in the world'). These contrasting approaches are represented in this volume most clearly in the chapters by van Dijk, Fairclough and Allan on the one hand, and by Greatbatch on the other.

Scannell bemoans the domination of media studies, as he sees it, by over-concern with ideology in place of more focus on what is unique about the media in relation to language and to the world. He draws attention to the ways in which the media deal with the here and now to show how media and language can benefit from a phenomenological approach, pointing to the work of Bell (e.g. this volume) on how the concepts of time and chronology feature in news stories, and to the work of Marriott (1995, 1996) on action replays. In Scannell's view, the worldlessness of some ideological approaches can lead to such characteristically media phenomena being overlooked.

Conclusion

We would like to conclude this introduction with two caveats. Firstly, although we have attempted to produce a volume of chapters that give readers practical demonstrations of some of the main approaches to media discourse, grasping and implementing these techniques requires time and commitment, and the complexity of some approaches can be daunting for students and even specialists.

We urge students, if they find frameworks hard to use at times, to keep in mind the following:

- the rewards from perseverance are worthwhile in terms of the perceptions they bring;
- all approaches have been taught to students;
- full-scale analyses are time-consuming – the originators are aware of this and conduct these on only a few texts, with more specific analyses on larger samples;
- the complexity of the frameworks is a reflection of the complexity of such texts as news stories (even if such stories appear simple on first impression).

Secondly, we would not like to leave readers with the impression that we believe this volume contains all of the main approaches to media discourse. We would not wish to make such a claim. There are three primary gaps which we see in this collection.

The first gap is individual: Roger Fowler, author of one of the three current texts on media language (Fowler, 1991), was unable either to attend the Round Table meeting or to contribute a chapter to this book. His analysis of language structures uses the tools of functional linguistics, including analysis of the transitivity of sentences, use of passives and nominalizations, and modality. With its emphasis on vocabulary (including a concern with how groups and individuals are labelled in the media) Fowler's approach is probably the most accessible among the main frameworks used to analyse media discourse. We regret his absence.

The second gap is disciplinary. Reception or comprehension of media texts is the focus of just one chapter in this book (Richardson's), although it also figures importantly in the contributions by Bell and Allan. Fairclough's concept of the 'lifeworld' also invites a concern with the contexts in which media are received, although he does not pursue this issue in this book. The understandings which audiences bring to print and broadcast media, their evaluative reactions to discourse styles, their preferences for other variables, the situations in which they receive media texts, are crucial to our approach to media discourse. While there is some work that links the media text and its reception (e.g. Morley, 1980, 1992; Meinhof, 1994), a close relating of the text and its reception is still relatively rare as yet in research. Richardson's contribution here and elsewhere does begin to redress the balance. The third gap is also disciplinary, but much wider. We have no chapter focusing on the production of media texts. This is not an accident. It reflects an almost total lack of research on how media texts are actually produced, of how the finished text is the outcome of the processes by which it was made. Most of the chapters in this book touch on the importance of production at some point. Allan treats it in relation to the 'encoding' moment of Hall's model, but offers no new data of his own. Bell touches on production practices as they are presumed to be revealed in the actual text, such as disagreements between news workers. On the basis of published layouts, Kress and van Leeuwen offer interpretations of the working concepts of those who make newspaper page layouts. One of the three components of Fairclough's approach, discourse practices, has production practices as a primary aspect. Yet none of the contributors has focused on this crucial area.

This lack of production research is no accident either. It is more difficult to research production than reception (while reception is more difficult than the text itself). That difficulty is not so much theoretical as practical and interactional. Access to and acceptance by media organizations and personnel is the central problem, as researchers have found for decades since Lazarsfeld (1948). Suspicion strong enough to jeopardize the conduct or outcome of research has dogged many studies including those by the Glasgow University Media Group (1976, 1980), Burns (1977), Schlesinger (1980, 1987) and Fenby (1986). Bell has in part bypassed the problem of being an outside researcher by also working as an insider, but until more journalists become researchers, or researchers journalists, scholars are going to need to devise acceptable means of approaching media organizations for their co-operation.

As well as introducing students to the available analytical approaches, this book serves as a state-of-the-art statement on media discourse. The future agenda for this kind of work must clearly focus more on reception, and particularly production, as well as and in relation to the texts themselves. There has been a convergence between the methods and interests of linguistic discourse analysis and European critical sociopolitical theory, literary criticism and cultural studies. Both strands share an interest in media texts as manifestation of and contributor to sociopolitical structures and. trends. The growing fusion of approaches from discourse analysis, cultural studies and media sociology reflected in this book is also a promising indicator of the way forward for media discourse studies. The obstacles include the access issue just highlighted, and also the nature of the analytical frameworks themselves. But the pay-off from overcoming those obstacles is, we believe, worthwhile.

Chapter 2

Opinions and Ideologies in the Press

Teun A. van Dijk

1 Aims

Editorials and op-ed articles in the press are generally expected to express opinions. (Op-ed articles are opinion pieces published on the page opposite the editorials.) Depending on the type and the stance of the newspaper, these opinions may vary considerably in their ideological presuppositions. This rather common formulation seems to imply that the ideologies of journalists somehow influence their opinions, which in turn influence the discourse structures of the opinion articles. Within the framework of a larger project on discourse and ideology, this chapter examines some of the theoretical properties of these complex relations between ideology, opinions and media discourse. For instance, we need to spell out what exactly we mean by 'ideology' here, what the nature is of the common-sense notion of an 'opinion', and by what discourse structures they may be expressed.

At one level of analysis, opinions and ideologies involve beliefs or mental representations, and our approach therefore first takes a *cognitive* perspective. On the other hand, the ideologies and opinions of newspapers are usually not personal, but *social, institutional or political*. This requires an account in terms of social or societal structures. In fact, we integrate both approaches into one *sociocognitive* theory that deals with shared social representations and their acquisition and uses in social contexts. And finally, since we examine in particular the sometimes subtle textual expressions of ideologically based opinions, this sociocognitive orientation will be embedded in a discourse analytical framework (for details, see van Dijk, 1995).

This approach is unique in rejecting the theoretical reduction that characterizes virtually all past and contemporary approaches to ideology. As is the case for language and knowledge, ideologies too are very complex social phenomena, which require independent conceptual analysis and empirical description at various theoretical levels. Thus, recognizing that ideologies are socially shared and used by groups and their members does not mean that they therefore cannot and should not *also* be described in cognitive terms. In that respect, ideologies are like knowledge and natural language (or rather like the grammars and discursive rule systems that underlie language use). Hence, our distinction between the mental and the social is a theoretical and analytical one, made to account for different dimensions of ideology.

Thus, in line with contemporary cognitive science, beliefs and ideological belief systems need to be accounted for *also, though not exclusively*, in terms of mental representations and eventually in terms of the neurobiological structures of the brain. This by no means implies a reduction to individualist, dualist or mentalist positions. On the contrary, what we are after is to show precisely how elements of societal structure (such as groups, institutions, power or inequality), as well as the everyday social practices of discourse and other forms of interaction among people as group members, are systematically related to the socially constructed dimensions of their minds.

For us, then, the mind is both a common-sense and a theoretical concept. It is no less (and no more) 'real' or 'material' than equally unobservable societal structures and social practices. The latter are no more 'all in the mind' than ideologies and other beliefs are all in interaction or discourse. In our view, only integrated sociocognitive theories are able to explain in detail how social ideologies 'monitor' the everyday practices of social actors like journalists, and conversely, how ideologies are formed and changed through the everyday interaction and discourse of members in societal contexts of group relations and institutions like the press.

Our examples will be taken from opinion articles in the *New York Times* and the *Washington Post*, which may be taken to express a variety of more or less liberal and more or less conservative opinions and ideologies, depending on the issues at hand, while at the same time probably exhibiting fragments of an overall 'American' ideological perspective on news events and the world.

2   Ideologies

The concept of 'ideology' is one of the most elusive notions in the social sciences, and this chapter will not even try to summarize the long theoretical debate about this notion (see, among many other books, Centre for Contemporary Cultural Studies (CCCS), 1978; Eagleton, 1991; Larrain, 1979; Thompson, 1984, 1990).

Rather, it is the aim of this chapter to make a further step in the (slow) development of a new theory of ideology aiming to replace the hitherto rather vague notions of ideology in philosophy and the social sciences. This new theory has three main components:

A   *Social functions.* A theory of the functions of ideologies for groups or institutions within societal structure. This theory answers the simple question of why people develop and use ideologies in the first place.

B   *Cognitive structures.* Within this framework, a theory is developed about the mental nature and the internal components and structures of ideologies, as well as their relations to other cognitive structures or social representations, such as socially shared values, norms, attitudes, opinions, and knowledge, on the one hand, and personal and contextual models (experiences, intentions, plans etc.), on the other hand. This theory answers the question of what ideologies look like, and how they monitor social practices.

C   *Discursive expression and reproduction.* A theory of the ways ideologies are expressed in, and acquired and reproduced by, the structures of socially situated text and talk. This theory is a special case of a broader theory of the ways ideologies are expressed and reproduced by social practices in general.

Social functions

Since the social functions of ideologies have been amply discussed in the classical literature, we shall be very brief about them. Contrary to the conventional view, however, we do not limit ideologies to their role in the reproduction and legitimation of class domination. To begin with, dominated groups also need ideologies, for example as a basis for resistance. This means, secondly, that ideologies in general are not wrong or right, but rather more or less effective in promoting the interests of a group. Thirdly, we shall assume therefore that the main social function of ideologies is the *co-ordination* of the social practices of group members for the effective realization of the goals of a social group, and the protection of its interests. This applies both to group-internal social practices as well as to interaction with members of other groups. Given this general function of ideologies, it is of course true that many ideologies develop precisely in order to sustain, legitimate or manage group conflicts, as well as relationships of power and dominance.

Cognitive structures

In order for ideologies to effectively sustain such social functions, their cognitive contents, structures and strategies should somehow be tailored to these social functions. In other words, what people *do* as group members should reflect what they *think* as group members, and vice versa, a relation studied in terms of 'social cognition' (Fiske and Taylor, 1991). Thus, social practices presuppose vast amounts of sociocultural and group-specific beliefs or social representations, such as knowledge, attitudes, norms, values and ideologies. Our theory proposes that ideologies are the 'axiomatic' basis of the mental representations shared by the members of a social group. That is, they represent the basic principles that govern social judgement – what group members think is right or wrong, true or false.

What do such ideologies look like? Despite the vast literature on ideologies, we do not know. But we may speculate about the typical contents and in particular the structure of ideologies. For instance, many group ideologies involve the representation of Self and Others, Us and Them. Many therefore seem to be *polarized* – We are Good and They are Bad – especially when conflicting interests are involved.

Such basic propositions of positive self-presentation and negative other-presentation may influence the myriad of opinions and attitudes We have about Them in more specific social domains. Racist ideologies featuring such axiomatic propositions may thus co-ordinate prejudiced social group attitudes about minorities or immigrants, for instance in matters of immigration, residence, employment or education. In other words, the main cognitive function of ideologies is to organize specific group attitudes. This does not mean that ideologies as well as ideologically based attitudes are consistent, although in another sense they may well be coherent in relation to the basic interests of the group.

More generally, we propose that ideologies reflect the basic criteria that constitute the social identity and define the interests of a group. That is, ideologies may be represented as group self-schemata, featuring such categories as *Membership* ('Who belongs to our group? Who may be admitted?'), *Activities* ('What do we do?'), *Goals* ('Why do we do this?'), *Values* ('How should we do this?'), *Position* ('Where are we? What are our relations to other groups?') and *Resources* ('What do we have, and what do we not have?'). Because these schemata are ideological, the way groups and their members represent themselves and others may of course be 'biased', when seen from the point of view of others (including our point of view as analysts).

For journalists as a group, these ideological categories will feature basic information about who is recognized as a journalist (e.g. through holding a diploma or licence), what journalists typically do (e.g. write news and editorials), their goals (e.g. to inform the public, to serve as a 'watchdog of society'), their values and norms (e.g. truth, reliability, fairness), their position with respect to their readers or the authorities, and their typical group resource (information).

Ideologies and other social representations of the mind are 'social' because they are socially shared. As is the case for grammar and other forms of knowledge, such shared representations should be seen as general and abstract. As a practical criterion, we may say that all representations that are routinely presupposed in discourse and other social practices are socially shared. Of course, throughout socialization, individual members may acquire slightly variable 'versions' of these social representations. Some members (e.g. the 'ideologues') of a group may have a more detailed and complete ideological system than others (see the discussion in Lau and Sears, 1986). This is the first source of individual variation in the enactment of ideologically based social practices, but it does not therefore mean (as is sometimes argued) that ideologies do not exist, any more than that grammars, discourse rules or sociocultural knowledge can be said not to exist because some members have more knowledge than others. In other words, as suggested before, the analysis of ideologies should take place at the abstract level of groups, and not at the level of individual cognition. Moreover, since individuals may belong to a number of social groups, they may have several ideologies, each variably influencing their social practices, depending on the situation. This also explains why personal uses of ideologies in concrete situations may be variable and often appear contradictory.

Models

General group ideologies and the specific group attitudes they organize may be expressed directly in discourse, for example by general expressions of opinions such as 'Women are less competent' in male chauvinist ideology. However, much opinion discourse, including that in the press, is more specific, and expresses not only group opinions, but also personal knowledge and opinions about specific people, events and situations ('I disapprove of this invasion'). Such personal and specific opinions derive from socially shared opinions or attitudes as well as from people's personal experiences and evaluations as these are represented in so-called *mental models*.

Models are the crucial interface between the social and the personal, between the general and the specific, and between social representations and their enactment in discourse and other social practices. Essentially, models represent people's everyday experiences, such as the observation of or participation in actions, events or discourse. Unlike social representations they are personal, subjective and context-bound: they feature what individuals know and think about specific events, and account for the fact that such events and actions are subjectively interpreted. Thus, models explain why interpretations of discourse are constructive.

People continually 'model' the events of their everyday lives, including the communicative events they engage in, or the news events they read about in the press. Thus, remembering, storytelling and editorializing involve the activation of past models, whereas intentions, plans, threats and announcements involve models about future events and actions. In sum, all our social practices are monitored (intended, understood) in terms of mental models.

Although such models as a whole are unique, personal and context-bound, large parts of them are of course social in the sense that the knowledge and opinions they embody are merely personal 'instantiations' of sociocultural knowledge and group opinions. In other words, models are indeed the interface between social representations, including ideologies, on the one hand, and social practices and discourse on the other hand.

From models to discourse

We now have the vital missing link between ideology and discourse. Ideologies organize specific group attitudes; these attitudes may be used in the formation of personal opinions as represented in models; and these personal opinions may finally be expressed in text and talk. This is the usual, indirect way of ideological expression in discourse. We have seen above, however, that in some forms of discourse, ideologies may also be expressed directly, that is, in general statements.

Because models represent what people know and think about an event or situation, they essentially control the 'content', or semantics, of discourse. However, since people know and think much more than they usually need to say for pragmatic reasons, only a fraction of the information in a model will usually be expressed in text and talk. This is of course also true for opinions: people do not always find it necessary or appropriate to say or write what they think. In many respects a text is merely the tip of the iceberg of what is mentally represented in models. And conversely, due to the construction of a model and the application of knowledge and attitudes in this construction, people usually understand much more of a text than it actually expresses.

We have already suggested that people form not only models about events they know about (through personal experience or through communication), but also specific models of the communicative events in which they participate. Such so-called context models will typically feature the overall definition of the situation (e.g. a lecture, talk with a friend, or reading the newspaper), as well as subjective beliefs about participants in different roles, about overall aims and goals, the setting, and so on. Context models are crucial in the production and comprehension of discourse. Whereas event models represent what is being communicated, context models largely regulate *how* this is being done, that is, the phonological, syntactic, lexical and other formal variation of text and talk. Like event models, such context models may of course also feature opinions, such as evaluative beliefs about other communicative participants, their roles, credibility, and so on. Thus, reading editorials usually involves the formation of opinions not only about what is said, but also about the writer, or the newspaper.

It should be stressed again that the sociocognitive framework presented here does not imply any primacy for the cognitive or the social dimensions of discourse or ideology. Rather, it aims to show the close relations between mind and society. It does, however, imply that, both theoretically and empirically, societal structures cannot be directly related in any way to discourse structures. This is only possible through social actors and their minds, that is, through the mental interpretations or constructions of social and situational structures by group members. All accounts that ignore cognitive analysis of the processes involved in the development and uses of ideology are in our view simplifications or reductions. Indeed, if social structures (such as those of domination) could directly influence (cause?) social practices and discourse, no ideologies or other shared social representations of the mind (such as knowledge) would be needed in the first place. And if individual experiences and interpretations (as represented in models) were ignored, this would imply that all social actors in a group would do and say the same thing.

3 Opinions

Before we examine in some detail the discourse expressions of opinions in editorials, we need briefly to attend to the rather elusive notion of 'opinion' itself. Above, we defined opinions as 'evaluative beliefs', that is, as beliefs that feature an evaluative concept. In many cases, this poses no problem. Any belief that presupposes a value, and that involves a judgement about somebody or something, is evaluative, such as 'X is good (bad, beautiful, ugly, honest, intelligent)', depending on the values of a group or culture. Some judgements are evaluative only indirectly or in specific situations, for example when someone or something is believed to be small or large, light or heavy, and when such a factual belief itself presupposes a value judgement (e.g. 'being a small X is bad').

The same is true for categorizations, for example when someone is believed to be a thief or a terrorist. These may be factual beliefs. If socially accepted, general criteria can be specified for such a categorization, such as the judgement of a court of law. On the other hand, if the factual criteria are less relevant, and the concept is used only or primarily to make a value judgement (someone is bad), then we are dealing with an opinion. Obviously, as is the case for all values and judgements, these may vary culturally and socially. And as soon as groups and conflicting group interests are involved, such opinions will be said to be ideological.

This highly simplified account has practical implications for discourse analysis. It hides fundamental problems of cognition and philosophy, such as the basis of knowledge and belief, evaluations and judgements (Kornblith, 1994; Lehrer, 1990). In the social psychology of opinions and attitudes, such issues are usually ignored (Eagly and Chaiken, 1993).

In a discussion of ideology in particular, the criteria of truth and falsity become relevant here. Thus, if we define opinions as evaluative beliefs, and contrast these with factual beliefs, as we have done, we are begging the question if we are unable to distinguish between evaluative and factual beliefs. Both involve a judgement, but simply saying that this judgement presupposes values in opinions, and truth criteria in factual beliefs, again needs further explication. Indeed, to take a contemporary example, is the belief 'smoking is bad for our health' an opinion or a factual belief? It features a typically evaluative concept ('bad') and as such seems to be an opinion, namely about smoking or smokers. On the other hand, when based on the conclusions of scientific research, then the belief may be seen as factual.

In other words, it depends on the grounds or criteria of judgement. If these grounds are merely a cultural or group norm or value ('it is bad to damage our health by smoking') then the belief is an opinion. However, if the grounds are socially shared criteria of truth (e.g. observation, reliable communication, valid inference, scholarly research, etc.), or other knowledge based on such criteria, then the belief is factual (true or false). Both types of judgement are socially, historically and culturally relative. Also, truth criteria may be different in different periods or for different groups. But for beliefs to be factual, it is only necessary that within each culture or group accepted criteria of knowledge are applied. And whenever these particularly favour a special group, the very system of knowledge and truth criteria may be ideologically based.

Note that we do not use the concept of 'opinion' here to refer to false beliefs, as is sometimes done in everyday language use. False beliefs are also factual if they can in principle be evaluated relative to a system of truth criteria. Conversely, opinions and ideologies are often said to represent the 'truth' for specific people or groups, but that does not make them factual in our sense. As soon as norms and values are involved, they are evaluative and not factual.

Many other relevant notions that are commonly used in the distinction between knowledge and opinions, such as subjectivity and objectivity, or consensus, are ignored here. Similarly, a more discursive definition of knowledge and beliefs will not be proposed either. Although opinions are usually the object of disagreement, and are debated in specific argumentative structures, the same may also be true for factual beliefs. That is, the claim defended in an argument may be either factual or evaluative. Nor do we accept the discursive reduction of opinions and knowledge. For us, as for most psychologists, these are mental representations, and not discursive structures. That is, people are said to 'have' and share opinions, whether they express them in discourse or not, and both within and across specific contexts. That beliefs are socially acquired, constructed, changed and used (also) through discourse is obvious, but that does not make them discursive in the usual sense of 'being a property of discourse'.

4 Discourse Structures

After this brief summary of our theory of ideology and opinion, we now need to examine in some more detail how these may be expressed in text and talk in general, and in opinion articles in the press in particular. A discourse analytical approach to this question will typically do this by examining the various levels and dimensions of discourse.

Lexical items

Traditionally best known in studies of ideology and language is the analysis of *lexical items*. Words may be chosen that generally or contextually express values or norms, and that therefore are used to express a value judgement (e.g. 'terrorist', 'racist'). But although there are many predicates that are normally used to express an opinion (e.g. 'beautiful', 'dirty' etc.), others may be used either factually or evaluatively (e.g. 'polluted', 'democratic', 'intelligent'), depending on whether a knowledge or value system is presupposed in their use, as discussed above.

However, in a discourse analytical approach in particular, we want to go beyond this obvious analysis of lexical items. Opinions may also be expressed in many other, much more complex, ways in text and talk: for instance in headlines, story structures, arguments, graphical arrangements, syntactic structures, semantic structures of coherence, overall topics, and so on. Let us examine some of these somewhat more carefully, and thereby focus on the various semantic structures of discourse, since they form the core 'content' of the expression of ideological opinions (van Dijk, 1995; for the semantic notions used here, see van Dijk, 1985). As a convention, we shall now refer to meanings, concepts and propositions (and hence to opinions) by using single quotes, and to the actual words, sentences and other expressions of such meanings with double quotes, or in italics.

Propositions

Concepts and their expressions in lexical items usually do not come alone, but combine into *propositions* expressed by clauses and sentences. Thus the occurrence of words that seem to imply opinions (such as "terrorist") does not mean much if we do not know the meaning of the sentences in which they occur (and, of course, of the whole text and context, to which we turn below). For instance, there is considerable difference between the proposition 'He is a terrorist' and its denial 'He is not a terrorist', even if they both contain the concept of 'terrorist', and although both may be taken as expressions of opinions.

Propositions are usually analysed in terms of a main predicate (usually interpreted as a property, event or action) and a number of arguments with different semantic roles, such as Agent, Patient, and so on, as in the proposition 'killed (Agent: terrorists, Patient: hostages)'. This proposition may be modified further by modalities such as 'It was necessary (possible, unlikely etc.) that'.

Each category of a proposition may be modified again by another predicate: for example 'desperate (terrorists)' and 'terrified (hostages)'. As discussed above, each of these concepts may feature implied opinions. Thus, choosing 'desperate' rather than 'cold-blooded' as a modifier for 'terrorist' implies another, less negative, opinion suggesting that the terrorist had no other option but to kill the hostages. This implication may also be inferred from the choice of modalities such as 'They were obliged to . . .'. We find such use of necessity-modalities quite often in strategies that limit the negative actions of the authorities of the We-group, as in 'The police had to act tough against the demonstrators' (for examples in news reports about police actions, see van Dijk, 1988a).

Interestingly, however, it is not merely the concepts involved in the proposition, but also the propositional structure itself that may express opinions. If negative acts are attributed to people appearing in the Agent role, then they are held (more) responsible for these actions than if they appear in other roles. Moreover, the *syntactic structure* of the sentence expressing such propositions may vary such that the agency of a particular person or group is de-emphasized, as is the case in passive constructions (e.g. "The demonstrators were killed by the police", or "Demonstrators (were) killed"). In this way, OUR people tend to appear primarily as actors when the acts are good, and THEIR people when the acts are bad, and vice versa: THEIR people will appear less as actors of good actions than do OUR people (for detailed analysis of these strategies, see e.g. Fowler, 1991; Fowler et al., 1979; van Dijk, 1991).

We find here a first general strategy for the expression of shared, group-based attitudes and ideologies through mental models. This strategy of polarization – positive ingroup description, and negative outgroup description – thus has the following abstract evaluative structure, which we may call the 'ideological square':

1 Emphasize our good properties/actions
2 Emphasize their bad properties/actions
3 Mitigate our bad properties/actions
4 Mitigate their good properties/actions.

These functional moves in the overall strategy of ideological self-interest, which appear in most social conflicts and actions (e.g. in racist, sexist etc. discourse), may be expressed in the choice of lexical items that imply positive or negative evaluations, as well as in the structure of whole propositions and their categories (as in active/passives etc.). Here 'our' may refer to the ingroup or its friends and allies, and 'their' to the outgroup and its friends or allies (for social psychological studies of these principles, for example in attribution, see e.g. Fiske and Taylor, 1991; for the dimension of impression management, see Tedeschi, 1981).

Implications

Opinions need not always be explicitly expressed in a proposition, but may be implied. Theoretically, this means that given an (expressed) proposition P, one or more propositions Ql, Q2, . . . may be inferred from P on the basis of an event model or context model.

These models may themselves embody instantiated knowledge or attitudes. Thus, in an editorial about the expulsion from Israel of 400 members of Hamas (an Islamist Palestinian movement), the *New York Times* concludes as follows:

(1) Whatever Israel's offenses, it mocks reality for Arabs to imply that the expulsion is equivalent to Saddam Hussein's crimes against Kuwait or Libya's complicity in state terrorism. By all means hold Israel to the letter of Geneva Conventions. But don't exaggerate the scale and nature of the infraction. (*NYT*, Ed., 29 Jan. 1993)

The first sentences imply the opinion proposition that the Arabs are exaggerating, whereas the last sentence implies that the "infraction" of the Israelis is in fact minor, which is also an opinion. Also the choice of the very concept of "infraction" is itself a form of mitigation. Since the Israelis are on OUR side, and Saddam Hussein and Libya are typically enemies and hence THEM, we also see the basic ideological framework being expressed that explains such a mitigating operation. as well as the implied propositions (in our detailed analysis of a mple opinion article below, we shall see how Saddam   may also be used by Us to characterize other enemies).

Presuppositions

Propositions may be implied because they are presumed to be known (to be true) or presupposed, given a model of an event. They may be strategically used to obliquely introduce into a text propositions which may not be true at all. This is also the case for presuppositions that embody opinions. Thus, in the previous example it was presupposed that the "Arabs" did indeed exaggerate the scale and nature of the "infraction", which by itself is a partisan opinion about the reaction of the Arabs. Earlier in the same editorial, we read the following passage:

(2) Israel's defenders justly argue that the world takes too little note of the terrorist crimes committed by Islamic

extremists, and of their fanatic determination to block any compromise settlement between Israelis and Arabs. (*NYT*, Ed., 29 Jan. 1993)

Since the *NYT* claims that Israel's argument is valid, it also espouses the presuppositions of that argument, namely that "Islamic extremists" commit terrorist crimes and block any compromise settlement. The phrasing of that presupposition, while not attributed (by quotes) to Israel, is that of the *NYT*, and hence also the opinions implied by the use of the lexical items "terrorist crimes", "extremists" and "fanatic determination". No such words are used to describe the expulsion of 400 Palestinians by Israel. On the contrary, the article explicitly claims that this "infraction" should not be exaggerated. Earlier in the article, it is therefore described as a "blunder", and not as a "terrorist crime" of the State of Israel, as the Palestinians probably would have done. We see again how opinions about friends and enemies are being described, implied and presupposed following the ideological square proposed above.

Descriptions

Moving now to the proper discursive level of *sequences* of propositions, we find that events may be described at various levels of generality or specificity, and with many or few propositions at each level (van Dijk, 1977). If we apply the ideological square to this phenomenon, we may expect that Our good actions and Their bad ones will in general tend to be described at a lower, more specific level, with many (detailed) propositions. The opposite will be true for Our bad actions and Their good ones, which, if described at all, will both be described in rather general, abstract and hence 'distanced' terms, without giving much detail.

Thus, again in the example from the *NYT* quoted above, the expulsion of Hamas members is evaluatively summarized with the predicate "blunder" and as "violating the Geneva Convention". Later, these Palestinians are described as "huddling in tents in a freezing no man's land in Lebanon", which may be read as implying something negative for the Israelis. However, this is the only negative way Israeli policies are described in this article, whereas those of the Palestinian "terrorists" and the "Arab" states are described in much more detail, as we have seen before in the description of the "terrorist crimes" and the "fanatic determination", as well as in the following passages:

(3)   But it would compound the blunder and jeopardise Middle East peace talks for Arab states to press for United Nations sanctions before President Clinton's team has even settled in.... (Palestinians huddling in tents...). That perfectly suits the banished Islamic militants, since their plight has effectively stalled the peace talks they vigorously oppose. (*NYT*, Ed., 29 Jan. 1993)

Thus, Palestinians are described as wanting to block talks "vigorously", and to be "fanatically determined" to do so, and this is also true for other parts of the text: negative Arab reactions are spelled out in detail (and emphasized) and negative Israeli actions given little attention, mitigated or structurally subordinated.

Methodologically, single examples like these do not prove much; additional quantitative demonstration would be needed in order to establish that the overall strategy indeed applies. The example given is merely illustrative for the *kind* of operation at work: what we want to know is how opinions and attitudes may be expressed in discourse. Other work may then examine how *often* this happens, and whether the empirical hypothesis (about the differential descriptions of ingroups and outgroups) may hold up in quantitative comparisons.

Local coherence

One of the crucial semantic conditions of textuality is coherence, that is, the property of sequential sentences (or propositions) in text and talk that defines why they 'hang together' or form a 'unity', and do not constitute an arbitrary set of sentences. Both in formal discourse studies and in our sociocognitive approach, coherence is defined relative to models. That is, roughly speaking, a sequence of sentences is coherent if a model can be constructed for it. This may involve causal or conditional relations between the facts as represented by a model. In other words, coherence is both relative and referential. That is, it is defined according to the relations between facts in a model which is referred to or talked about.

If coherence is based on models, and models may feature opinions, which in turn may be ideological, it should be expected that coherence too may involve opinions and ideologies. If Dutch employers believe, as many of them do, that immigrant workers do not work hard enough, or have insufficient knowledge of the language or lack education, these are all opinions, but since they are believed to be 'true', they may function as the causal part of explanations, and thus make the texts of employers coherent (from their ideological perspective at least). Others might prefer to attribute high minority unemployment to the discrimination of the employers, rather than to blame the victims, and the 'ideological coherence' of their explanatory discourse would therefore be rather different (for detailed analysis of such biased talk by corporate managers, see van Dijk, 1993).

Besides this form of referential or extensional coherence, sequences of propositions may also be related by intensional or functional relations. One proposition may be a Generalization, Specification, Contrast or Example of another proposition. Since meanings rather than models seem to be involved here, it is hard to see how such relations can be ideologically controlled by opinions. Yet, the use of such functional relations may have strategic, argumentative or rhetorical functions. Thus, it is one thing for an editorial to describe a 'riot' in terms of black 'violence', but quite another to add the Generalization that this is 'always the case', as also happens in many negative conversational stories about minorities (van Dijk, 1984, 1987a). Similarly, in the same story, a storyteller may point out that We have to wait years for an apartment, but that *They* get a new apartment right away. Storytellers thus may make a general claim, for example about the lack of cultural adaptation of immigrants, and then add an example (which may turn into a complete story). In sum, the intensional relations too may accurately reflect conflicting relations between groups, cognitive operations of generalization and specification, of comparison and contrast, and so on, which may also obviously be imbued by ideological opinions. This is the case in the example discussed above concerning the political consequences of the expulsion of 400 members of Hamas from Israel:

(4)   The greater challenge now is to revive the stalled peace talks. To do so, the Administration will need Arab help. Now that Israel has compromised on an issue of principle, are Arab leaders willing to do the same? (*NYT*, Ed., 3 Feb. 1993)

The opposition and comparison between Israelis and Arabs become particularly clear in the last sentence, which is based on a contrast between Israel's 'positive' action (having granted the return of 100 of 394 expelled Palestinians) and scepticism about any positive action by Arab leaders. In both cases, opinions are involved, and opposing the two parties as in this example is one move in the broader strategy of positive self-presentation and negative other-presentation (indeed, the following sentence is "Predictably, the PLO has rushed to say no.").

Global coherence and topics

Local coherence between propositions of text or talk is a necessary, but not sufficient, condition for discursive coherence. Another unifying principle is at work, namely that of overall or global coherence, as it is defined by 'topics' of paragraphs, large stretches of text or whole discourses. Such topics may be formally described as semantic macrostructures that are derived from local microstructures by specific mapping rules. In actual discourse processing, these rules take the form of efficient (but fallible) macrostrategies for the construction or local execution of topics (van Dijk and Kintsch, 1983).

Since propositions may be belief propositions, macropropositions may represent opinions, as is typically the case in editorials. Locally and globally, an editorial will express local and global opinions, respectively, as would typically become clear in summaries. Indeed, the *NYT* editorial of which we just analysed a fragment, is summarized as follows in the Lexus database from which it was downloaded:

(5)   An editorial congratulates President Clinton for his first Middle Eastern foreign policy success in extracting con-

cessions from Israel on the issue of its deportation of 400 Palestinians, concluding that Arab countries can best promote the new seriousness about international law by returning to the peace talks. (*NYT*, Ed., 3 Feb. 1993)

Thus, the speech act of congratulation first presupposes that Clinton did something well (an opinion), and the (summary of the) recommendation at the end also involves an opinion about what Arabs should do. Thus, more generally, we may expect editorials of course to express, presuppose or imply opinions at the overall, macro level too.

That such opinions reflect partisan positions and ideologies may be concluded from the same example. We can infer which side of the Middle East conflict the *NYT* editors stand on by the fact that they congratulate Clinton for "extracting" a concession from Israel, instead of blaming him for being unable to force the Israelis to comply with the resolution of the UN Security Council (ordering the return of all those who were illegally expelled). This stance is despite their criticism of Israel, which is also evident in this editorial. Indeed, a locally critical opinion about Israel is not the same as an overall, macro opinion about Israel that is negative. On the contrary, negative opinions about Israel typically occur in lower-level, subordinate sentences.

Semantic moves

Overall ideological strategies of positive self-presentation and negative other-presentation may also be implemented at the local level of sentences and sentence sequences. In this way, one clause may express a proposition that realizes one strategy, and the next clause a proposition that realizes the other strategy. This is typically the case in the local semantic moves called disclaimers: "I have nothing against blacks, but . . .". In this so-called Apparent Denial, the first clause emphasizes the tolerance of the speaker, whereas the rest of the sentence (and often also the rest of the text) following the *but* may be very negative. In the same way, we may encounter Apparent Concessions in the same racist paradigm ("There are also intelligent black students, but . . ."), or Apparent Empathy ("Of course refugees have problems, but . . ."), and so on.

The very strategies on which such local moves are based are intended precisely to manage opinions and impressions, that is, what our conversational partners will think of us. Thus to avoid the negative impression of being an intolerant, ignorant bigot, the disclaimers are used as strategic prefaces to the negative part of the text. This does not mean that such moves are merely rhetorical. Obviously, speakers may well be convinced, on the basis of other (humanitarian) ideologies, that one *should* not have anything against blacks (Billig, 1988).

At the end of example (1), we find two Apparent Concessions in which Israel's "infraction" and obligations are conceded (in initial but subordinate clauses), but the main focus is placed on ridiculing the claims of the Arabs (comparing Israel with Saddam Hussein). Of course, such moves may also apply to other parties, such as when the *NYT* criticizes Premier Rabin for acceding to the expulsion, as follows:

(6)   Whatever the domestic political costs for Mr. Rabin, magnanimity would better serve Israel's wider interests. (*NYT*, Ed., 29 Jan. 1993)

Thus, the concession part pays tribute to the reality of the internal opposition to lifting the ban on the expelled Palestinians, but the main thrust of the argument focuses on what the *NYT* thinks is best for Israel. Incidentally, also note the style of the recommendation, namely the choice of the very positive "magnanimity", which hardly seems compatible with undoing the expulsion of 400 citizens and complying with UN resolutions. Would the *NYT* describe a terrorist who releases some of his hostages as 'magnanimous'? That is, a critical position towards friends may also use kid gloves, and in fact express ideologically based opinions. This is a typical example of the strategy of emphasizing Our good actions.

Integration?

Having reviewed the mapping of opinions on several semantic structures, we may ask ourselves whether some general principles may be derived from our analyses. Is there some 'logic' in the way ideological (or other) evaluations tend to manifest themselves in discourse meaning?

To answer this question, let us briefly retrace the theoretical itinerary that brought us from ideologies to discourses. Discourse meanings derive from mental models of events, controlled by context models. These models may embody both personal and instantiated social opinions about events or about any of their relevant aspects (participants, their properties and actions, etc.). The social opinions 'applied' to a specific event and context may be organized in attitudes, which in turn may be based on ideologies shared by groups. These ideologies are mental representations whose categories schematically code for the major social dimensions of groups (identity, activities, goals, position, value, resources), and involve interest-based selections of values that underlie the evaluations and the social practices of group members.

Thus, despite personal and contextual variation, opinions about events may be expected to express underlying ideological frameworks that also monitor social practices, and hence discourse, in strategic, self-interested ways. Especially in institutional and public discourse, it will generally be in the interest of a group if information is selected from a model and emphasized in discourse that is positive about the group of the speaker, and negative about opponents or Others. The converse is equally true: it will not be in our best interest to select and emphasize information that is negative for/about Us, or positive for/about the Others. This is precisely what the ideological square, discussed above, suggests as an overall strategy in mapping models on text and talk.

How does such an overall strategy influence discourse semantics? What semantic strategies does it entail at all levels of discourse meaning? We may try to answer these questions by distinguishing various dimensions of the moves that translate overall ideological strategies into semantic structures.

Volume   Models are generally much more detailed than the texts that express them. We usually know more than we say, and the same is true for our opinions, which we may often 'keep to ourselves', for good contextual reasons. This means that we are able to say either more or less about an event. We may describe it in a few general propositions, or use many propositions that characterize the event (and our opinions about it) in detail. Obviously, such variation may be constrained by the ideological square in an obvious way: say a lot about Our good things and Their bad things, and say little about Our bad things and Their good things.

Importance   Models, like most mental schemata, are hierarchically organized: they have overall propositions (macrostructures) at the top, and more specific propositions at the bottom; for the same reason, some information is important, other information less important, conceptually speaking, in the overall representation of an event. Since people may understand and hence model each event differently, the hierarchical structures of events may be different too. Similarly, for strategic ideological reasons, such differences of importance may be manipulated in discourse meaning. Some propositions will only appear at the lower-level microstructure, others typically may function as overarching macropropositions. Thus, a 'race riot' may be mainly conceptualized as an act of 'black mob violence', as conservative white politicians and media will conceptualize it, or as a form of 'urban resistance', as black or white radicals might conceptualize it. Macrostructural organization of models (how the event is globally interpreted) will thus influence the topicalization of discourse, and hence its global coherence and what is presented as important or as less important information. The same may be true at the micro level, where importance may translate in prepositional (and then clausal) structure, as is the case with topic–comment or focus organization. As a strategy, then, we will expect that information that is favourable about/for Us and unfavourable for Them will be construed as important or topical macro-information, and vice versa.

Relevance   The pragmatic dimension of relevance is about the utilitarian importance of information for (language) users or participants, and is therefore controlled by context models. Important information may still be less relevant for the readers or the audience, and conversely, unimportant details may well be relevant for them, if we measure relevance in terms of the seriousness or the scope of consequences for its users. Trivially, we may expect Our discourses to feature information and opinions that are particularly relevant for Us, and irrelevant for Them, and vice versa. For instance, information about white racism, though important, may be found less relevant by white newspaper editors and hence be accorded less newsworthiness, as is indeed the case (van Dijk, 1991).

Implicitness/Explicitness   The presence or absence of model information may be semantically construed as explicitness or implicitness. The influence of the ideological strategic square is obvious here: make explicit the information and opinions that are good for Us, and bad for Them, and vice versa. Again, this may be at the overall level of the discourse (as we have seen for Volume), or at the level of words and sentences.

Attribution   In explanatory contexts, acts may be variously attributed to actors, and explained in terms of their properties or the situation (Antaki, 1988; Jaspars, Fincham and Hewstone, 1983). Agency, responsibility and blame may also be attributed as a function of ideological orientation: good acts will usually be self-attributed to Ourselves (or our allies) and bad acts other-attributed to the Others (or their allies), and in both cases these groups are assigned full control and responsibility for their acts. The converse is true for Our bad acts and Their good acts: Our bad acts will be de-emphasized and attributed to circumstances beyond our control, and the same is true for Their good acts ("they were just lucky"). These various attribution strategies may appear at all levels of action description, and also appear in word order (responsible agency may be preferentially expressed by grammatical subjects and in initial position).

Perspective   Inherent in the notions of ideology, attitudes and the specific opinions based on them is the notion of 'position'. Events are described and evaluated from the position, point of view or perspective of the speaker. This perspective may be cultural, social, personal or situational, and may apply to all levels and dimensions of discourse. That is, judgements are by definition relative, as the concept of 'standpoint' (a synonym of 'opinion') suggests. This is true for the subjective point of view of the individual, as much as for the shared, inter-subjective opinions of group members. Situational perspective is expressed, first of all, in context-dependent deictics (pronouns, demonstratives and adverbs like 'here', 'now' and 'today'), verbs (like 'come' and 'go') and position- or relation-dependent nouns (such as 'home', 'sister' and 'neighbour'), among other expressions. Personal perspective trivially manifests itself in fixed expressions such as 'from my point of view', 'in my opinion' or 'as far as I am concerned'. The plural forms of such expressions may indicate social perspective ('from our point of view' etc.), which however may also simply be expressed by first person plural pronouns, as in the well-known ethnocentric example "We are not used to that here", used to express negative opinions about the acts of foreigners. A well-known slogan expressing a sociopolitical (and geographical) perspective (an anti-American one) is of course "Yankee, go home!". Implicitly this is also the case in the racist slogan of the National Front in France: "Les Français d'abord", which of course suggests that the person who is speaking is French.

In sum, given a mental model of an event, and a context model of the current communicative event, the overall strategic principles examined above allow language users to express their opinions not only through explicitly evaluative words, but also through:

- the generality vs. specificity and quantity of model propositions used in descriptions of events;
- the explicitness vs. the implicitness of model propositions;
- the importance assigned to propositions relative to others;
- the contextual relevance assigned to propositions;
- the attribution of agency, responsibility and blame for actions;
- the perspective from which events are described and evaluated.

These different discursive strategies have several functions, such as enhancing the vividness of descriptions or the credibility of accounts, and for our analysis they are particularly relevant in expressing the ideological perspective and the opinions of groups and their members. In each case, then, the strategy applies 'via' the ideological square: the type of description (general, or explicit etc.) must be in Our favour, in Our interest, or in any other way contribute positively and persuasively to Our self-presentation and impression management, or conversely, contribute to the negative presentation of our opponents, enemies or the Others in general.

Surface structures

In the previous sections we focused on the mapping of opinions and ideologies on semantic structures of discourse. Meanings are, however, expressed in various 'forms' or 'surface structures', that is, in concrete lexical items, clause and sentence structure, syntactic categories, word order, discourse intonation, graphical structures, and the organization of macrostructures in canonical schemata, such as those of narration, argumentation or news reporting.

Many of the semantic structures examined above, as well as the opinions embodied in them, thus need to be inferred from such surface structures. However, these structures or forms may also play their own role in the expression of opinions. One of the ways they do this is by the formal implementation of the ideological square. Meanings, and therefore opinions, may also be emphasized or de-emphasized by their expressions. They may be expressed on top (as in headlines), earlier in the text (as in leads of news reports), in topical (initial) positions in sentences, or through a complex system of rhetorical 'figures of speech' (repetition, parallelism, metaphor, comparison, irony, litotes etc.), or vice versa for meanings/opinions that need to be de-emphasized. We shall not further investigate the details of these expression structures of opinions in this chapter, but it should be borne in mind that many of the discursive strategies of ideological expression are formal. Conversely, in text comprehension, these expression structures influence semantic interpretation, and hence also the construction of opinions in models.

5   An Example

To illustrate the theoretical analysis proposed above, let us at this point examine in some detail how ideologies and opinions may be expressed and combined at the different levels of a typical 'opinion article'. Here we take an op-ed piece in the *Washington Post* (15 December 1993), written by Jim Hoagland (© 1997, Washington Post Writers' Group; reprinted with permission):

GADHAFI: SINISTER POSTURING

[1] A moment comes when a tyrant crosses a line of no return. In the grip of megalomania, he is incapable of making rational calculations of cost and gain. He strikes out in fury and in fear, intent on destroying even if it means destruction will visit him in turn.

[2] Iraq's Saddam Hussein crossed that line in the spring of 1990. But the outside world paid little heed until he invaded Kuwait that summer. Libya's Moammar Gadhafi now has crossed that line. The international community should not repeat the mistake it made with Saddam.

[3] On Sunday Gadhafi invited the world's two most notorious Palestinian terrorists, Ahmed Jibril and Abu Nidal, to visit Tripoli, perhaps to set up headquarters there. The Libyan leader told a cheering crowd in the town of Azizia that the invitations were meant to defy the United Nations.

[4] Gadhafi has shown that he no longer values the cloak of silence or acquiescence in his evil that he sought to purchase or extort. He is on the attack, pushing his long confrontation with the West back to the breaking point.

[5] For months Egyptian diplomats, fearful of the damage Gadhafi could do their country, and European oil executives and Washington lawyers, enamored of the lucre Gadhafi could send their way, have spoken of Gadhafi's new 'moderation' and have urged the international community to treat him with reasonableness and patience.

[6] He was, the lawyers submitted, about to change his spots on terrorism. He was, the Egyptians said, misunderstood and in any event a lesser evil than the Islamic fundamentalists who have declared war on the Egyptian regime. He was, the oil men claimed, a leader they could do business with, on favorable terms.

[7] Their pleas for patience lie in ruins now that Gadhafi has renewed his public embrace of terrorism, in word and deed. He has responded with vitriol and menace to the mild economic sanctions placed on his regime by the U.N. Security Council.

[8]   The Security Council has demanded that Gadhafi turn over for trial abroad two of his security aides, who are accused by the United States of carrying out the bombing of Pan Am Flight 103 on Dec. 21, 1988. His refusal to do so triggered sanctions that restrict air travel to and from Libya and freeze Libya's oil revenues banked abroad.

[9]   Intelligence reports link Jibril and his General Command organization to the planning of the Pan Am massacre, which cost 270 lives. Although Jibril's exact role is not clear, Gadhafi's invitation strips away the pretense that the Libyan is interested in seeing justice done in this case.

[10] As sinister as his invitation to the two managing partners of Terror Inc. is Gadhafi's suspected involvement in the kidnapping over the weekend in Cairo of Mansour Kikhiya, his former foreign minister, who broke with Gadhafi over terrorism to become a leading dissident – and a resident of the United States, due to become a U.S. citizen next year.

[11] Kikhiya's associates tell me he had gone to Cairo reluctantly and only after receiving personal guarantees from senior Egyptian officials of safe passage. He was well aware of the presence of Libyan secret police and of the Egyptian government's effort to shield Gadhafi from international punishment by arguing against sanctions.

[12] But on Dec. 10 Kikhiya disappeared from his hotel room in Cairo. Left behind in the room were the insulin and syringe Kikhiya needs every eight hours to treat his diabetes.

[13] Politically sensitive visitors like Kikhiya are routinely kept under surveillance by Egypt's internal intelligence service. His disappearance raises the question of Egyptian complicity in or tolerance of a Libyan plot to eliminate the Libyan exile movement. The movement has begun to worry Gadhafi, who brands the exiles as 'stray dogs and dollar slaves.'

[14] Gadhafi stands at a crossroads similar to the one that Saddam confronted in the spring and summer of 1990. He

responds with a similar lashing out at those who would
thwart him, even at the cost of embarrassing an Egyptian
government that has defended him.

[15] Libya is not broke or gravely weakened by a long war, as
Iraq was. But Gadhafi is boxed in and embarrassed by
sanctions. Sanctions show the Libyan population that
Gadhafi is not the omnipotent, respected leader he claims
to be.

[16] Rather than sink into impotence, Saddam went to war.
Gadhafi does not have the ground army to do that. But he
does have an army of international terrorists, including
those who carried out his orders to bomb Pan Am 103 five
years ago this month.

[17] Abu Nidal has also favored the Christian and Jewish year-
end holiday seasons as moments for terrorist outrages. His
men shot up the airports in Rome and Vienna in December
1985.

[18] It is impossible to know if Gadhafi was simply reminding
the world of his sinister capabilities, or foreshadowing new
atrocities with his public welcome of terrorists. But he has
warned the world that he must be watched and confronted
anew after a season of phony peace.

Let us analyse the evaluative and ideological strategies of this
article paragraph by paragraph, beginning with the headline.

GADHAFI: SINISTER POSTURING

In this headline, as well as in the rest of the text, the main target for
Hoagland's attack is of course Gadhafi, generally known as the
devil incarnate of conservative US foreign policy (for details, see
Chomsky, 1987). Structurally, the importance of Gadhafi is first
emphasized by his appearance in the title, which means that he is
the actor of a macroproposition. Secondly, fronting his name in the
title further emphasizes his agency and responsibility for the
nominalized verb "posturing", an effect that would be less obvious
in the normal ordering for this sentence: 'The sinister posturing of
Gadhafi'. Then, Hoagland's negative opinions are explicitly expressed in the choice of "sinister" and "posturing", the first predi-

cate being associated with secret and dark forces, and the second with affectation and a pose, and as having a big mouth, but really being nobody. Both predicates are obviously intended in the political sense, and hence express not so much Hoagland's personal opinion, but a shared US evaluation of Gadhafi. Note also that *what* Gadhafi has done is not topicalized in the headline, but only the *way* he does it, so that it is the evaluation itself that is thus emphasized. In the system of the ideological square, this is a clear example of negative other-presentation, as well as an example of emphasizing these negative properties of the Other.

1. *A moment comes when a tyrant crosses a line of no return. In the grip of megalomania, he is incapable of making rational calculations of cost and gain. He strikes out in fury and in fear, intent on destroying even if it means destruction will visit him in turn.*

The relevant opinions expressed here appear first of all in the lexical style, that is, in words such as *tyrant, megalomania, strikes out, fury,* and *destroying*, all predicated of an imaginary dictator, but (after the title) clearly meant as a generic description that fits Gadhafi. The political evaluation becomes obvious in the choice of *tyrant*, which categorizes him not only as undemocratic or even as a dictator, but also as someone who viciously oppresses his people. Moreover, the choice of *tyrant* is part of a long tradition of Western descriptions of Eastern 'despots', also applied, for example, to Saddam Hussein, but seldom to 'Western' dictators, such as Batista of Cuba, Pinochet of Chile or Stroessner of Paraguay. That is, there are various types of denomination, and the most important, political criterion for the choice of opinion pre-dicates is whether dictators are 'Ours' or 'Theirs', following the ideological principle that Our bad things tend to be mitigated, and Theirs emphasized (see also Herman, 1992; Herman and Chomsky, 1988).

Another evaluative sequence or 'opinion line', continuing the idea of *posturing* in the title, is picked up by the use of *megalomania*. Again, Gadhafi is negatively being described as someone who thinks he is bigger than he is, but the specific term also implies a form of mental deficiency: he is a lunatic. This personal evaluation of someone who 'has lost his mind' also appears in the statement that Gadhafi is unable to make rational calculations, that he strikes out in fury and fear and is self-destructive.

Thus, whereas Gadhafi is first politically placed beyond the pale of democracy and humanity, he is now also excluded from the world of 'us, sane' people. These various evaluations presuppose that Hoagland speaks from the point of view of Western, US, rational, democratic people(s), and the usual ideological polarization here therefore opposes this group with one of its main enemies, while Gadhafi is the incarnation of anti-Western, anti-US, anti-democratic (etc.) forces.

Thirdly, Gadhafi is not only a tyrant (over his own people) and a lunatic, but also a threat, since he is said to be "intent on destroying", which brings in the relevant international perspective already addressed above. Note that the opinion about his being a threat is not itself expressed, but based on an inference, namely from the explicit opinion that he is destructive, and the implicit knowledge that he is a head of state: violent, crazy dictators are a threat to the world, as was already suggested by the use of the concept of 'destruction' later in this paragraph.

Perhaps most interesting in this paragraph is the seemingly innocent phrase "even if it means destruction will visit him in turn", since the international dimension of Gadhafi's aggressiveness here seems to suggest a legitimation of retaliation, following the maxim derived from militarist ideologies: we are allowed to destroy someone who is bent on destroying us. It was precisely this legitimation, of course, that Reagan used when the US air force bombed Tripoli some years earlier, killing a large number of civilians, among them a child of Gadhafi. (In that case, incidentally, Gadhafi's alleged posturing, rather than his destructiveness, was seen as sufficient reason to attack Tripoli.)

> 2. *Iraq's Saddam Hussein crossed that line in the spring of 1990.*
> *But the outside world paid little heed until he invaded Kuwait*
> *that summer. Libya's Moammar Gadhafi now has crossed that*
> *line. The international community should not repeat the mistake*
> *it made with Saddam.*

As may be expected, a 'tyrant' like Gadhafi invites comparison with the other demon of US foreign policy: Saddam Hussein. The same metaphor used in the Gulf War (about the line drawn in the sand of the desert) is now applied to the case of Libya, in order to accentuate the similarity of the threats posed by both dictators to the international community. Note that "the outside world paid little heed" seems a factual statement, but in fact implies an opinion, namely that according to Hoagland the outside world *should* have paid more attention, which is a normative implication, as is also clear from the last sentence of this paragraph ("should not repeat the mistake"). Here we encounter the typical recommendation speech act that is a standard part of editorials and op-ed articles: after an analysis of what is wrong (an opinion), it is concluded what should be done, which semantically is also an opinion, and pragmatically an act of advice or recommendation.

3. *On Sunday Gadhafi invited the world's two most notorious Palestinian terrorists, Ahmed Jibril and Abu Nidal, to visit Tripoli, perhaps to set up headquarters there. The Libyan leader told a cheering crowd in the town of Azizia that the invitations were meant to defy the United Nations.*

After the evaluative introduction of the editorial, we here find the newsworthy 'facts' that form the immediate cause or 'peg' of the opinion piece, namely Gadhafi's invitation to two Palestinians. The evaluation implied by the use of *notorious* and *terrorist* is standard fare, and is part of the overall opinion-coherence of the article, representing fragments of the attitude of Hoagland and many of his colleagues towards the Middle East conflict. The last sentence of this paragraph is more interesting. As such, it is a factual statement, and not an opinion; indeed, it may be true or false, and the truth criteria are non-subjective (although there may be some dispute about when a group of people is a 'crowd' and when their actions are called 'cheering'). And Gadhafi might indeed have defied the United Nations, although there may be some doubt about whether he actually said it that way. Given the authority of the UN, however, defying the UN would normally be a negative act (although the USA itself has defied UN resolutions many times). This means that, by stating this, there may be at least an implicit opinion, based on the general evaluative belief that defying legitimate institutions is wrong. This description ties in with the earlier characterization of Gadhafi as a dangerous megalomaniac, and at the same time provides the 'proof' of such a characterization: he who defies the UN must be both aggressive and a fool.

4. *Gadhafi has shown that he no longer values the cloak of silence or acquiescence in his evil that he sought to purchase or extort. He is on the attack, pushing his long confrontation with the West back to the breaking point.*

The opinions here are very explicit, as is most obvious in the standard way of describing the most terrible of opponents: they are *evil*, just as Reagan famously described the former USSR as the 'evil empire'. The words *extort, attack* and *confrontation* are similarly borrowed from a lexical repertoire designed to describe the acts of the enemy. Note, however, that the opinion does not merely imply a negative evaluation of aggression. There is a lot of aggression in the world that Jim Hoagland and the *Washington Post* do not routinely write about. The crucial point, as also expressed by the earlier verb *defy*, is that Gadhafi confronts *Us* in the West (and especially Us, Americans). That is, the ideological polarization between Us and Them (or in this case between Us and Him) is being activated here to influence the organization of opinions in this article. As the theory predicts, this will usually happen through specific negative attitudes about the Others, in this case about 'Their' violence and aggression in general, and their terrorism in particular. Hoagland follows this standard evaluative scenario rather faithfully.

5. *For months Egyptian diplomats, fearful of the damage Gadhafi could do their country, and European oil executives and Washington lawyers, enamored of the lucre Gadhafi could send their way, have spoken of Gadhafi's new 'moderation' and have urged the international community to treat him with reasonableness and patience.*

Hoagland's opinion discourse now shifts to those who are prepared to accept Gadhafi, and the choice of *enamored of the lucre* implies that being overly fond of profits is viewed negatively here – not, of course, because this is out of line with the basic tenets of capitalism both Hoagland and the *Washington Post* undoubtedly espouse, but rather because this means doing business with the enemy. The use of quotes in the description of Gadhafi as being 'moderate' implies that Hoagland does not agree at all with such a characterization, as indeed his earlier epithets in this piece show rather unambiguously.

Here the old rule seems to apply that the friends of our enemy are also our enemy, so that oil executives and lawyers in this case are evaluated accordingly.

6. *He was, the lawyers submitted, about to change his spots on terrorism. He was, the Egyptians said, misunderstood and in any event a lesser evil than the Islamic fundamentalists who have declared war on the Egyptian regime. He was, the oil men claimed, a leader they could do business with, on favorable terms.*

The arguments of those who have a less negative view of Gadhafi are replayed, but again the lexicalization of these arguments does not seem to imply agreement. The use of the verbs *submitted* and *claimed* suggests as much, and also the expression *about to change his spots on terrorism* reveals Hoagland's serious doubts about Gadhafi's change. The rhetorical parallelism of the sentence structures of this paragraph further stresses this doubt about the claims of those Hoagland criticizes. Interesting for our analysis is that opinions also appear when people evaluate others' opinions.

7. *Their pleas for patience lie in ruins now that Gadhafi has renewed his public embrace of terrorism, in word and deed. He has responded with vitriol and menace to the mild economic sanctions placed on his regime by the U.N. Security Council.*

The justification of Hoagland's scepticism follows in this paragraph. A new enumeration of Gadhafi's evils is used to belie those who wanted to placate him: *embrace of terrorism, vitriol and menace*. These opinions fit the overall negative characterization of Gadhafi as a dangerous terrorist. In light of such an opinion, being patient is clearly found an inadequate response. For our analysis this is interesting, because it shows that words that usually imply positive opinions are used here in a critical way.

8. *The Security Council has demanded that Gadhafi turn over for trial abroad two of his security aides, who are accused by the United States of carrying out the bombing of Pan Am Flight 103 on Dec. 21, 1988. His refusal to do so triggered sanctions that restrict air travel to and from Libya and freeze Libya's oil revenues banked abroad.*

These factual statements simply appear to explain the historical background of the (mild) economic sanctions against Libya, and do not explicitly express opinions. Yet, mentioning the fact that Gadhafi is accused of bombing an aircraft is in line with, and supports, the earlier qualification of Gadhafi as a terrorist, whereas referring to his refusal to comply with the demands of the Security Council is a specification of the earlier evaluative description of defiance. In other words, factual statements about negative actions (bombing an aircraft) may not express an opinion, but strongly suggest such an opinion, which in this case might be that of the reader. Moreover, factual statements may support opinion statements: bombing an aircraft is a form of terrorism, and refusal to comply with demands of the international community (and especially of the UN), a form of megalomania.

9. *Intelligence reports link Jibril and his General Command organisation to the planning of the Pan Am massacre, which cost 270 lives. Although Jibril's exact role is not clear, Gadhafi's invitation strips away the pretense that the Libyan is interested in seeing justice done in this case.*

A similar negative description of the 'facts' is given here of another enemy, Jibril, and the selection of *massacre* and *cost 270 lives* is clearly monitored by a strongly negative opinion. Note also the disclaimer *Although Jibril's exact role is not clear*, which keeps some journalistic distance from the evidence of the intelligence reports, but which also suggests that what follows is evaluated negatively.

10. *As sinister as his invitation to the two managing partners of Terror Inc. is Gadhafi's suspected involvement in the kidnapping over the weekend in Cairo of Mansour Kikhiya, his former foreign minister, who broke with Gadhafi over terrorism to become a leading dissident – and a resident of the United States, due to become a U.S. citizen next year.*

The key-word of the title, *sinister*, appears again to qualify Gadhafi's actions as threatening and ominous, along with the rest of his portrayal as a terrorist. The picture is completed here by Gadhafi's (suspected) involvement in kidnapping a former associate. Inviting two terrorists, and important ones at that, is by itself a negative act, and calling it 'sinister' merely emphasizes the point. To mark the usual Us vs. Them articulation of ideological discourse, Kikhiya is now promoted to the status of dissident: the enemies of our enemies become our friends, and may be awarded citizenship. In other words, Gadhafi is not merely suspected of kidnapping a former associate (indeed, why would that be relevant to 'Us'?), but in fact of kidnapping a (near) US citizen, and hence attacking the USA.

11. *Kikhiya's associates tell me he had gone to Cairo reluctantly and only after receiving personal guarantees from senior Egyptian officials of safe passage. He was well aware of the presence of Libyan secret police and of the Egyptian government's effort to shield Gadhafi from international punishment by arguing against sanctions.*

12. *But on Dec. 10 Kikhiya disappeared from his hotel room in Cairo. Left behind in the room were the insulin and syringe Kikhiya needs every eight hours to treat his diabetes.*

The only expression of opinion in these two paragraphs may be the reference to Libya's secret police: only dictatorships have a secret police, so Libya is a dictatorship. Note also the reference to a source, a rather unusual move in an opinion article, but here strategically effective, while making the accusations more credible. Similarly indirect is the reference to Kikhiya being a patient in need of regular medication, but having left his medicine in the hotel room, which suggests that he must have been kidnapped. This 'proof' of abduction at the same time emphasizes the negative characteristics of the Others: they even abduct sick men and do not give them their medication.

13. *Politically sensitive visitors like Kikhiya are routinely kept under surveillance by Egypt's internal intelligence service. His disappearance raises the question of Egyptian complicity in or tolerance of a Libyan plot to eliminate the Libyan exile movement. The movement has begun to worry Gadhafi, who brands the exiles as 'stray dogs and dollar slaves'.*

Note that the security force of 'our friend' Egypt is not called a 'secret police' but an "internal intelligence service", thus lexically differentiating those associated with Us, and those associated with Them. The use of *brand* in the last sentence implies that Hoagland does not agree with the way Gadhafi describes his opponents, and the nature of the description itself is so preposterous that merely mentioning it is sufficient to qualify it. That exiles are called "dollar slaves" by Gadhafi further exacerbates the polarization between Us and Them, since 'dollars' are associated with the West or the USA.

14. *Gadhafi stands at a crossroads similar to the one that Saddam confronted in the spring and summer of 1990. He responds with a similar lashing out at those who would thwart him, even at the cost of embarrassing an Egyptian government that has defended him.*

15. *Libya is not broke or gravely weakened by a long war, as Iraq was. But Gadhafi is boxed in and embarrassed by sanctions. Sanctions show the Libyan population that Gadhafi is not the omnipotent, respected leader he claims to be.*

Paragraph 14 paraphrases earlier parts of the text, using the same comparison with Saddam Hussein, and *lashing out* continues the phrase "He strikes out in fury and in fear" used in the first paragraph. Both have negative implications. The opinion at the end of paragraph 15 is complex and interesting. The use of the verb "to show that" implies that the speaker holds the proposition to be true, so that Gadhafi in fact is *not* omnipotent and respected by his people, and hence he is a dictator. Similarly, since they hurt Gadhafi rather than his people, the use of sanctions is also legitimated, which is an indirect opinion.

16. *Rather than sink into impotence, Saddam went to war. Gadhafi does not have the ground army to do that. But he does have an army of international terrorists, including those who carried out his orders to bomb Pan Am 103 five years ago this month.*

17. *Abu Nidal has also favored the Christian and Jewish year-end holiday seasons as moments for terrorist outrages. His men shot up the airports in Rome and Vienna in December 1985.*

Although Saddam Hussein and Gadhafi are not comparable in military terms, Gadhafi makes up for this by his "army of terrorists", and his directing the bombing of Pan Am flight 103. What earlier in the text was a US accusation of Gadhafi's involvement is here presented as fact. And as before, since Gadhafi associates himself with the terrorist Abu Nidal, he is himself a terrorist. These examples hardly express explicit opinions, but the description of the people he associates with as "terrorists" and their actions as "terrorist outrages" clearly reveals a negative evaluation.

18.   *It is impossible to know if Gadhafi was simply reminding the world of his sinister capabilities, or foreshadowing new atrocities with his public welcome of terrorists. But he has warned the world that he must be watched and confronted anew after a season of phony peace.*

In this concluding·paragraph, the evaluative description *sinister* is used again, and *atrocities* continues the line of negative descriptions of the acts of Gadhafi. The final recommendation (that he must be watched) is, of course, itself based on norms and values informing this piece, and hence a political opinion. Even the positive concept of 'peace' associated with Gadhafi may be converted into "phony peace", thus making Gadhafi unreliable even when he keeps quiet: he can never be trusted.

6   Summary

Having briefly commented on the various types of opinion expression in a typical conservative op-ed article in the US press, we may at this point try to summarize our observations more analytically in light of the earlier theoretical framework.

Polarization

Opinions may be organized following an ideological pattern that polarizes ingroups and outgroups, Us vs. Them. This principle also has a number of corollaries in the form of maxims, such as 'The Enemy of Our Enemy is Our Friend'. In this case, the basic dual ideologies used are the familiar ones of Western superiority and Arab inferiority, whereby *We* are associated with positive values such as democracy, rationality and non-violence, and *They* with dictatorship, violence and irrationality. More specifically, the ideology of Arab inferiority here focuses on attitudes to terrorism, organizing a set of socially shared opinions about various aspects of terrorism and their associations (such as bombing, kidnapping, killing innocent people etc.). Moreover, following the logic of Ingroup–Outgroup relations, the Others are also presented as a threat.

Opinion coherence

Specific opinions about specific terrorists (Gadhafi, Nidal, Jibril) may follow the application of this general attitude. Together with conceptions about terrorist attacks and abductions of political opponents, this instantiation of an attitude also sustains what we have called the 'opinion coherence' of discourse in that various aspects of terrorism are being discussed.

Attribution

Attributions of negative actions to our enemies require that our enemies are described as responsible agents, who are consciously, intentionally and cynically aware of what they do and of the consequences of their actions, even if these actions may be branded as irrational or even crazy at the same time. On the other hand, those of Us who are too friendly towards our enemies do not fully realize what they are doing, and hence they may be advised to mend their ways.

Description

The identifying descriptions of groups or institutions related to Us and Them also follow the principle of ideological polarization. Thus, Their security forces are called the 'secret police', whereas Ours are an 'intelligence agency'.

Interest

Positive or negative opinions about Our or Their actions basically follow an evaluative logic based on a construction of what Our best interests are. Thus, Gadhafi's 'posturing' is not primarily judged to be evil as such (indeed, many of Our friends, such as Israel, do likewise), but it is judged to be evil in that it is seen to threaten our (US, Western) interests in the world.

Implicitness

Opinions may be explicit and implicit, direct and indirect. Some opinions in this op-ed article may be derived from a combination of factual statements with the norms, values and positions of the author. Thus "crossing a line" is, as such, not an evaluative predicate, but in the present context it expresses the opinion that Gadhafi has gone too far. Similarly, the factual description of terrorist acts (such as bombing an aircraft) does not express an opinion either, but shared social attitudes about such acts allow readers to derive the appropriate opinions.

Meta-opinions

Opinions may be opinions about other opinions. Thus, (too) positive opinions about our enemies are disqualified (as too moderate, too mild). Similarly, opinions may apply to speech acts of others. Doubts about the contents of the assertions of others may thus be expressed by discrediting them as mere 'claims' or 'submissions'.

Expression

The expression of opinions may be enhanced in several stylistic and rhetorical ways. Words describing negative acts may be taken from the repertoire of mental health, and opponents may be described as irrational, lunatic and megalomaniac. Another strategy is to compare a target enemy with another, certified enemy, e.g. Gadhafi with

Saddam Hussein, and Saddam Hussein with Hitler, and all of them with devils and demons. Negative characterizations are also enhanced by rhetorical contrasts: by opposing negative actions by Them with positive ones by Us (e.g. mild sanctions of the UN are met by sinister posturing and threats of terrorist warfare). Also alliterations (*fury and fear*), parallelisms and especially lexical repetition (*sinister*) may attract attention to specific opinions. Similarly, negative opinions about Them tend to be detailed, repeated and illustrated with concrete examples: thus the terrorism of Gadhafi, Jibril and Nidal is detailed by reference to the bombing of the Pan Am flight, the kidnapping of a Libyan dissident, and so on.

Unmentionables

Negative information and hence negative opinions about Us (i.e. self-critique) may be left completely unsaid in violent ideological confrontation. Not only is Gadhafi totally evil, but We (the USA, the West etc.) are totally good. We have done nothing to provoke Gadhafi. Thus, the equally terrorist bombing of Tripoli by the US air force, killing innocent children, is not even mentioned, although hinted at with a phrase like "destruction will visit him". Thus, our attacks on our enemies are always provoked and hence justified.

Arguments

Opinions usually need support. That is, they are preceded or followed by a sequence of assertions that make them more plausible by various rules of inference, based on attitudes and values. Similarly, possible negative opinions about us are forestalled by implicit counter-arguments against such opinions. Opinions in op-ed articles are usually formulated as evaluative support for a speech act of advice, recommendation or warning, which define the pragmatic point or conclusion of an opinion article.

Using history

Ideological opinions selectively invoke and hide history. Thus, terrorism is presented as a timeless evil. No historical background or explanation for Their violence against Us is given, no reference to the Middle East conflict made, not even a brief disclaimer about the plight of the Palestinians. On the other hand, it is necessary to show historical continuity, so that we learn from history: hence the reference to the Gulf War and Saddam Hussein. Similarly, from a more cultural angle, we need continuity in presenting Arabs as the enemy of the West by describing them in terms of ideological opinions that are part of a long tradition of Western superiority and Arab inferiority.

We have summarized the findings of our analysis in terms of a number of rather specific moves that are typical for the expression of underlying ideologies in opinion articles. These moves generally enact the major overall strategies of ideological discourse, namely those of positive self-presentation and negative other-presentation. At the same time, the discourse structures involved enable us to witness 'at the surface' some of the underlying trajectory that relates ideologies to discourse, such as the values involved in ideological statements, their polarization, their implementation in domain-related attitudes (in this case about international politics), their influence on specific models about specific events and participants (what Gadhafi did), and the ways these are presented as a function of a context model (of Hoagland writing in the *Washington Post*, especially for US citizens, and more specifically addressing US politicians and other elites, such as business people).

7   Suggestions for Ideological Analysis

There is no one, standard way to do critical discourse analysis, nor to do ideological analysis of editorials or other types of text or talk. However, from the discussion in this chapter, as well as from our other work, the following practical suggestions may be derived for doing ideological analysis: (a) examine the context of the discourse, (b) analyse which groups, power relations and conflicts are involved, (c) look for positive and negative opinions about Us and Them, (d) spell out the presupposed and the implied, and (e) examine all formal structures that (de)emphasize polarized group opinions.

Backgrounds

No serious ideological analysis is possible without at least some knowledge of the 'facts', about the historical, political or social background of a conflict, its main participants, the grounds of the conflict and preceding positions and arguments. Many ideological moves closely involve the self-serving use and abuse of the 'facts'.

Context

In order to understand the ideological position of the author (writer or speaker), describe the communicative context: group membership(s) of the author, the aims of the communicative event, the genre, the intended audience(s), the setting (time, location), the medium, and so on. Through the contextual occasioning or functions of the discourse, its ideological functions may be spelled out. For instance, an editorial may function as a critique and advice to specific (often elite) groups or institutions, and hence involves (power) relations between the media and media writers on the one hand, and these other groups, on the other. This context also defines the ideological dimension of the speech acts involved (e.g. warnings as a means of enacting power).

Ideological categories

Ideologies are the basic 'axioms' of socially shared representations of groups about themselves and their relations to other groups, including such categories as membership criteria, activities, goals, values, and crucial group resources. Look for expressions in the text that refer to these basic *categories* defining the *interests or identity* of the group the author belongs to.

Polarization

Many ideologies sustain and reproduce social conflict, domination and inequality. This conflict may involve any type of interest (typically symbolic or material resources) mentioned above, and is characteristically organized in a polarized way, that is, represented as Us vs. Them. This polarization is at the basis of much ideological discourse, that is, as the strategy of positive self-presentation and negative other-presentation. Since ideologies involve values, they typically surface as evaluative beliefs or opinions. Find all *opinions* in the text that enact such *polarized evaluation* of Us and Them. Little discourse analytical expertise is necessary to do such an ideological 'reading' of the text.

The implicit

Ideological opinions, however, are not always expressed in a very explicit way. That is, very often they are implied, presupposed, hidden, denied or taken for granted. Hence it is necessary to examine more systematically the *semantic structure* of the text for various forms of implication, indirectness or denial, as shown above. Indeed, seemingly non-evaluative, non-ideological descriptions of 'facts' may imply positive opinions about Us and negative opinions about Them. Also the ways the sentences of the discourse cohere (e.g. on the basis of causality) may be part of this implicit manifestation of ideology. Similarly, the overall coherence of the discourse in terms of topics or themes indicates what information (and what ideological opinions) are deemed more or less important, thus reflecting the structures of the underlying ideological mental models, attitudes and ideologies.

Formal structures

Indirectly, the various forms of a discourse may also be involved in the expression or signalling of ideological positions. The ideological square of polarization applies here too. Structural features may emphasize or de-emphasize information or opinions about Us and Them: sound structures in talk (e.g. intonation, stress, volume, 'tone', applause, laughs); graphical structures in printed text (headlines, columns, placing, letter type, photos etc.); the overall (schematic) organization of the discourse (e.g. argumentation); lexical choice and variation in the description of Us vs. Them; and the syntactic structure of clauses and sentences.

Chapter 3

The Discourse Structure of News Stories

Allan Bell

1 On Analysis

This chapter offers and exemplifies a framework for analysing the discourse structure of news. Why would one want to undertake such an enterprise? Why analyse news story structure? What is the pay-off for the labour-intensive analysis of the text of news stories?

Stories are central to human nature. The stories people tell are a core part of their social identity, and the construction of a life story is crucial to our self-identity. The idea of the story is also central to news media. Journalists do not write articles, they write stories – with structure, order, viewpoint and values. So the daily happenings of our societies are expressed in the stories we are told in the media.

In addition, the media are important social institutions. They are crucial presenters of culture, politics and social life, shaping as well as reflecting how these are formed and expressed. Media 'discourse' is important both for what it reveals about a society and because it also itself contributes to the character of society. Linguistic research on the media has always emphasized this last concern, focusing where issues of ideology and power are closest to the surface. But prerequisite to all such questions is a sound discourse analysis, and this is something that students of media – in their eagerness to get to the 'real meat' of ideological detective work – have sometimes skimmed over at their peril.

To the linguist, a first answer to a question about why undertake such a study is 'because it is there'. News is a major register of language. Understanding how it works is important to understanding the functioning of language in society. Such a study also enables us to compare news with other kinds of stories, such as the ones people tell in face-to-face conversation. And we can compare the discourse structure of news with other media genres such as editorials, and one type of news medium with another, for instance tabloid and broadsheet press, or newscasts on different television stations.

The text is central to news. News content is not independent of its expression, and we can only hope to have a clear understanding of the nature of news content by close analysis of the news text. A close, linguistically proficient analysis of the text needs to be the foundation for all attempts to unpack the ideologies underlying the news. Such an analysis shows that even simple-looking news stories are often rather complex, and the events they describe rather less distinct than we supposed. It also illuminates how stories are made. This is important for news audiences – to know something of how the news products they consume are manufactured. The very idea that the news is a 'product' may itself come as something of a surprise, and analysis can show something of the make-up of the product.

My approach to news discourse focuses on the question 'what does this story actually say happened?'. It begins by taking the news media's concentration on factuality on its own terms, together with the ordinariness of our acceptance, as readers, of such stories and what they tell us (cf. Scannell, this volume). It is not a question – at least initially – of whether these reports represent what 'really' happened. What we are *told* happened is important in the news just as it is in courts of law, which devote much of their time to scrutiny of accounts of events.

This analytical framework seeks chiefly to deduce an 'event structure' for a story – that is, to reconstruct, from the often fragmented information presented, what the story says actually happened. It thus concentrates on the basics of storytelling, which in the news are encapsulated by the journalist's 'five Ws and an H': who, what, when, where, why, how. Only after we are clear what the story says will we be in a position to see what it does not say. We will find, as shown below, that news stories are regularly not saying what we think they say on first reception. They are not telling a simple, clear tale, but are replete with ambiguity, unclarity, discrepancy and cavity.

Such close analysis is prerequisite to a more sophisticated approach to questions of ideology in news texts. It makes us aware of the complexity and ambiguity of news. It enables us to examine whether a headline fairly represents the story it accompanies. It shows who are the sources of information in the news – and which information has no explicit source at all. It leads us to consider why these particular events have been reported at all, and why they have been gathered together into a single published news story.

This chapter is organized thus: first I outline a framework for analysing the discourse structure of news, then exemplify it briefly through examining a number of single-sentence newspaper stories. I then present detailed guidelines for analysis of discourse structure, and proceed to close analysis of one news story. Lastly, I examine one of the most important and interesting aspects of news story structure – time – again with an example analysis of press stories.

2   The Framework

The approach to media discourse analysis used in this chapter was developed in Bell (1991). It draws on elements from general frameworks of story analysis, especially Labov's analysis of narratives of personal experience told in conversation (Labov and Waletzky, 1967; Labov, 1972), as well as from van Dijk's framework for analysing news discourse (1988b). The analysis of time in news stories derives from Bell (1995b, 1996). The frameworks used to analyse the structure of different kinds of stories have a lot of their elements in common (e.g. Labov, 1972; Rumelhart, 1975; van Dijk, 1988b). Labov's is one of the most familiar and contains six elements: abstract, orientation, action, evaluation, resolution and coda (see Bell, 1991 for application of this framework to news stories).

Figure 3.1 shows the elements needed to describe the discourse structure of news stories. A story normally consists of attribution, an abstract, and the story proper. Attribution of where the story came from is not always made explicit. It can include credit to a news agency and/or a journalist's byline, and may also state place and time ('dateline'). The abstract consists of the lead sentence or 'intro' of the news story and – for press news – also a headline. The lead covers the central event of the story, and possibly one or more secondary events. This necessarily entails giving in the lead itself some information on actors and setting involved in the event. The body of the story itself consists of one or more episodes, which in turn consist of one or more events. Events must describe actors and action, usually express setting of time and place, and may have explicit attribution to an information source. Episodes are clusters of events which share a common location or set of news actors (and need only be specified when a single story contains two or more clearly distinct sets of events).

As well as the above elements which present the central occurrences, there are three additional categories of material in a news story: background, commentary and follow-up. These represent the past, the (non-action) present, and the future of the events described in the main action of the story.

The category of *background* covers any events prior to the current action – story past time. These are frequently previous events which probably figured as news stories in their own right at an earlier stage of the situation. If the background goes back beyond the near past, it is classed as 'history'. Example 3 of the one-sentence stories below contains just such background.

Commentary provides the journalist's or news actor's present-time observations on the action, assessing and commenting on events as they happen (rather than the actual narration of the events themselves, or other parties' verbal reaction to them). It may provide context to assist understanding of what is happening, or evaluative comment on the action, or expectations of how the situation

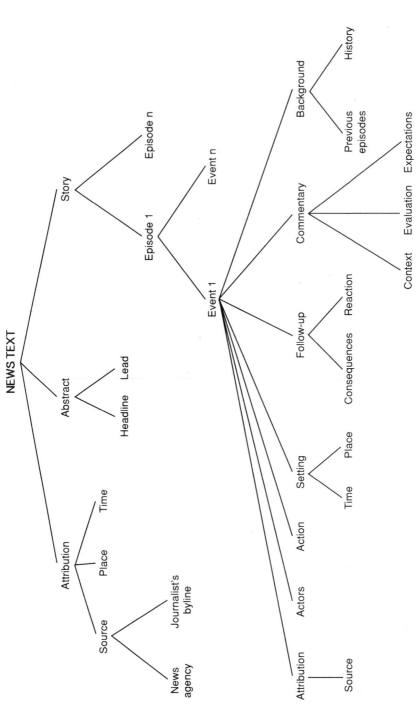

Figure 3.1 Model discourse structure for news texts (after Bell, 1991: 171)

will develop. The story in figure 3.4 analysed below contains both context (S9: S = Sentence) and evaluation (S1, S3).

Follow-up covers story future time – any action subsequent to the main action of an event. It can include verbal reaction by other parties or non-verbal consequences. Because it covers action which occurred after what a story has treated as the main action, follow-up is a prime source of subsequent updating stories – which are themselves called 'follow-ups' by journalists. The story in figure 3.6 below contains follow-up material in S2.

3 Analysing the Single-Sentence Story

This chapter deals with the structure of press news only, and a specific kind of press news: the 'hard' or 'spot' news which we recognize as the staple diet of daily media – stories of fires, wars, accidents, disasters, dangers and all manner of the mayhem that befalls human life. The minimal well-formed hard news story is just one sentence long. Many newspapers publish one-sentence stories, either to fill odd corners, or gathered in a column of news briefs. In a lot of broadcast news, many stories may consist only of a single sentence. The single-sentence story is also an appropriate proxy for examining the structure of longer stories in general. The news story is always focused in its first sentence – its lead or intro (Bell, 1991). We can see this most clearly when the story itself is reduced to just that sentence, but the lead is itself a microstory even when a full story follows. It compresses the 'news values' that have got this story through to publication.

The single-sentence story is therefore a good place to start as an introduction to analysis. Here are the texts of five one-sentence spot news stories published in British daily newspapers in February 1994. They are all from the international news agencies – Associated Press, Reuters and Agence France Presse – which act as models of Western journalistic style.

(1) **Clashes kill eight**
At least eight people have died in tribal fighting in the Bimbila region of northern Ghana. – AFP

(2) **Fumed out**
Tokyo: Two *sake* brewers were seriously ill after being over-come by fumes when one fell into a half-full vat and the other was trapped trying to rescue him. – Reuter

(3) **Deportation setback**
Storms over Iceland delayed the deportation from Norway yesterday of 12 American anti-abortion activists who had allegedly planned to stage demonstrations during the Winter Olympics and were detained by police when they arrived at Oslo's airport. – AP

(4) **Icicle horror**
A woman was fighting for life last night after a giant icicle fell 30 storeys from a New York skyscraper and speared her.

(5) **Awaiting the end**
Communist North Korea is building an underground mauso-leum and waterproof glass coffin to await the death of its "Great Leader", President Kim Il-sung, a South Korean press report said. – AFP

Example 1 covers a single event and can be diagrammed as in figure 3.2 (in this and subsequent figures, some nodes of the structure are omitted to simplify the tree diagrams). It has a headline – 'Clashes kill eight' – as have all these single-sentence stories, and an attribu-tion to the source agency, Agence France Presse. It consists of a single event, which specifies:

*   actors – 'at least eight people'
*   action – 'have died in tribal fighting'
*   setting, specifically place – 'in the Bimbila region of northern Ghana'.

The structure of this story is as minimal as it can be. Yet, of course, even here it is quite likely that we are not dealing with just a single action – the eight victims may well have perished in widely sepa-rated incidents.

Example 2 compresses a chain of five actions into one sentence:

1   first *sake* brewer falls into vat
2   second brewer goes to save him

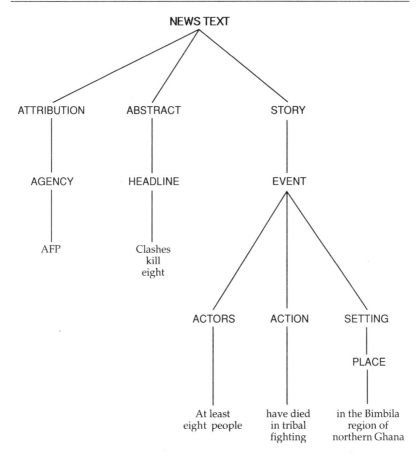

Figure 3.2 Discourse structure of the one-sentence story in example 1 (some nodes of the structure are omitted for simplification)

3 second brewer also gets trapped
4 both brewers overcome with fumes
5 both now seriously ill.

The most notable thing about example 2 is the order in which it tells these. My list above is in chronological order, that is the time sequence in which things actually happened, beginning at (1) and ending at (5). But the news typically begins with the most recent main happening (as also in examples 3 and 4). So the narrated order of the actions in story 2 is 5-4-1-3-2. It starts with the most recent happening, then the next most recent, then goes back to the first and causal action, then fills in the remaining steps (again in reverse chronological order). The story is thus told in a radically non-sequential fashion – an issue we will return to in detail later in the chapter.

Most of these single-sentence stories overtly narrate more than one event. In terms of the model story structure indicated in figure 3.1, their structure is therefore complex. Example 3 contains a sequence of four events, with a complex embedding of background involving multiple time points and locations. The four events are (in chronological order):

1   Anti-abortion activists had allegedly planned to stage demonstrations during the Winter Olympics
2   detained by police when they arrived at Oslo airport
3   had been scheduled for deportation from Norway yesterday
4   deportation delayed by storms over Iceland.

Three of these events have their own different place specification. Each has a different time specification: event 1 includes a future ('planned to stage demonstrations') which did not in fact happen, and event 3 is as yet a 'non-event' which has still not occurred – deportation. Figure 3.3 diagrams the discourse structure of this example (again with some of the potential nodes of the tree diagram omitted to reduce complication). It shows some of the complexity of action, place and time that can be covered by even a single-sentence story. Such a story offers a considerable challenge to the reader's comprehension, as I shall discuss further below, particularly because of its multiple embedding of disparate events, some of which have not in fact (yet) happened. There is also obviously a lot more to be told about what has happened 'behind the scenes' of this story, the factuality of which will doubtless be in dispute between the different parties. The story also has one notable gap that readers have to fill from their world knowledge – why storms over Iceland should delay a deportation from Norway. We are probably to understand that the storms delayed or diverted an incoming aircraft on which the activists were meant to leave.

Looking across these five example stories, we can see patterns in their discourse structures. Firstly, all of them specify main event,

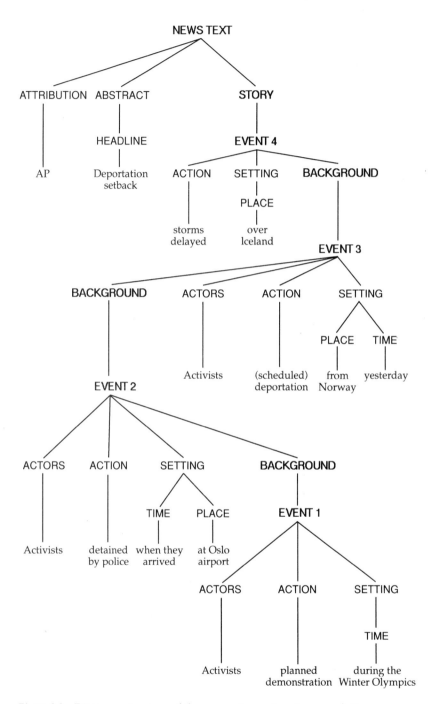

Figure 3.3 Discourse structure of the one-sentence story in example 3

news actors and place – the journalist's *what, who* and *where*. Example 1 contains only those elements. Time is expressed in most of them. News agency attribution is present in all except (4), and (5) also credits a local agency. But none attribute their information to any other source such as bystanders, spokespeople or officials. Secondly, these stories proclaim their news value. As single-sentence stories, they probably originated as the lead paragraphs of longer stories from the international agencies. Their role is therefore to concentrate the news value of the whole story. News values are those factors which take a story into the news. They include attributes such as negativity, immediacy (or recency), proximity, lack of ambiguity, novelty, personalization and eliteness of the news actors (Bell, 1991). A story's news value focuses in the lexicon of newsworthiness in its lead sentence. In (4), for instance, almost every word makes a claim to news value: 'fighting for life', 'giant icicle', 'fell 30 storeys', 'New York skyscraper', 'speared'. Most of the stories contain death, violence, or the imminent threat of these. The facticity of the stories is stressed through the detail of person, place and time already mentioned, and through the use of figures.

Thirdly, all but one story (3) begin with *who* – the main news actor. The stress on personalization and elite news actors guides the order of constituents within the sentence, even if this will result in a passive-voice verb. News-writing mythology holds that verbs should be active, but passivization is quite common as the only means of getting the main news actors to the start of the sentence. We thus have a *grammar* of news value as well as a lexicon. Syntactic rules such as passivization are applied to serve the values of news discourse, as is linkage through temporal conjunctions such as *after* and *as* (2, 4). In most cases one event is the sequel to or result of another, as also in examples 3 and 4.

Fourthly, time is sometimes expressed directly in these stories as 'yesterday' or 'last night'. But often there is no direct reference to current calendar time. We interpret these stories as 'reported within the past day'. But this immediacy criterion may not always be the case, and some of these stories could well be days-old news (e.g. 1, 2) and we readers would be none the wiser.

Fifth, since these are all international agency stories, they often carry explicit place of origin in the dateline (2). Otherwise place is sometimes expressed in the canonical form of a prepositional phrase, such as 'in the Bimbila region of northern Ghana' (1).

Lastly, information content, brevity and clarity can be seen tussling with each other. Sometimes, as in (3), clarity is the loser and the result is a sentence or a story in which the degree of layering and the dispersion of the events reported jeopardizes comprehension. This accords with van Dijk's finding (1988b: 77) that lead sentences in news stories can often be syntactically and informationally complex.

4   What Does the Story Actually Say?

I now turn to consider in more depth one longer news story, subjecting it to close analysis of its discourse structure. The Guide to analysis below presents a step-by-step procedure for establishing what a story says happened – that is, the *event structure* of the story. The fruit of analysing the discourse structure of stories in this way is an understanding of what the story says actually happened. At least at this stage, I am concerned only with what the story says, not with whether or how closely that corresponds to 'the facts' of what happened.

The event analysis takes into account not just the overt specifying of events themselves, but what the story says about news actors, locations and times of occurrence in order to tease out the structure of the story. Moving through each of these aspects, we will commonly have to modify our conception of what happened as further specification of persons, time or place makes it clear that our earlier models were inadequate.

Figure 3.4 contains the text of a very routine news story from the (UK) *Daily Mirror*. I chose such a story because it is common rather than exceptional. The first group of analyses seek to uncover what the story is telling us actually happened – what events occurred, where they occurred and when, and who was involved (that is, four of the journalistic five Ws and the H, with the exception of 'why' and 'how': cf. Manoff and Schudson, 1987). This analysis yields structures for these four aspects: events, times, places and news

Guide

How to analyse and interpret the discourse structure of a news story. First number the sentences of the story. The first steps listed under each numbered point below (in roman type) are basic analytical moves. The later steps under each point – indented and in italics – are the more interpretive procedures.

What

1 **Headline**
   What events take place in the headline? Summarize and number each event.

2 **Lead**
   What events take place in the lead or intro? Summarize and number.

3 **Events**
   What events take place in the story? Summarize and number, then enter numbers alongside each sentence of the story (as in figure 3.6).
   Re-categorize events in headline and lead as necessary to correspond with the fuller picture you now have from the story as a whole.
   What is the central event of the whole story? (Usually the main 'hard' news event in the lead.)

4 **Headline, lead and story**
   What is the relationship of the headline to the lead?
      What events in the lead are included/excluded in the headline?
      What news values lie behind these inclusions and exclusions?
      Is the headline a valid representation of the lead?
   What is the relationship of the lead to the story as a whole?
      What events in the story are included/excluded in the lead?
      What news values lie behind these inclusions and exclusions?
      Is the lead a valid representation of the whole story?

Is there any information that is given in the lead but not returned to in the rest of the story?

How does the lead begin telling the story as well as act as an abstract for it?

Who

5 **Story attribution**

Is the story as a whole attributed? To whom (agency, journalist)?

6 **Sources attribution**

Is there any attribution within the story? Who is attributed? (list)

Beside each sentence, note down whom it is attributed to (if anyone).

Precisely what is attributed and to whom?

What speech verb is used in the attributions? (list)

What claims do the attributed sources have to authority?

Who is quoted directly? Indirectly?

Why have the particular speech verbs been used?

What parts of the story are not attributed? Why?

Where is attribution unclear or ambiguous? Does this have any repercussions?

7 **News actors**

What news actors are mentioned? (list: people, organizations, nations, etc.)

How are they labelled or referred to? (list)

What kinds of people or entities are mentioned in the story?

Why are they in the news? Are the news actors elite?

Is the news story personalized?

Are there patterns in the way the story refers to them or labels them?

Does specifying who the news actors are modify the event structure you developed earlier?

Where

8 **Places**
What place expressions are used? (list)
Where do they occur in the story? (sentence number)

9 **Place structure**
What locations does the story take place in? (list)
Does the story stay in one location or move from place to place and back? Why?
Is it clear what is happening in which location?
What sort of places are the events happening in? Is there a pattern to this?
Does specifying locations in this way modify the event structure you developed earlier?

When

10 **Times**
What time expressions are used in the story? (list)
Where do they occur in the story? (sentence number)

11 **Time structure**
What is the time structure of the story? Take the time of the central event as Time 0. Label earlier events as Time -1, -2 etc., and later events as Time $+1$, $+2$ etc. in the chronological sequence in which they actually occurred.
Beside each sentence, note down the number of the time or times at which the actions mentioned there occurred.
How does the order in which the story is told relate to the chronological order of events?
Why has the story been written in this order? What values lie behind the order?
Does the order help or hinder a reader in understanding what is going on in the story?
Does specifying times of occurrence in this way modify the event structure developed earlier?

12 Background
Is any background given (events prior to the central action – either recent previous events or more historical events)?
Does any of the background indicate any particular ideological frame behind the story?

13 Commentary
Is there any commentary on events? – evaluation of events (editorializing)? Context for what has happened? Expectations of how the situation will develop?
Does any of the commentary (especially evaluation) indicate any particular ideology behind the story?

14 Follow-up
Is there any follow-up to the central action of each event (subsequent events, either reaction (verbal) or consequences (non-verbal))?
Does any of the follow-up indicate any particular ideology behind the story?

Event and Discourse Structure

15 Event structure
Collate your successive re-categorizations of what happened in the story, drawing on news actors, place and time as well as the actions themselves.
List in chronological order the events and their associated actors, times and places and the sentence numbers in which they occur (as in table 3.1 example). This represents the event structure as you finally assess it to be.
Note any alternatives, which represent discrepancies or unclarities in the story itself.
Is the story told in instalments? That is, do the events follow one after another or are they interspersed with each other?

16 Discourse structure
At this stage you can draw a tree diagram of the discourse structure (e.g. figures 3.2, 3.3, 3.5). Note that the apparent

order which these example figures display is only arrived at after a succession of rough drafts! Such a structure is also idealized in the sense that it masks ambiguities and unclarities.

17 **Cohesion**
What linkages are expressed or implied between the sentences or events in the story? How? (list)
What linkages are omitted? (list)
What do the linkages (or their absence) between sentences or events mean for understanding the story?
Is a cause-and-effect relationship between different events implied by the way they are ordered?
Does the story flow smoothly, or does it jump about? Why?

18 **Confusion**
Has it now been possible to say precisely what happened in the story?
Or are there still ambiguities, gaps or confusions, as exemplified in the possibility of alternative event or discourse structures? (list, explain)

actors. In theory, these four should all mesh into a unified picture of what the story says happened. In practice, they often do not quite fit together, and it is precisely these differences which may cast the most interesting light on the story. The category labels I use below are from Bell (1991), reproduced earlier as figure 3.1, the model tree diagram of news story structure. Working through this example, I follow the sequence of steps indicated in the Guide, although not all the points listed there are useful for analysing this – or any individual – story. There is a logic to the order in which I have listed the steps, but not all steps are necessarily going to contribute equally to an understanding of every story. Neither are they necessarily always best followed in this particular order or independently of each other – it may often make sense to carry out some later steps before those I have listed here as earlier.

EVENT STRUCTURE			TIME STRUCTURE
3	HL	**2 held as IRA blitz is foiled**	+2
1			0
1 (2?)	S1	POLICE and MI5 agents have swooped in an undercover operation which netted bomb-making equipment – and may have foiled a major IRA blitz on the British mainland.	0 (+1?)
1 (2?)	S2	They recovered enough Semtex explosive to devastate a large office block.	0 (+1?)
1? (2?)	S3	And security services believe they have intercepted a highly-placed IRA quartermaster who supplies equipment to terror cells.	0? (+1?)
3	S4	Last night two men were being held in London under the Prevention of Terrorism Act.	+2

Pistol

1	S5	One, in his 30s, was arrested at Accrington, Lancs, with between 10 lb and 15 lb of high explosives, bomb-making equipment, a pistol and ammunition in his car.	0
1	S6	Plain-clothes police wearing flak jackets and carrying semi-automatic weapons seized the suspect in a car park next to Charlie Brown's Auto Centre.	0
2	S7	Within two hours another man, in his 50s, was held at Wembley in North London.	+1
1	S8	A terraced house in Accrington was under police guard last night.	+2
3	S9	The suspects can be held for up to seven days before being charged or released.	+3

Figure 3.4 Example story with Event and Time Structures (*Daily Mirror*, London, 23 February 1994; reproduced by permission of Mirror Group Newspapers)

1 Headline

The headline appears to narrate two events – (1) the holding of two suspects, and (2) the foiling of an IRA blitz. The two events are clearly closely linked, or may even in effect be the same action – the blitz may have been foiled precisely through the capture of the two people. The journalistic 'as' of the headline would thus not be an accident; it would specify precisely the temporal and causal relationship between the two events. Alternatively, there may have been action which foiled the blitz, and then led to the capture of two suspects. We cannot tell from the headline alone. We must read on.

2 Lead

The lead appears to tell of one event: a security service 'swoop' which discovered bomb-making equipment. This action is clearly related to, but not quite identical with, the two events in the headline. The 'foiled' statement in the headline is now shown to be an evaluation of the significance of the raid rather than a separate action of any kind. We thus find that the lead sentence clarifies the ambiguity of the headline, but it of course remains possible that the operation consisted of raids on more than just one location.

3 Events

We can now move to tease out the event structure of the story as a whole. The lead and the following three sentences (i.e. S1–4) invite the interpretation that there has been a single raid. But the second half of the story tells of two suspects being arrested in widely separated locations. It takes until S7 to become clear that we are dealing with quite separate events, and it remains unclear whether they were in some sense part of a single security operation, or whether they coincided by chance. The central action of both events is clearly the respective raids (assuming that Wembley involved a raid – we are told only that the man was 'held', in a strangely active use of a stative verb, akin to 'arrested'). To this point, it seems we can describe the story as being about a total of three events, assuming we treat the continuing detention of the two suspects as a separate event:

1   Accrington arrest
2   Wembley arrest
3   detention of two suspects.

The Accrington arrest seems to be the central event of the story and most of the story apparently concentrates on it (see figure 3.4 for Event Structure).

4   Headline, lead and story

We have already seen that the content of the lead in this story disambiguates the headline. But a closer look at the headline shows that the '2 held' statement with which it begins does not derive from the lead at all but rather from S4. This is an infrequent pattern, since a majority of headlines are derived solely from lead sentences and not from information further down a story (Bell, 1991).

There is also a contrast in the modality of the verbs used in the headline and the lead. The lead hedges its evaluation as 'may have foiled', but the headline presents this as unvarnished fact – 'is'. The central event of the lead, the raid, is represented in the headline *only* by the gloss of 'foiled' – that is, the tentative evaluation expressed in the lead has become the unhedged description of action in the headline. This is a classic news 'over-assertion' of a kind I found commonly in a study of editing changes made to news copy (Bell, 1983, 1984). The original lead sentence would have been written by a journalist, and the headline by a copy-editor. The shift is driven by the attempt to make a story as definite as possible ('unambiguity' is one of the classic news values: Galtung and Ruge, 1965; Bell, 1991). So it appears that the headline is not a valid representation of the story as a whole to the extent that through omitting the modal verb, the headline overstates the certainty of the evaluation contained in the lead. Modality is probably rarely expressed in headlines.

Further, we are not told whose opinion it is that a major IRA blitz may have been foiled. There is no sourcing of the evaluation. It is not mentioned again in the body of the story. We are probably to assume the source is the 'security services' quoted in S3, but it may in fact be the product of the journalist who wrote the story. A more likely possibility is that this statement is a gloss inserted by the copy-editor in order to raise the news value of the story – to 'beat it up'. Evidence for this is the fact that it appears in S1 after a dash – an avoided piece of punctuation that betrays late and hasty addition of the second half of S1.

5   Story attribution

This story attributes no journalist as author nor agency as provider. We must assume it is written by a staff reporter who was not 'bylined'.

6   Sources attribution

More importantly, the story does not directly specify the source of its information. The nearest we get to sourcing is in S3 where we are told what 'security services believe' in relation to the results of their actions. We can presume they were also the source of some of the information about the event itself, as well as possibly of the evaluation in S1. The use of 'believe' rather than 'say' in S3 is probably significant, indicating either that the security services were not prepared to provide information 'on the record' for the media, or that this was a chance comment that the journalist has built into more than the source would have wanted. We can note that the S9 background about detention powers probably comes from the journalist's own knowledge rather than any source.

7   News actors

The news actors specified in the story are:

security services (S3)
   police (S1, S6, S8)
   MI5 agents (S1)

two IRA suspects (S4)
   one arrested in Accrington (S5)
   second arrested in Wembley (S7).

There is also another reference to an IRA member – 'a highly-placed IRA quartermaster' (S3). The way the reference is phrased in S3 implies that this character is not the same as the person/s involved in the events of S1–2. Use of co-ordinator 'and' to introduce the sentence, plus indefinite article 'a . . . quartermaster', implies a different person. If it was the same person we would rather expect a phrasing like 'security services believe the suspect is a highly-placed IRA quartermaster . . .'.

On the other hand, given the detail of weaponry listed with the Accrington suspect in S5, S3 seems more likely to also refer to him. But since that would entail S1–2 referring to the Wembley suspect, this interpretation is not entirely satisfactory either. The remaining possibility is that this refers to a third person not otherwise mentioned, but that seems least likely of all.

Notice how we are gaining more information as our analysis moves into the story, and that new information modifies our understanding of earlier information. But it does not always *clarify* that understanding, and at this point we have to say that the identity of the quartermaster is unclear. Such questions of reference identity are not uncommon in news. In studies of editing practice (Bell, 1984), I have found cases where editors were obviously unable to decode whether expressions in different sentences were meant to refer to the same or different places or people. Their attempts to clarify reference sometimes took the wrong interpretation, and converted a second reference to a city already mentioned in a story into a first reference to another city.

8   Places

The story uses expressions of place in the following:

blitz on the British mainland (S1)
held in London (S4)
arrested at Accrington, Lancs (S5)
with . . . ammunition in his car (S5)

seized the suspect in a car park next to Charlie Brown's Auto Centre
(S6)
held at Wembley in North London (S7)
a terraced house in Accrington (S8).

What is not said is more striking than what is said: there is no
specification of where the raids and arrests took place until S5 and
below. This contributes to our unclarity about what has taken place.
We may also wonder why the story details 'Charlie Brown's
Auto Centre', since this is unlikely to be known to anyone beyond
the immediate Accrington area. For locals, however, the description
might signify that the raid was in a central, busy area of the town,
for example. This may be a clue that the origin of this part of the
story was in a local Accrington reporter's account which has not
been appropriately edited for national readership. In contrast,
Wembley – which no Briton needs an introduction to – is glossed as
being in North London, presumably for international readership. So
within two sentences we have conflicting indications of the presumed readership, local versus international, through the kind of
shared knowledge that is and is not presupposed.

9 *Place structure*

It seems then that the story has (at least) three locations – raids in
Accrington, Lancashire, and in Wembley, North London, plus the
site or sites in London where the two suspects are being held pris-
oner. So we can confirm our specification of probably three events
in the story. If we had more detail, we might wish to regard other
actions – such as the guarding of a terraced house in Accrington (S8)
– as further separate events, since it seems likely that the house was
not located at the car park which was the scene of the Accrington
suspect's arrest.

What is most striking, however, is that the further we get into the
analysis, the less clear it becomes exactly what we are being told
happened. What on the surface appeared a simple little story turns
out to be rather complicated and opaque. In particular, it is by no
means obvious which of the two sets of news actors, locations and
actions detailed in S5–7 are actually being referred to in S1–3,

because those first three sentences contain no unambiguous references to persons, and no reference to place at all. For instance, we cannot be sure which place the Semtex explosive was found in (S2), or which (if either) suspect is the quartermaster of S3.

10   Times

The specification of time is often surprisingly sparse in a news story (aside from tense and aspect marking on verbs). It is frequently left to the inference that 'this must be recent because it is news'. The time expressions in this story are:

last night (S4)
within two hours (S7)
last night (S8)
for up to seven days (S9).

No time is expressed until the fourth sentence of the story, with the presumption of recency governing our reading up to that point. There is no specification of the time of day when the two arrests were made, although we know there was no more than two hours between them. We presume the arrests took place during the day before the story was published – certainly before 'last night'. But in fact it is possible that the news is older than this, dating from the night before last or even earlier. It is not uncommon for stories to remain silent on the time of their events. Occasionally it becomes obvious that the presumption of recency is wrong – and sometimes this silence on timing appears to serve the misleading implication of immediacy.

11   Time structure

Closely related to teasing out the event structure of a story is specifying its time structure: what happened in what order, what is the story's chronology? The time structure of this story is rather straightforward except for the lack of clarity over absolute timing, and what actions are part of what event.

Time structure is shown on the right of figure 3.4. We take the time of the main news action as T0 – the operation described in S1, which I will assume to refer to the Accrington raid (though it may cover both). Thus S1, 2, 5 and 6 all describe aspects of the raid. I will interpret S3 as also referring to Accrington. All these are therefore T0 events. S7 occurs at the time of the Wembley raid 'within two hours', therefore at T + 1: the next time point after T0. S4 and 8 both refer to 'last night', subsequent to both arrests, that is T + 2. S9 can be considered subsequent again, therefore T + 3.

This is a comparatively simple time structure, as even a short news story can easily involve ten or more actions in non-chronological order, as we will see in a later example. This story is also unusual in not leading with the most recent event, perhaps because of the staticness of 'held' that I noted earlier. But we can also note that the headline *does* in fact major on the most recent event – the detention of the two suspects. There has thus been a difference of opinion over what constitutes the central news event in this story. The journalist who wrote the story, including the original lead, thought it was the raid. The copy-editor who edited it and wrote the headline thought it was the detention of two suspects. Such disagreements are a common locus of newsroom anguish.

Because time is such an important element in news stories and merits more discussion and illustration, I will return to it below with examples where it plays a more important role.

12   Background

The category of background (cf. figure 3.3) covers events prior to the central action of the story, and may include either recent past events or more remote history. This story contains no background.

13   Commentary

Commentary concerns context, evaluation or expectations for events that are happening. In this story we have already noted the evaluative comments concerning foiling an IRA blitz (S1, headline), and the assessment of the significance of the security services' discoveries (S3). In addition, there is context given about the Prevention of Terrorism Act (S4), which spells out (S9) the provisions under which the suspects can continue to be detained.

14 Follow-up

If we take the raids to be the central event of the story, then the detention of the two suspects counts as follow-up to that event. Follow-ups commonly become the lead in subsequent stories, and we have noted already that the headline (written later than the story, of course) tends in this direction.

15 Event structure

We have noted the ambiguity and lack of clarity in the *who* and the *where* of this story. The left side of figure 3.4 shows the event structure as best I can judge it. Usually it is *time* that is the problematic factor in understanding what happened in a story. In this case it is the place structure which is the more confusing, and to a lesser extent the identity of the news actors, because it is by no means clear which place is referred to in different parts of the description – Accrington or Wembley. Table 3.1 schematizes this event structure, linking action, actors, place and time for each event.

Table 3.1 Event structure of IRA story (figure 3.4)

Event	Sentence	Actors	Place	Time
1 Raid, arrest, seizure	Headline S1, 2, 3, 5, 6, 8	Security services, IRA	Accrington	0 +2
2 Arrest	S7 (S1? 2? 3?)	Security services, IRA	Wembley	+1 Within 2 hours
3 Detention ('held')	Headline S4, 9	2 IRA members	London	+2, +3 Last night

16   Discourse structure

Figure 3.5 diagrams the discourse structure of the story in accordance with the interpretation I have offered, again omitting some of the detail so that an already complex diagram does not get more complicated still. The neatness of the eventual tree should not disguise the fact that it presupposes a series of (albeit increasingly refined) rough drafts. Event 3 is placed as a follow-up to both events 1 and 2. The constituents of each event are the straightforward ones of actors, action and setting, plus commentaries and follow-ups.

If we take other interpretations of the ambiguous information in the story, it will mean shifting some constituents to other points of the diagram. So, if we understand the 'blitz foiled' comment as applying to both the Accrington and Wembley raids, we will attach that Evaluation to both events 1 and 2 (or possibly to the Story as a whole). If we decide the quartermaster was the Wembley suspect rather than the Accrington one, we will re-attach that Evaluation to event 2.

17   Cohesion

News stories are standardly written as a series of one-sentence paragraphs, and commonly express little linkage between the sentences. With each news sentence usually also its own paragraph, there is no larger unit of text organization. There is routinely no flow of time sequence from one sentence to the next, and a lack of devices such as adverbs expressing linkages between sentences. It is common for cohesion between sentences to be unclear or non-existent, and we may be genuinely doubtful what actions within the story belong together, at what point location actually shifted, or what material is attributed to whom.

It is the lack of such signposting, together with the mix of locations, that contributes to the ambiguities of this story. In the absence of any indications to the contrary, we would normally take S1–3 to be describing a single set of happenings, although there are no explicit linkages to mark this. Things become clearer after S4 where links are expressed: 'one' at the start of S5 links the news actor back into S4, and 'the suspect' in S6 continues the thread of reference. The signposting in S7 equally clearly indicates that this is a different event – 'another man' in another place at another time. However, the jump back to Accrington again in S8 is rather disconcerting to a reader.

18 Confusion

I have noted a number of points where it is unclear, ambiguous or confused what actually happened in this story, to whom, and where. To list these as questions (such as a journalist doing a follow-up story might ask a source):

Were the two arrests part of a single operation or coincidental? (S1)
Which arrest did security forces consider represented a 'foiled IRA blitz'? (S1)
Was Semtex recovered at Wembley as well as Accrington? (S2)
Was the Accrington or the Wembley suspect the quartermaster? (S3)

The grounds for confusion in this story are possible because of the lack of cohesion and specific reference across the story. This is commonly a source of problems for accuracy of both reporting and understanding. In a study of reporting of climate change (Bell, 1994), I found that the practice of not expressing cohesive links between sentences of a story enabled one journalist to refer alternately to the greenhouse effect and ozone depletion between successive sentences of a story in a way that seriously confused these two basically distinct atmospheric phenomena.

The packaging of the two raids in one story implies that they and the suspects were closely linked. However, we are told so little about the Wembley arrest that we cannot be sure of this. In fact, when we examine the role of the security services as news actors in the story, 'police' are twice specified in relation to Accrington (S6, S8), but MI5 are mentioned only generally in the lead sentence. It seems possible that Accrington involved only the police, Wembley involved only MI5, and the timing was coincidence rather than a single operation. This unclarity of reference in fact serves to enhance news value through co-option of a minor story into a bigger

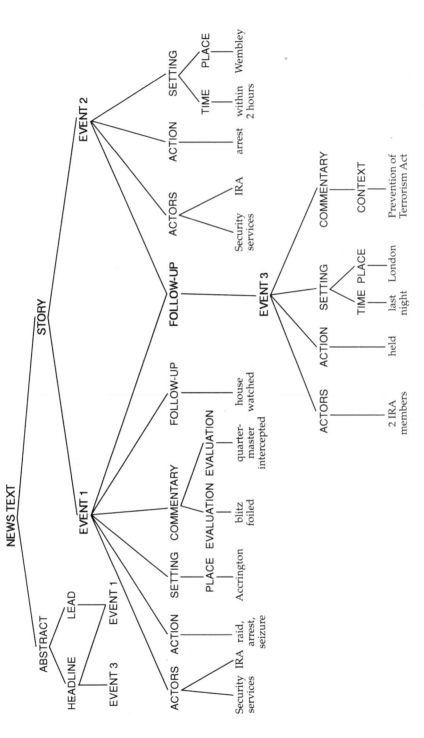

Figure 3.5 Discourse structure of IRA story in figure 3.4

story (Bell, 1991). One reading of the story is that most of the serious action is linked to Accrington, and very little to Wembley. The ambiguity of reference therefore enables the Wembley event to be co-opted to the Accrington raid, building it into more than it would be just on its own – when it might not have been reported at all.

The detailed analysis I have run through in this section has shown us a good deal about the character of this story – indications of how it was made, evidence of inconsistencies and gaps, and manifestations of the news values behind it. We can see the claims it makes to be newsworthy mainly in the negativity of its content – in the presence of conflict, discoveries of weapons and explosives, use of force – together with involvement of elite news actors (the security services), co-option of possibly separate stories to reinforce each other, reduction of ambiguity over the significance of the arrests, and possibly enhanced immediacy.

The journalist's own ultimate abstract of a story is the one-word 'slugline' by which each story is identified in the news processing system – now in practice also presumably the filename under which the story is saved in the computer. The slugline is often a good guide to news value, and it is instructive to speculate what slugline a particular story might have carried. The likely candidates on this example story seem to me to be: 'swoop', 'blitz' or 'foiled'.

5   News Time

Time, as we have seen in the analyses so far, is an important dimension of news stories and merits more discussion in its own right. Time is expressed in stories at different levels of language – in the morphology and syntax of the verb phrase, in time adverbials whether lexical or phrasal, and in the discourse structure of stories above the sentence. One characteristic of all kinds of stories appears to be so shared across genres and cultures that it has been called 'canonical' – events tend to be told in the chronological order in which they occurred.

Time in story has interested widely different groups of scholars (Toolan, 1988) – literary theorists, and cognitive psychologists researching discourse comprehension, as well as text and discourse linguists. Literary theory tends to treat chronological order as the unmarked or basic form underlying fictional narrative, and identifies the time structure of a novel as interesting just where it departs from chronology. Genette's general theory of narrative discourse (1980) developed in relation to Proust's *À la recherche du temps perdu* is primarily devoted to time. Time order is his dominant category, analysed in terms of 'anachronies' – departures from chronological sequence. Cognitive psychologists make the distinction between *event structure* and *discourse structure* (Brewer, 1985) – between the order in which events actually happened and the order in which they are told in a story (my own framework above allows for an event structure in discourse which is non-chronological). There is only one real-world event structure but many possible discourse structures. The chronological is apparently the 'natural' order because it matches its discourse structure to the event structure.

Fairy stories are typical – even archetypal – of the canonical time ordering of stories. So, in 'The Three Little Pigs':

> The first little pig meets a man carrying straw, buys the straw, and builds a house out of it. The big bad wolf comes, huffs, puffs, blows the house of straw down and eats up the pig.

> The second little pig meets a man carrying sticks, buys the sticks, builds a house, and ends up getting eaten too by the wolf.

> The third little pig meets a man carrying bricks, . . . etc.

> But the wolf fails to blow the brick house down, the pig puts a pot on the fire to boil, the wolf climbs down the chimney to get at the pig, but instead gets boiled for dinner.

> End of story.

Analysis of a story's time structure

News is by nature time-bound – it is a perishable commodity. Time is a defining characteristic of the nature of news, a major compulsion in news-gathering procedures, and an influence on the structure of news discourse. Figure 3.6 shows the text of a typical agency story, as published in Wellington's *Evening Post* newspaper. The time structure of the story's events is listed down the right-hand

TIME
STRUCTURE

Protest cut short

S1   Lima, Jan 18. – The estranged wife of Peru's   0
President Alberto Fujimori was taken to
hospital today just 24 hours after she began   −2
a hunger strike to protest at her party's
elimination from congressional elections.   −3

S2   Doctors said she was suffering from tachycardia,   +1
or an accelerated heartbeat.

S3   Earlier, [deposed first lady Susanna] Higuchi,   −1
sitting under an umbrella in a scorching
summer sun outside the National Electoral
Board's headquarters, had pledged to press
on with her protest.

S4   The electoral board said on Monday Higuchi's   −3
Armonia-Frempol party had not qualified
for the April Congressional vote because   +2
it failed to present a full list of candidates   −4
for the 120-member legislature.

S5   Board member Manuel Catacora said today   0
that since Higuchi had presented her party's   −4
congressional slate just 10 minutes before the
filing deadline, a provision allowing parties
five days to correct any error did not apply.   0

S6   Higuchi, a 44-year-old civil engineer, has been   −5
estranged from Fujimori since August when   −6
she protested an election law that banned her from
running from [*sic*] public office. – Reuter

Figure 3.6   International news agency story as published in the *Evening Post*,
Wellington, 20 January 1995 (reproduced by permission of Reuters)

side. Time zero is the story present, the time of the lead event in the
lead sentence. Times prior to this are labelled Time −1 for the event
immediately preceding, moving back up to Time −6 in this story,
the earliest occurrence in the reported background. The story also
reports on events subsequent to Time 0, labelled Time +1 (the

diagnosis), and so on. Here I report only briefly for illustrative purposes on a more detailed analysis drawn from Bell (1995b). The lead sentence covers three temporally and causally sequential events, but in reverse chronological order. The result (Higuchi's departure to hospital) precedes cause (hunger strike), which itself precedes prior cause (disqualification from elections). They are linked by temporal expressions, usually *after* for a sequence as in examples 2 and 4 of the single-sentence stories analysed earlier, or *as* for simultaneous events (as in the headline in figure 3.4). The temporal expressions commonly imply a causal link, even though this may not always seem warranted.

In figure 3.6, Time Zero is explicitly identified in the lead sentence – 'today' – with other earlier or later time points signposted in the later sentences. Some of the time references situate events in calendar time (*since August* in S6), others in relation to each other (*just 24 hours after . . .* in S1, *earlier* in S3), still others are deictic with the present as reference point.

Labov found that a defining characteristic of personal narrative as a form is the temporal sequence of its 'clauses'. That is, the action is invariably told in the order in which it happened, what I have labelled canonical order – 'matching a verbal sequence of clauses to the sequence of events' (Labov, 1972: 360). News stories, by contrast, are seldom if ever told in chronological order. The time structure of the story in figure 3.6 is very complex, with nine points in time identified in the analysis. The story as a whole divides into three sections: S1–2, S3–5, S6. The lead sentence alone covers three events and times, as we have seen. Each of the three sections represents a cycle through events taking us further back in time, presenting in reverse order of actual occurrence (plus a couple of excursions into story future time) the chain of events which have culminated in the lead event of this story. The earliest events are reported last of all, with the final sentence describing events from some six months previously which are the antecedents to the present occurrences.

In the body of the story, perceived *news value* overturns temporal sequence and imposes an order completely at odds with linear narrative. It moves backwards and forwards in time, picking out different points on each cycle or giving more detail on previously mentioned matters (S4 and S5). This violation of our expectations that narratives usually proceed in temporal succession is a distinctive feature of news stories – the inverted pyramid structure. Van Dijk has called this the instalment method (1988b: 43), by which an event is introduced then returned to in more detail two or more times. The radical discontinuity of time between sentences imparts a general lack of syntactic, semantic and discourse cohesion within the news story, as we have seen in the figure 3.4 IRA story. The reverse-chronological structure has a direct pay-off (and in part doubtless an origin) in journalistic practices – stories are routinely cut from the bottom up to fit into available space. The important information must therefore come as early as possible, and the story should be capable of ending at any sentence. So, in the IRA story, at least the last two sentences could be cut without affecting the earlier part of the story (for more discussion of this question, see Bell, 1991).

Earlier forms of news telling

As news consumers we are so accustomed to this approach that we forget how deviant it is compared both with other narrative genres and with earlier norms of news reporting. Figure 3.7 shows a story from the *New Zealand Herald* of 11 June 1886. It reports the eruption of Mount Tarawera, a volcano located some 200 km to the south-east of Auckland, where the *Herald* is published. The eruption caused significant loss of life and reshaped an extensive area of the New Zealand landscape.

It is a typical disaster story which would run in any modern newspaper, but here it is narrated in absolute chronological order. Events are told from the viewpoint of the readers in Auckland – first hearing the sounds of the distant eruption and speculating on their cause, then eventually receiving the news of the real cause. Where the historical story begins at the beginning, the modern lead sentence would run something like this:

'Mount Tarawera erupted last night killing at least 30 people and sending hundreds more fleeing . . .'

Research on the development of modern news narrative style indicates that the inverted pyramid structure developed in

AT an early hour on Thursday morning a noise as of the
firing of cannon was heard by many Auckland residents.

From the continuousness of the firing, the loudness of the
reports, and the apparent occasional sound resembling
salvoes of artillery, many people both here and at Onehunga
were under the impression that a man-of-war, probably the
Russian Vestnik, had run ashore on the Manukau bar and
that these were her signals of distress.

Vivid flashes, as from the firing of guns, were also seen
both at Onehunga and also from the cupola of the Herald
Office, which served to almost confirm the impression that
there had been a marine disaster. At about 8.30 a.m.,
however, it began to be circulated about town that a
catastrophe, far surpassing in horror even the most terrible
of shipwrecks, had taken place.

The first news was, through the courtesy of Mr Furby, the
officer in charge of the telegraph department, issued by us
in an extra and consisted of the following message, sent
from Rotorua, by Mr Dansey, the telegraphist there, who
manfully and bravely "stuck to his instrument" in the face
of the most dreadful danger:

"We have all passed a fearful night here. At 2.10 a.m.
there was a heavy quake, then a fearful roar, which made
everyone run out of their houses, and a grand, yet terrible,
sight for those so near as we were, presented itself. Mount
Tarawera suddenly became active, the volcano belching out
fire and lava to a great height. A dense mass of ashes came
pouring down here at 4 a.m., accompanied by a suffocating
smell from the lower regions.

"Several families left their homes in their nightdresses
with whatever they could seize in the hurry, and made for
Tauranga. Others more lucky, got horses and left for
Oxford."

Figure 3.7 News as chronological story: *New Zealand Herald*, 11 June 1886

American journalism at the end of the nineteenth century. Schudson
(1982, 1989) found that until the 1880s, stories covering presidential
State of the Union addresses did not summarize the ,key points
at the beginning. However, by 1910 the lead as summary was
standard.

News time and news comprehension

The discontinuous, non-chronological nature of the time structure of contemporary news stories invites the question of how well readers and hearers understand them. Introducing their study of narrative comprehension, Ohtsuka and Brewer (1992: 319) state: 'If the reader is to comprehend a narrative text, the reader must be able to derive the underlying event sequence from the given text sequence.' If this is strictly so, then it has dire consequences for the comprehensibility of news. The example analyses in this chapter show it takes considerable effort for the academic analyst – let alone the casual audience – to unravel the time structure.

Psychological research on the comprehension of narratives[1] has illuminated both the time structures of different kinds of stories, and the effects which different orderings have on audiences' comprehension. Ohtsuka and Brewer (1992) found that readers understood the canonical/chronological version of a story most easily. There was a significant drop in comprehension level for a second version of the same story which was presented in directly reverse chronological order, and for a third version which told some of the events using flashbacks. A final version contained 'flashforwards' which could not be immediately related to what had already been narrated, and here comprehension was little better than chance.

Relating these principles and findings to news stories, we can see that while the canonical/chronological pattern is not used in modern news, nor is the backwards pattern used in its pure form of telling an entire story from last event back to first. However, sections of news stories do run events in reverse order. Flashback appears to be the staple time structure of news stories, and this is abundantly evident in the stories examined in this chapter.

The findings to date on comprehension of news stories are equivocal on whether the non-linear time sequence of standard news writing is in fact harder to comprehend, or whether chronological order is easier. Lay readers clearly have some ability to reproduce news formats. Lutz and Wodak (1987) tested the form in which subjects retold news stories, asking them to write a lead sentence themselves. They found that most middle-class students reproduced a standard, reverse-chronology news format. But while some lower-class informants included much of the desired information, their retellings did not follow news style.

In another study, Duszak (1991) had readers reconstruct the randomized sentences of a news story. Most identified the lead sentence correctly, but there were two relevant tendencies in how they ordered sentences after the lead. Informants appeared to be avoiding the radical discontinuousness of news formats by grouping apparently cohesive sentences together. And they tended to reassemble events in a more chronological order than the original had, for instance putting background material earlier in the story rather than at the end. It seems that readers have a default strategy by which – in the absence of cues to the contrary – they re-impose chronological order on events in the discourse. Duszak rightly interprets this as a 'powerful drive' to retell events chronologically, clashing with readers' knowledge of the ordering promoted by news schemata.

More research is needed on the effects of time structure on news comprehension. The hypothesis that the non-canonical news format does adversely affect understanding is a reasonable one on the basis of comprehension research into other narrative genres, but the degree to which familiarity with news models may mitigate these problems is unclear.

Brewer hypothesizes that certain discourse genres are particularly intended for comprehension. In these, 'the order of events in the discourse will map the order of the underlying events' (Brewer 1985: 187) – that is, they will be written in chronological order. Among the genres supposedly designed for comprehension he explicitly and rightly includes news stories – with no comment on the fact that news stories virtually never follow the easily comprehensible canonical order. They consist of series of flashbacks, flashforwards and reverse tellings which, when they are used in films or novels, challenge the audience's powers of decoding.

So why do journalists write in an order which we know to be less easily comprehended, when one of their declared goals is reader comprehension? Ohtsuka and Brewer (1992: 331) ask the same question of non-chronological orderings in any kind of narrative: 'why don't authors always write texts in canonical form?' Their answer is that authors have purposes – and narratives have functions – other than just comprehension. They serve to entertain and persuade, for

example. With news stories, however, the questio
sharp, because comprehension by the audience is o
explicit aims of news writing. The answer lies in
journalistic values, journalistic practices and technol
ment, which is strong enough to overturn the drive
sibility.

The values of media control the way in which news is presented.
We can account for the way news stories are structured only with
reference to the values by which one 'fact' is judged more newsworthy than another – and so more worth remembering and
understanding. In particular the value of immediacy, as we have
seen, is a powerful force in news discourse. The reason for this is
the dominating role that time plays in the practice of news-work
(Bell, 1995b). Time rules news-work in a way it does few other
professions: the product must be finished by a set time or it is
useless. Schlesinger's study of BBC newsroom practices rightly
characterizes news-work as 'a stop-watch culture' (1987: 83).
Newsrooms operate against the clock, measuring daily achievement by the ability to produce a required number of stories for the
deadline. The drive to get the news first is embedded deep in the
news ethos, and radically affects the structure of the news text – to
the extent of motivating attempts to disguise the age of news
which is less than fresh. These work practices both drive and are
reinforced by technological development. From the invention of
the telegraph, which gave rise to modern news coverage as we
know it, to the presentation of live news as it happens through the
satellite and the cable, innovation in technology has been aimed at
reducing the time between the occurrence of a news event and its
telling.

6   Conclusion: Application and Applicability

The detailed analysis of news stories presented in this chapter
has told us a lot about the character of the stories – indications of
how they were made, evidence of discrepancies and gaps, and
manifestations of the news values behind them. There is
considerable pay-off from a comparatively straightforward dis-

course structural analysis of this kind. It can open up a subtext of the news, for instance of implied linkages which may not stand up to scrutiny. It can lead us closer to 'what the story actually says happened'.

In the IRA story, for example, we have been able to infer a good deal about its production and potential reception as well as about the text itself. We have seen the joins between the different input texts that have gone to make this one story; the divergent local and international readerships at which these inputs were targeted; and the conflicting views held by journalist and copy-editor over what was really the story in these events. We have noted the unspecificness of much of what we have read, reflected in alternative possible discourse structures for the story, which make it impossible from this text alone to determine exactly what were the persons, places and events involved. We have seen how the routinely jumbled time structure and lack of cohesion between sentences has served to make some things un-clear, and looked at some of the repercussions that may have for comprehension of news stories. We have been able to assess the validity of the headline, and the reliability of evaluations put forward in the story.

It is particularly salutary how our specification of events, persons and places changed as the analysis moved further down the story. The interpretation based only on the headline and lead was rather misleading. If this had been a single-sentence story of the kind analysed earlier in the chapter, the level of unclarity and ambiguity would have remained very high. Projecting this experience back on to the earlier examples, it seems likely that the interpretations I offered of their event and discourse structures would be proved quite mistaken if we had access to the full text of the stories from which they have been cut.

The system of analysis I presented in the Guide earlier covers most of what we might want to know about a story's discourse structure, but there are other questions we might ask in relation to it, such as:

- What vocabulary is used in the lead to claim news value for the story?

What is the order of sentence constituents within the lead? What news values lie behind that order?

Is there a conflict between the journalist's goals of brevity and clarity in the lead?

- What figures or similar 'hard facts' does the story contain? How does the story use these to buttress its news value?

- How much of the story consists of talk? What kind of talk – statement, accusation, reaction, announcement?

- What are the news values which have made this a published news story?

The analytical framework concentrated on the journalist's five Ws and an H. But it is significant that two of those did not figure explicitly – 'how' and particularly 'why'. 'How', of course, is in many ways represented as the detail of 'what', but 'why' is not overtly addressed in the IRA story – or in many others. It is no accident that Carey characterizes 'how' and 'why' as the 'dark continent' of journalism (Carey, 1987; cf. Bell, 1996). Secondly, while there is good insight to be gained from an understanding of a profession's own understanding of its work (Manoff and Schudson, 1987), it must not be forgotten that such categories should themselves be subjected to analysis and deconstruction.

The analytical work involved in this framework is not small. The demand is in fact a true reflection of the real complexity of texts such as news stories, which sometimes appear deceptively simple. In doing such work, it is essential to move systematically, picking off the analysis point by point.

Yet while we need to be selective in our analyses and know what is an appropriate point to cut off at, it is evident to me that many of the insights yielded come only near the end of detailed work following a pattern such as that outlined in the analysis Guide. Because the analyses are time-consuming if undertaken at all comprehensively (cf. van Dijk, 1991: 10), we need to complement full-scale work on a few texts with more piecemeal, specific analyses on larger samples. But the reward of such work is a better knowledge of what the stories of our time are saying, and an understanding of the way they may be produced and received.

Notes

This chapter is in large part the fruit of a fellowship I held in 1994 at the Centre for Language and Communication Research, University of Wales Cardiff. So also was the idea for the Cardiff Round Table as a whole and this publication of a range of approaches to media discourse. I am grateful to the Centre – and particularly to its Director, Nikolas Coupland – for support and warm hospitality on that and later occasions. During the fellowship, I taught a course on news language and discourse, and much of the present chapter grew from that material and experience. I work normally as a researcher and journalist rather than a teacher, and it was salutary how hard the students found it to understand and apply these analytical approaches. This was a main motivation behind the Round Table meeting and this collection. I am greatly indebted to co-editor Peter Garrett for the encouragement and insight he brought to my chapter and to the book as a whole.

1 In this section, I report at second hand the findings of other researchers on story 'comprehension' which are relevant to my concern with temporal order. This begs methodological and theoretical questions that are beyond my scope to address in this chapter – such as the relationship between recall and comprehension, and between written and oral channels, and the dynamic way in which audiences interpret meanings in everyday life. Compare Richardson's and Allan's chapters in this volume.

Chapter 4

News from NowHere: Televisual News Discourse and the Construction of Hegemony

Stuart Allan

1 Introduction

News from NowHere? This title signals from the outset my aim to displace the 'view from nowhere' indicative of much postmodern theorizing about televisual news in order to address the ways in which this form of discourse constructs a politicized configuration of the 'now-here'. That is to say, I wish to render problematic the means by which televisual news seeks to implicate its audience in a specific relationship of spectatorship, ostensibly that of an unseen onlooker or witness. Televisual news claims to provide an up-to-the-minute (now) narrative which, in turn, projects for the viewer a particular place (here) from which she or he may 'make sense' of the significance of certain 'newsworthy' events for their daily lives. This process of representation, far from being a neutral reflection of 'the world out there', works to reaffirm a network of conventionalized rules by which social life is to be interpreted. Accordingly, I argue that televisual news accounts encourage us to accept as *natural*, *obvious* or *commonsensical* certain preferred definitions of reality, and that these definitions have profound implications for the cultural reproduction of power relations across society.

This chapter's discussion draws primarily on enquiries into televisual news discourse undertaken in the area of cultural studies. Efforts to discern the contours of cultural studies need to recognize that its formal definition as a discipline of study and research is characterized by constant debate. Differences in opinion regarding 'what counts' as cultural studies are becoming ever more pronounced due, in part, to an increasing recognition of the need to avoid prescriptivist definitions of what constitutes 'culture' as an object of analysis (particularly in different national contexts). Nevertheless, and despite the sometimes heated nature of the ensuing discussions, these different voices typically share a crucial presupposition, namely that all definitions of cultural studies are necessarily partial, provisional and selective in their claims. With this in mind, I make the general suggestion that cultural studies be understood as being inclusive of a variety of different approaches (conceptual and methodological) which endeavour to explicate the cultural dynamics of everyday experience in relation to the *naturalization* of social divisions and hierarchies, especially those of class, gender, race, ethnicity and sexuality. That said, of course, where culture is understood as a formation of material signifying practices by which norms, rules, values, beliefs, meanings, subjectivities and identities are held to be representative of 'a whole way of life' (Williams, 1961), the boundaries which delimit the scope of exploration for cultural studies will necessarily be under continuous renegotiation.

It is against this backcloth of change and renewal, then, that I shall proceed to situate the broad imperatives of cultural studies research on televisual news discourse. If the origins of cultural studies, at least in Britain, are routinely defined in relation to the work of Richard Hoggart, Raymond Williams and, to a lesser extent, E. P. Thompson, it was the interventions of Stuart Hall and his colleagues at the Centre for Contemporary Cultural Studies (CCCS) at the University of Birmingham during the 1970s and 1980s that were most relevant to the emergence of a cultural studies 'approach' to news discourse.[1] In order to map a number of the most salient features of this research terrain, and in this way to help advance an evaluative assessment and critique of this approach for future applications, this chapter will assume the following form. First, the discussion commences with a consideration of the issue of 'hegemony' as it pertains to the mass media, for in my view this is the principal point of departure for cultural studies analyses of news discourse. Next, attention turns to specify the precise mechanisms by which televisual news operates to render its preferred truth-claims *authoritative, credible* and *factual* – and, in this way, potentially hegemonic. To this end, the three primary 'moments' of the communicative process, as identified by Hall (1980) in his encoding–decoding model, are highlighted: specifically, the production or 'encoding' of the news message, followed by the moment of the 'news text' itself (an illustrative analysis is provided), and then its negotiation or 'decoding' by the news audience. Each of these respective moments is then examined with an eye to its importance for investigating how televisual news discourse articulates the fluidly contradictory dynamics of hegemony as being inferentially consistent with the dictates of 'common sense'. Finally, the chapter concludes by briefly outlining a basis for possible future elaborations of this mode of enquiry.

2   News and Common Sense

Much of the early cultural studies work concerned with the analysis of news discourse sought to intervene against the traditional orthodoxies of empirical, positivistic social science. In the 1970s, social science research into televisual news tended to prioritize quantitative models of content analysis, whilst the attendant approaches to the 'audience effects' derivative of this content were often framed in terms of public surveys and questionnaires. Researchers routinely sought to identify the singular 'message' of televisual news as it was transmitted (ostensibly in a unilinear direction) from sender to receiver. The complexities of textual meaning production, to the extent that they were directly problematized at all, were usually described using a language of 'bias' and 'objectivity'. That is, attention would often focus on whether a given news account had portrayed a news event in an impartial, politically neutral (nonpartisan) manner. The principal conceptual issue would then be whether the account had successfully 'reflected' reality or, alternatively, had actually served to 'distort' what had really taken place. Studies could then be undertaken to determine the 'societal impact' of the news coverage of different threats to the established social order, thereby allowing for an assessment of any concomitant dangers for the proper maintenance of the larger 'pluralistic consensus'. The news media were generally viewed as part of the 'system of checks and balances' for the smooth running of the governmental sphere, so their performance *vis-à-vis* this functionalist role was a matter of considerable concern for these social scientists.

Cultural studies researchers took issue with these conceptual commitments from a number of different angles. In their view, the most serious of the limitations engendered by social scientific lines of enquiry was their acute failure to adequately address the implication of the news media in the cultural reproduction of oppressive relations of power across society. In contrast, then, cultural studies researchers sought to identify the ways in which the news media systematically extend and reinforce the interests of economic and political elites. An emphasis was placed on the need to elucidate the routinized logics by which these institutions reproduce hierarchical relations indicative of everyday life in capitalist societies such as Britain (especially those of class in the early research, followed by a later shift to address gender, racial, ethnic and sexual divisions). To the extent that the news media contribute to the *naturalization* of these relations, they were deemed to be working to confer ideological justification, to varying degrees, on to a multiplicity of social inequalities.

This meant that televisual news, far from being characterized as a 'reflection' of reality, was to be theorized as a complex assemblage of signifying conventions in which a preferred 'map of social reality' has been inscribed. That is to say, whereas news discourse is presented by its makers as an objective, impartial *translation* of reality, it may instead be seen to be providing an ideological *construction* of realities. Cultural studies researchers could then attempt to show how only certain definitions of reality are aligned with 'common sense', with what 'everyone knows to be true'. Such definitions may then be analysed as instances of discursive power, for to the degree that they naturalize a preferred range of truth claims (to the detriment of alternative ones) as being the most *obvious, reasonable* or *rational* ones available, they are working to reproduce the imperatives of hegemony.

Not surprisingly, then, the concept of 'hegemony' came to occupy a central place within cultural studies approaches to news discourse. Most attempts to define the concept attribute its development to Antonio Gramsci, a radical Italian philosopher who died in 1937 after more than a decade in Mussolini's prisons. Very briefly, in his critique of power dynamics in modern societies, Gramsci (1971: 12) describes hegemony as a relation of:

> . . . 'spontaneous' consent given by the great masses of the population to the general direction imposed on social life by the dominant fundamental group; this consent is 'historically' caused by the prestige (and consequent confidence) which the dominant group enjoys because of its position and function in the world of production.

In this way, Gramsci is recognizing a crucial distinction between coercion and persuasion. In the case of the former, he underlines the point that it is the 'apparatus of state coercive power which "legally" enforces discipline on those groups who do not "consent" either actively or passively' (1971: 12). This type of coercive control is the exception rather than the rule, however, as power is much more commonly exercised over subordinate groups by means of what he terms 'political and ideological leadership'. It follows that a ruling group is hegemonic only to the degree that it acquires the consent of other groups within its preferred definitions of reality. More specifically, these subordinate groups are directed to negotiate reality within what are ostensibly the limits of 'common sense' when, in actuality, this 'common sense' is consistent with dominant norms, values and beliefs. Hegemony is to be conceptualized, therefore, as a site of ideological struggle over this 'common sense'. In Gramsci's (1971: 348) words, at stake is 'a cultural battle to transform the popular "mentality" and to diffuse the philosophical innovations which will demonstrate themselves to be "historically true" *to the extent that they become concretely – i.e. historically and socially – universal'* (emphasis added).

Raymond Williams sought to elaborate upon Gramsci's approach for cultural studies research by foregrounding the lived culture of hegemony. Of utmost importance, in his view, was the need to address hegemony as 'a lived system of meanings and values', that is, as 'a whole body of practices and expectations, over the whole of living: our senses and assignments of energy, our shaping perceptions of ourselves and our world' (1977: 110). In this formulation, hegemony constitutes 'a sense of reality for most people in the society' and, as such, is the terrain upon which the 'lived dominance and subordination' of particular groups is struggled over in day-to-day cultural practices. Far from being a monolithic system or structure imposed from above, then, lived hegemony is a process: 'It is a realised complex of experiences, relationships, and activities, with specific and changing pressures and limits' (1977: 112). Consequently, no one group can maintain its hegemony without adapting to changing conditions, a dynamic which will likely entail making certain strategic compromises with the forces which oppose its ideological authority. Dominance is neither invoked nor accepted in a passive manner: 'It has continually to be renewed, recreated, defended, and modified. It is also continually resisted, limited, altered, challenged by pressures not at all its own' (1977: 112). Williams' emphasis on the countervailing determinants of hegemony thus encouraged researchers to accentuate what are contending, and at times contradictory, processes of transformation and incorporation.

Efforts within cultural studies to extend the concept of hegemony via specific analyses of the news media are discernible in a wide variety of different theoretical and methodological contexts. As noted above, however, I would suggest that the work of Hall and his CCCS colleagues, during the 1970s and 1980s, has proved to be the most influential. The CCCS research succeeded in demonstrating a number of ways in which a Gramscian approach to hegemony could facilitate a radical rethinking of how news discourse contributes to the daily renewal of the pernicious logics of class, sexism, racism, homophobia, ageism and nationalism, amongst others, across different societies (several agenda-setting essays are contained in collections edited by Cohen and Young (1981); Curran, Gurevitch and Woollacott (1977); Gurevitch, Bennett, Curran and Woollacott (1982); Hall, Hobson, Lowe and Willis (1980)). Significantly, this shift to address the problem of hegemony displaced a range of different formulations of 'dominant ideology', most of which held the news media to be complicit in the cultural reproduction of capitalist relations of production in direct accordance with the interests of a ruling class or bloc. News discourse was often theorized in these formulations as 'concealing' or 'masking' the 'true' origins of economic antagonisms, that is, their basis in the class struggle, thus the question of audience effectivity tended to be framed as a matter of 'false consciousness'. Aware of the limitations associated with theorizing the dynamics of news discourse in such reductionistic terms, cultural studies researchers were able to see in Gramsci's writings the means to develop a far more sophisticated mode of critique.

In the early cultural studies literature, the collective project which informs the book *Policing the Crisis* is broadly representative of the major emergent themes (see Hall, Critcher, Jefferson, Clarke and Roberts, 1978). Briefly, in this study's investigation into how 'mugging' was 'discovered' by the news media as 'a frightening new strain of crime' in the early 1970s, and the ensuing ideological rupture which led to severe state interventions 'in the interests of law and order', the appearance of a *crisis of hegemony* is identified. In their words:

> A crisis of hegemony marks a moment of profound rupture in the political and economic life of a society, an accumulation of contradictions. If in moments of 'hegemony' everything works spontaneously so as to sustain and enforce a particular form of class domination while rendering the basis of that social authority invisible through the mechanisms of the production of consent, then moments when the equilibrium of consent is disturbed, or where the contending class forces are so nearly balanced that neither can achieve that sway from which a resolution to the crisis can be promulgated, are moments *when the whole basis of political leadership and cultural authority becomes exposed and contested.* (Hall et al., 1978: 217)

The role of the news media, especially the daily press, in the creation of a 'moral panic' which would subsequently lead to a reconfiguration of the public consensus about crime along far more authoritarian lines, is carefully documented. Crime control agencies, in seeking to secure popular approval for more coercive measures (for example, the length of sentences for 'petty street crime' rose dramatically), had much to gain by having the news media accept their definition of a 'mugging epidemic'. Hall et al. examine a variety of the strategies employed, to varying degrees, by the daily press to re-inflect the language of crisis being generated by these agencies. This focus on how certain frameworks of interpretation were set in motion allows them to show, in turn, how the limits for much of the political debate about what constituted this 'breakdown of public morality' and who was to blame for it (and, moreover, which measures would be necessary to end the crisis) were established. Particular attention is thus given to the means by which news organizations, for a number of administrative, bureaucratic, professional, technological and ostensibly practical reasons, routinely reproduce the social definitions of the powerful. This is achieved largely – but not entirely – at the expense of those definitions advanced by oppositional or counter-hegemonic voices.[2]

Accordingly, in recognizing that the professional demands of 'impartiality' impose a series of constraints on the televisual newsworker (in Britain, it is a statutory requirement enforced by Parliament), attention has been directed to the specific mechanisms by which this over-accessing of powerful voices as news sources works to underwrite the ideological rules of 'objectivity' and 'balance'. Cultural studies researchers have attempted to highlight for interrogation the exclusionary imperatives of routine, 'commonsensical' news values and judgements. In order to develop this line of critique, however, it was clear that a new conceptual vocabulary would be required to lend their explorations a greater degree of analytical specificity. It was with this aim in mind that some researchers began to 'borrow' a range of categories from other approaches to textual analysis, most notably from semiotics or semiology (these terms were generally regarded as being interchangeable). As will be discussed in the next section, this shift allowed for a new emphasis to be placed on elucidating how the 'encoding' of televisual news accounts structures the hegemonic rules by which social reality is to be 'decoded' by the news audience within the continually evolving limits of 'common sense'.

3   The Codification of Hegemony

The contribution made by semiotics profoundly shaped the development of cultural studies. The semiotic project offered the promise of breaking with those approaches which reduced language to a 'neutral' instrument through which 'reality' is expressed. By foregrounding the textual relations of signification, it suggested fascinating new ways to think through Williams' theses concerning the lived hegemony of 'common sense'. Moreover, semiotics allowed for the opening up of what had become a rather empty postulate, namely that televisual news texts are inherently meaningful, so as to unpack the *naturalness* of the 'codes' implicated in their representations of reality.

Briefly, the notion of 'code' was re-inflected within cultural studies to specify a systematized arrangement of meanings organized in accordance with certain rules or conventions. Given that the 'polysemic' (Barthes, 1967) potential of the message is never fully realized in practice, it is the mobilization of certain meanings in the place of others which interests the analyst. In the case of a televisual newscast, then, it cannot present an 'unmediated' event to the viewer. Rather, as Hall (1980: 129) writes:

> Events can only be signified within the aural-visual forms of the televisual discourse. In the moment when a historical event passes under the sign of discourse, it is subject to all the complex formal 'rules' by which language signifies. To put it paradoxically, the event must become a 'story' before it can become a *communicative event*.

This is to suggest that the televisual news account, far from simply 'reflecting' the reality of an event, is actually working to construct a codified definition of what should count as the reality of the event. This constant, always dynamic process of mediation is accomplished in ideological terms, but not simply at the level of the televisual text *per se*. Instead, the complex conditions under which the text is both produced and consumed or 'read' will need to be accounted for in a cultural studies approach to news as a form of hegemonic discourse.

To clarify how analyses may best discern the extent to which the codes of televisual news discourse are embedded in relations of hegemony, Hall (1980) introduced a new conceptual model.[3] The 'encoding–decoding' model, as it was quickly dubbed, remains to this day the singularly most influential attempt to come to terms with these issues within cultural studies (see Ang, 1996; McGuigan,

1992; Morley, 1992; Seiter et al., 1989; see also Hall, 1994a). Central to Hall's agenda is the aim of showing why the televisual text, as an object of investigation, needs to be situated within the larger processes of its 'encoding' and 'decoding'. Turning first to the question of 'encoding', Hall seeks to underscore the fact that the production practices helping to construct the televisual message possess highly varied discursive aspects. Specifically, the production process 'is framed throughout by meanings and ideas: knowledge-in-use concerning the routines of production, historically defined technical skills, professional ideologies, institutional knowledge, definitions and assumptions, assumptions about the audience and so on frame the constitution of the programme through this production structure' (1980: 129). Moreover, the encoding of a televisual newscast, once again in his words, will 'draw topics, treatments, agendas, events, personnel, images of the audience, "definitions of the situation" from other sources and other discursive formations within the wider socio-cultural and political structure of which they are a differentiated part' (1980: 129).

It follows, according to Hall, that whilst the encoding and decoding of the televisual message are differentiated moments (that is, they are not perfectly symmetrical or transparent), they are related to one another by the social relations of the communicative process as a whole (1980: 130). Before this form of discourse can have an 'effect', however, it needs to be appropriated as a personally relevant discourse by the televisual viewer, that is, it has to be 'meaningfully decoded'. For Hall, it is this set of decoded meanings which 'influence, entertain, instruct or persuade, with very complex perceptual, cognitive, emotional, ideological or behavioural consequences' (1980: 130). The ideological form of the message thus occupies a privileged position *vis-à-vis* the *determinate* moments of encoding and decoding. These moments each possess their own specific modality and 'conditions of existence', for while their respective articulation is necessary to the communicative process, the moment of encoding cannot 'guarantee' that of decoding. In other words, the moments of encoding and decoding are 'relatively autonomous': they are inextricably bound up with one another, but there will be highly varied degrees of symmetry ('understanding' and 'misunderstanding') between the encoder-producer and the decoder-receiver.

Hall outlines three hypothetical positions (derived, in part, from Parkin, 1971) from which decodings may be constructed. These 'ideal-typical' reading positions, all of which are 'available' at the moment of decoding, are to be distinguished as follows:

1   When the viewer of a televisual newscast decodes its message in alignment with its encoding, she or he is occupying the 'dominant-hegemonic position'. From this position, Hall argues, the *authoritative, impartial* and *professional* signification of the news event is being accepted as perfectly *obvious* or *natural*; the compliant viewer, operating inside the dominant subjectivity it confers, thereby reproduces the hegemonic 'definition of the situation' in ideological terms.

2   In what Hall characterizes as the 'negotiated position', the viewer recognizes as *appropriate* the general legitimacy of the preferred definition, but identifies certain discrepancies or 'exceptions to the rule' within a specific situational context.

3   The final reading position is that which is consistent with an 'oppositional' code. That is to say, the viewer directly counters the logic of the dominant-hegemonic position in such a manner that the authority of its definition is directly challenged. Hall offers the example of a viewer who follows 'a debate on the need to limit wages but "reads" every mention of the "national interest" as "class interest"' (1980: 138). In this way, the dominant code has been re-inflected within a resistant, counter-hegemonic framework of reference.

Here it is important to note that these 'ideal-typical' reading positions are being marked for purposes of analytical clarity, and that they are not to be conflated with actual empirical or lived positions (see Corner, 1980; Morley, 1992; Richardson, this volume; Scannell, 1991; Silverstone, 1994; Wren-Lewis, 1983). The viewer's engagement with an actual televisual news programme is likely to engender a complex range of (often contradictory) positionalities as the activity of negotiating meaning is always contingent upon the particular social relations of signification in operation. Despite the rather abstract nature of its postulates, then, the encoding–decoding model allows for the issue of textual determination to be addressed as a fluidly heterogeneous process without, at the same time, losing sight of the ways in which it is embedded in relations of power. The status of the viewer is not reduced to that of a victim of false consciousness (one who passively acquiesces to the dictates of a 'dominant ideology' being imposed via the text), nor is it to be celebrated such that the viewer is to be accorded with an ability to identify freely with multiple interpretations of the text in a wildly immaterial fashion. Instead, by situating this dynamic activity as a *negotiated* process within certain conditional, but always changing, parameters, the encoding–decoding model succeeds in highlighting a spectrum of potential positions to be occupied, however fleetingly, in a determinant manner.[4]

4   Televisual News as Discourse

Central to the encoding–decoding model, then, is a recognition that the codification of meaning in televisual news discourse is constitutive of a particular politics of signification. What is at stake is the need to clear the conceptual space necessary for the investigation of the specific cultural relations at work in the discursive legitimation of certain hegemonic definitions of reality. From this vantage point, the communicative strategies utilized in televisual news to construct a sense of the very taken-for-grantedness of hegemony may be shown to be structuring 'in dominance' what is, at least in principle, a polysemic text. More to the point, once it is acknowledged that the full range of meanings potentially associated with a given message do not exist 'equally' (true polysemy), then new questions arise as to why particular meanings are being preferred over other possibilities. The ideological dynamics of hegemony may therefore be explicated, at least in part, through an examination of the visual and aural devices in and through which the newscast encourages its audience to apprehend these preferred meanings as being the most *truthful, credible* or *rational* ones available.

For our purposes here, we shall address, in turn, each of the three 'moments' or phases of the communication circuit implied by the encoding–decoding model in relation to televisual news discourse. Special attention will be given to how the consensual politics of hegemony are implicated in the codification (rule-guided) processes at issue in each of these interrelated moments. In so doing, I am seeking to elucidate how cultural studies researchers situate the televisual news text in relation to its conditions of production and consumption in order to account fully for the attendant complexities of its discursive configuration.

Turning firstly to the 'encoding' moment, then, it is apparent that whilst the inscription of hegemonic 'common sense' in the televisual message is always provisional (absolute closure is an impossibility), it is nevertheless being operationalized in the encoder's attempt to 'win the assent of the audience' (Morley, 1992) to a preferred reading of the message. The range of presuppositions about what is (and what is not) 'common sense' for the news audience – that is, what the encoder believes is 'simply too obvious for words' – thus takes on a distinctly ideological significance.

Encoding televisual news

Cultural studies research challenges the assertion that journalists are participants, knowingly or not, in some sort of wilful conspiracy to encodify the dictates of a dominant ideology in the newsroom.[5] Instead, by prioritizing for investigation the institutionalized routines and practices in and through which televisual news is produced, this approach offers an important vantage point for analysing the contradictory imperatives by which the meanings of televisual news are encoded. A key assumption is that it is the very visual and aural codes of televisual news that are regarded as the most 'natural', as the most representative of 'reality', which are actually the most ideological. It is the aim of the newsworker, of course, to engineer as strong a degree of correlation between the inflection of a news topic in a specific account and the audience member's 'purchase' or reading of it as is possible under the circumstances. To the extent that the newsworker is able to secure ideological closure such that the encoding and decoding moments are brought into near alignment, the parameters of a 'preferred meaning' of the topic will have been enforced.

To date, there has been much discussion within cultural studies concerning the hegemonic dynamics enmeshed in these communicative forms, with a number of studies seeking to discern the types of strategies encoders use to achieve 'the effect of immediacy-to-reality' while preserving, at the same time, the newscast's claim to impartiality. In particular, attention has focused on how processes of encodification are organized to set down the inferential 'rules' by which the imagined decoder (discursively posited as a 'witness') is to reconstruct the 'preferred meaning' afforded by the text. In what is in many ways a programmatic essay, Hall, Connell and Curti (1976: 65) point out:

> The facts must be arranged, in the course of programming, so as to present an intelligible 'story': hence the process of presentation will reflect the explanations and interpretations which appear most plausible, credible or adequate to the broadcaster, his [or her] editorial team and the expert commentators he [or she] consults. Above all, the known facts of a situation must be translated into intelligible *audiovisual signs, organised as a discourse.* TV cannot transmit 'raw historical' events as such, to its audiences: it can only transmit pictures of, stories, informative talk or discussion about, the events it selectively treats.

The technical and communicative competencies of the encoder will therefore help to determine the likelihood of a preferred meaning of the topic being established. Still, ideological closure is always a precariously unstable achievement, for no encoder is able to ensure that her or his intended message will be 'accepted' by the decoder. Following Hall, Connell and Curti (1976: 68), although the message is '*structured*, and aims for a certain kind of ideological *closure*, it can only be *relatively* closed up around any one reading: and that partial closure is, precisely, the result of the *work* – the ideological work – to which the signifying systems and their preferred *use* in any one instance, contribute, and what, in effect, *they sustain.*' The encodification of hegemony, conditional as it is upon contending processes of transformation and incorporation for its renewal, always risks coming unravelled (see also Allan, 1995).

In order to better account for the journalist's lived engagement with these normative dynamics, cultural studies researchers necessarily draw on a range of analyses concerning the cultural imperatives of news production, especially those conducted by sociologists, criminologists and ethnomethodologists (see, for example, Chibnall, 1977; Cohen and Young, 1981; Elliott, 1972;

Ericson, Baranek and Chan, 1987, 1989, 1991; Fishman, 1980; Gans, 1979; Gitlin, 1980; Halloran, Elliott and Murdock, 1970; Jacobs, 1996; Pedelty, 1995; Reeves and Campbell, 1994; Schlesinger, 1987; Tuchman, 1978; van Zoonen, 1991). These empirically driven investigations tend to be examined with an eye to what they can reveal about the culture of everyday interactions within specific news institutions. Of particular interest to cultural studies researchers are those enquiries which help to generate insights into the means by which the ideological character of news is encoded through the discursive norms and values of reporting.

Here the work of Philip Schlesinger (1987), for example, has been incorporated into cultural studies theorizing about the routinization of encoding practices. Specifically, in his enquiry into the occupational ideologies of broadcast journalists at the BBC, he describes several significant constraints shaping the contradictory logics of encodification. One of the most critical of these constraints is the time pressure of daily deadlines, hence his use of the phrase 'stopwatch culture' to pinpoint how temporal relations are interwoven throughout the production process (see also Bell, this volume; Schlesinger, 1990; Curran, 1990). Journalists, he argues, possess an exacting time-consciousness due, in part, to their constant need to co-ordinate and synchronize a range of news-work activities. The visualization of 'immediacy', so important for televisual news, is thus largely seen as a technical (and to some extent aesthetic) problem to be overcome in conjunction with negotiating the normative logistics of impartiality on a day-to-day basis.

The uncertainties of televisual news production, Schlesinger maintains, are marked by a range of tensions as journalistic values (competition, professionalism, speed in relation to deadline pressure) are brought into daily conflict with organizational values (accuracy, prestige, production values, audience reach). These tensions are indicative of the severe institutional constraints being placed on journalists as they strive to determine what counts as 'genuine' news and who is to be accredited as an indisputable source of 'facts'. This need to control a scarcity of time (duration of time-slot) and space (placement in the 'running order'), amongst other resources, leads to the routinization of the methods necessary to predict the potential trajectory of news events. The mediation of these methods through the 'strategic rituals' (Tuchman, 1978) of news-work ensures, where possible, that any 'unexpected' developments will be quickly processed in a manner which is consonant with the (largely internalized) 'journalistic standards' appropriate to the organization's bureaucratic rationales. Professional ideals, such as those of impartiality and objectivity, are likely to be operationalized in ways which privilege this institutional ethos and its priorities. Even the legitimacy of the 'news values' informing these routinized methods of encodification finds justification in the ongoing compromises made necessary, in part, by the dictates of these temporal requirements. As Schlesinger (1987: 105) writes:

> Production is so organised that its basic dynamic emphasises the perishability of stories. Where a story carries over from one day to the next, it is assumed that the audience will, after one day's exposure, be adequately familiar with the subject-matter to permit the 'background' to be largely taken for granted. It is always *today's* developments which occupy the foreground. The corollary of this point is that there is an inherent tendency for the news to be framed in a discontinuous and ahistorical way, and this implies a truncation of 'context', and therefore a reduction of meaningfulness.

This question of the 'framing' of news discourse, particularly with respect to the establishment of a mode of address deemed suitable for its assumed audience, has further implications for the encodification of normative truth claims. Todd Gitlin (1980) extends his reading of the encoding–decoding model in relation to an ethnomethodological notion of 'frame' to argue for a consideration of how the daily routines of journalism strive to *naturalize* the social world in accordance with certain discursive conventions. News frames, he argues, make the world beyond direct experience look natural; they are 'principles of selection, emphasis, and presentation composed of little tacit theories about what exists, what happens, and what matters' (1980: 6). The subject of often intense negotiation between journalists and their editors, as well as their sources, frames help to render 'an infinity of noticeable details' into practicable repertoires, thereby facilitating the ordering of the world in conjunction with hierarchical rules of inclusion and exclusion. As Gitlin (1980: 7) contends:

... largely unspoken and unacknowledged, [frames] organise the world both for journalists who report it and, in some important degree, for us who rely on their reports. Frames enable journalists to process large amounts of information quickly and routinely: to recognise it as information, to assign it to cognitive categories, and to package it for efficient relay to their audiences. Thus, for organisational reasons alone, frames are unavoidable, and journalism is organised to regulate their production.

Once a particular frame has been adopted for a news story, its principles of selection and rejection ensure that only that 'information' material which is seen to be *legitimate*, as *appropriate* within the conventions of newsworthiness so defined, is to appear in the account. 'Some of this framing', Gitlin (1980: 28) argues, 'can be attributed to traditional assumptions in news treatment: news concerns the *event*, not the underlying condition; the *person*, not the group; *conflict*, not consensus; the fact that *"advances the story"*, not the one that explains it.'

The operation of a hegemonic frame is not to be viewed, however, as a means to preclude the encoding of 'information' which might explicitly politicize the seemingly impartial definitions of social reality on offer. Rather, the very authoritativeness of the hegemonic frame is contingent upon its implicit claim to objectivity, which means that it needs to regularly incorporate 'awkward facts' or even, under more exceptional circumstances, voices of dissent. The hegemonic frame's tacit claim to comprehensiveness dictates that it must be seen as 'balanced' and 'fair' in its treatment of counter-hegemonic positions: indeed, after Gitlin (1980: 256), 'only by absorbing and domesticating conflicting values, definitions of reality, and demands on it, in fact, does it remain hegemonic'. Accordingly, it is through repetition, through the very everydayness of news discourse, that the prevailing frames (neither arbitrary nor fixed) acquire an ostensibly natural or taken-for-granted status.

The televisual news text

The 'moment' of the televisual news text is clearly a fluid one; its meanings are dispersed in ways which analyses of actual newscasts as static constructs or artifacts cannot adequately address. By situating this genre of text in relation to the variable conditions of its encoding and decoding, cultural studies modes of enquiry provide us with a far more dynamic understanding of meaning production than those efforts which treat it as an object in isolation, removed from its ideological context.

Of particular interest to much of the cultural studies work on the textuality of televisual news are the discursive strategies which render it recognizable as a relatively distinct form of cultural knowledge. For a news narrative to be 'read' as an impartial 'reflection' of 'the world out there', its explanations of the social world need to be aligned with the lived experiences of its assumed audiences in such a way that the rules conditioning 'what can and should be said' (Pêcheux, 1982) are ratified (see also Montgomery and Allan, 1992). As Ian Connell (1980) points out, it is primarily in and through the practical implementation of the very 'editorial criteria' by which 'topics' for news stories are defined that traces of these ideological processes are discernible. This shaping of topics is indicative of the attempt to generalize the mode of explanatory narrative on offer so as to make it appear to provide the 'best sense' of a given situation. The basis of these explanations, he argues, are those definitions of reality articulated by newsworkers and sources which can be categorized as what 'most' (or at least 'many') people think. Also interwoven into the fabric of these explanations is the presupposition that the newscast is itself a 'neutral' space within which such definitions are able to circulate for the viewer, positioned as onlooker, to evaluate independently. In Connell's (1980: 154–5) words:

> This is a *sense of witnessing* (that is, of being present at, but not directly involved in) a 'reality' which is, in and through this visual mode, made to seem 'out there', separate from and independent of those positioned as witnesses. The relation in which the 'audience' is cast by this visual mode is that of *onlooker*; the proceedings of protagonists are 'looked in on'. Whether the social beings who watch television news programmes, who are themselves sites of intersection of a multiplicity of discursive practices, actually assume this position is, of course, another matter. The point to be stressed here, however, is that the mode of vision currently in dominance presents the relation in this form – that is, as a relation between the 'involved' and the 'uninvolved'.

This construction of a televisual space, where 'the audience is constantly hailed as witness of, but not participant in, the struggle and argument over issues' (1980: 140), is to be upheld by delimiting the meanings of the events being conveyed to those which consolidate the facticity of the news narrative. Of course, it is the very *naturalness* of the discursive strategies by which this 'will to facticity' (Allan, 1995) is being narrativized that makes it so difficult to critique.

With this aim in mind, however, we may turn to highlight several such discursive strategies as they are employed in British national televisual newscasts (those of the BBC, a public service broadcasting system, and ITN, its commercial counterpart). Specifically, I shall limit my illustration to the opening minute of the newscasts. This schematic reading is advanced against the current of televisual 'flow' (Williams, 1974), so to speak, in order to pinpoint, if in a necessarily partial and highly subjective manner, several conceptual issues for further, more rigorous examination.[6]

In the first instance, the opening sequence may be read not only as a means to establish a sense of urgency for the newscast, but also as a way to anchor a declaration of 'nowness' and 'liveness' for its claim to authoritativeness. The commencement of the newscast signifies, by definition, the imminent threat of potentially distressing information (most news, after all, is 'bad news'), thus the opening sequence needs to announce its realignment of televisual flow at a number of different levels. Apparent across the range of the different BBC and ITN newscasts under consideration are several common features: the opening sequence tends to be a 15- to 20-second segment of brightly coloured computer-animated graphics, which rapidly unfolds to a sharply ascending piece of theme music (the use of trumpets is typical). Each of these segments privileges specific formulations of temporality (ticking clocks are used by both the BBC and ITN, which signal the up-to-the-minuteness of the news coverage) conjoined with those of spatiality (images of revolving globes spin to foreground an image of the British nation as defined by geography, in the case of the BBC; whilst for ITN's *News at Ten*, a London cityscape at night is slowly panned until the camera rests on a close-up of the clock-face of the main parliamentary building, the apparent 'seat of political power'). Implicit to this progressively narrowing focal dynamic is an assertion of the comprehensiveness of the news coverage: the news is 'live', it is being monitored from around the world, and 'we' are located as an audience within the 'imagined community' (Anderson, 1991) of the British nation. The final shot in the succession of graphic sequences (ostensibly sounded by the 'gong' of 'Big Ben' in the case of ITN) brings 'us' into the televisual studio, a pristine place of hard, polished surfaces (connotations of efficiency and objectivity) devoid of everyday, human (subjective) features.

The camera smoothly glides across the studio floor while, in the case of the *ITN Lunchtime News*, a male voice-over sternly intones: 'From the studios of ITN (.) the news (.) with Nicholas Owen and Julia Somerville.' (A dot in parentheses indicates a pause of less than a second.) Both newsreaders are situated behind a shared desk, calmly organizing their scripts. Serving as a backdrop for them is what appears to be a dimly lit (in blue light) newsroom, empty of people but complete with desks, computer equipment, and so forth. Similarly, for the *News at Ten*, as the male voice-over declares: 'From ITN (.) News at Ten (.) with Trevor McDonald', the newsreader appears in shot seated behind a desk, typing an invisible keyboard with his left hand as he collects a loose sheaf of papers with his other hand (which is also holding a pen). Connotatively representing an institutional forum of legitimized debate and controversy, the news studio may be read as the public embodiment of democratic principles and values which the newsreader, in turn, claims the right to represent on 'our' behalf.

As a result, the mode of address utilized by the respective newsreaders at the outset of the newscast needs to appear to be 'dialogic' (Bakhtin, 1981) in its formal appeal to the viewer's attention (see also Allan, 1994). This dialogic strategy of co-presence is to be achieved, in part, through the use of direct eye-contact with the camera (and thus the inscribed viewer). As Margaret Morse (1986: 62) observes, 'the impression of presence is created through the construction of a shared space, the impression of shared time, and signs that the speaking subject is speaking for himself [or herself], sincerely' (see also Hartley and Montgomery, 1985; Marriott, 1995). The impersonally professional space of the studio is, in this way, personalized in the form of the newsreader who, using a language which establishes these temporal and spatial relations of co-presence with the viewer, reaffirms a sense of shared participation.

Nevertheless, these dialogic relations of co-presence are hierarchically structured. The *direct* address speech of the newsreader (note that the 'accessed voices' will be restricted to *indirect* speech and eye-contact) represents the 'news voice' of the network: she or he stands in for an institution charged with the responsibility of serving a public interest through the impartiality of its reporting. For this reason, these relations of co-presence need to be organized so as to underwrite the signifiers of facticity and journalistic prestige, as well as those of timeliness and immediacy.

In addition to the steady gaze of expressive eye-contact, the visual display of the newsreader's authority is further individualized in terms of 'personality' (white males still predominate), as well as with regard to factors such as clothing (formal) and body language (brisk and measured). This conventionalized appeal to credibility is further enhanced through aural codes of a 'proper' accent (almost always 'received pronunciation') and tone (solemn and resolute). Such factors, then, may not only help to create the impression of personal integrity and trustworthiness, they may also ratify the authenticity of the newsreader's own commitment to upholding the truth value of the newscast as being representative of her or his own experience and reliability. Personalized terms of address, such as 'good afternoon' or 'good evening', may similarly work to underscore the human embodiment of news values by the newsreader as she or he seemingly engages in a conversational discourse with the viewer. The immediacy of the implied discursive exchange is thus constrained by the need to project a sense of dialogue where there is only the decisive, if inclusionary, voice of the newsreader (cf. Fairclough,* this volume). As Robert Stam (1983: 28) writes:

> The newscaster's art consists of evoking the cool authority and faultless articulation of the written or memorised text while simultaneously 'naturalising' the written word to restore the appearance of spontaneous communication. Most of the newscast, in fact, consists of this scripted spontaneity: newscasters reading from teleprompters, correspondents reciting hastily-memorised notes, politicians delivering prepared speeches, commercial actors representing their roles. In each case, the appearance of fluency elicits respect while the trappings of spontaneity generate a feeling of unmediated communication.

In play are a range of deictics which anchor the articulation of time ('now', 'at this moment', 'currently', 'as we are speaking', 'ongoing' or 'today') to that of space ('here', 'this is where', or 'at Westminster this morning') such that the hierarchical relationship of identification for the intended viewer is further accentuated.

Contingent upon these relations of co-presence is what may be characterized as the regime of the 'fictive We'. That is, the mode of address employed by the newsreader, by emphasizing the individual and the familiar, encourages the viewer's complicity in upholding the hegemonic frame (see Doane, 1990; Holland, 1987; Morse, 1986; Stam, 1983; Wilson, 1993). To the extent that the newsreader is seen to speak not only 'to us', but also 'for us' ('we' are all part of the 'consensus'), then 'we' are defined in opposition to 'them', namely those voices which do not share 'our' interests and thus are transgressive of the codified limits of common sense. As Stam (1983: 29) points out, there needs to be a certain 'calculated ambiguity of expression' if a diverse range of viewers are to identify with the truth claims on offer: 'The rhetoric of network diplomacy, consequently, favours a kind of oracular understatement, cultivating ambiguity, triggering patent but deniable meanings, encouraging the most diverse groups, with contradictory ideologies and aspirations, to believe that the newscasters are not far from their own beliefs.' As a result, in attempting to authorize a preferred reading of the news event for 'us', the newsreader aims to frame the initial terms by which it is to be interpreted.

The rules of the hegemonic frame, whilst in principle polysemic, are typically inflected to encourage a relation of reciprocity between the viewers' and the newsreader's 'personal' sense of 'news values'. The voice-over of the newsreader, in seeking to specify 'what is at issue' in each of the headlined news stories, begins the work of organizing the news event into a preferred narrative structure for us. Words are aligned with images to affirm, and then reinforce, the interpellative appeals of the news voice and the strategy of visualization: viewers can 'see for themselves' a range of the elements constitutive of what journalists often call the five Ws (who, what, where, when and why) and H (how) of the news lead. Moreover, as Mary Ann Doane (1990: 229) writes, 'the status of the image as indexical truth is not inconsequential – through it the "story" touches the ground of the real'. The extent to which these news headlines are made to 'touch the ground of the real' is thus dependent upon the degree to which hegemonic relations of reciprocity are established such that it is *obvious* to the viewer that these are the most significant news events of the day for her or him to know about, and that it is *self-evident* how they are to be best understood.

In order to illustrate this line of argument further, we may briefly consider the 'news lead' of the 'top story' for two newscasts, namely the BBC's *Nine O'Clock News* and ITN's *News at Ten*, broadcast on 3 September 1996.

Excerpt 1: BBC *Nine O'Clock News*, 3 September 1996

00:00 [newsreader] President Clinton says America may strike at Iraq again to make Saddam Hussein pay a price for his brutality	*Head and shoulders shot of newsreader, BBC logo over his right shoulder*
twenty-seven cruise missiles were fired this morning to check what he called the clear and present danger Iraq poses to its neighbours	*Video footage (single shot) of cruise missile being fired from a warship*
here the government plans to test every child as they start school	*Video footage (single shot) of two young boys, in school uniforms, seated at work table with learning cards*
and England's rugby team will boycott tomorrow's training session in the latest crisis to hit the rugby football union	*Video footage (three shots) of rugby team at practice*
00:26	*Opening sequence*

00:41 good evening (.) America says it is prepared to repeat this morning's cruise missile attack on Iraq to counter the clear and present danger it says Baghdad poses to the Gulf and the west's oil supplies (.) more than two dozen missiles were fired at military targets in southern Iraq (.) President Clinton said it was to make Saddam Hussein pay a price for his offensive against Kurds in the north of his country (.) Iraq said five people were killed and nineteen wounded	*Head and shoulders shot of newsreader, BBC logo replaced by still image of cruise missile being fired from a warship*
01:08 the US response (.) code named operation desert strike (.) began in the early hours of this morning . . .	*Animated image of Europe, nation states outlined, evolves until Iraq is centred*

Excerpt 2: ITN *News at Ten*, 3 September 1996

00:00	*Opening sequence*
00:10 [male voice-over] from ITN (.) News at Ten (.) with Trevor McDonald	*Moving shot of newsreader at desk in studio*
00:18 [newsreader] American missiles pound Iraq (.) Saddam remains defiant	*Video footage (single shot) of cruise missile being fired from a warship*
Clinton explains reckless acts have consequences	*Video footage (single shot) of Clinton standing at speaking podium, White House*

Tom and Jody's parents talk of their tragedy in a million	*Video footage (single shot) of two parents, seated*
and why the spotlight shines on a reluctant Mrs Major	*Video footage (single shot) of Norma Major, seated with man at a table, toasting one another with wine glasses*
00:35 good evening (.) President Clinton has been explaining to America and the world today his decision to unleash the biggest attack on Iraq since the Gulf War (.) he said it was to make Saddam Hussein pay for his brutality (.) and to reduce his ability to threaten his neighbours and America's interests (.) the Pentagon said America reserves the right to strike again (.) the attack was in response to President Saddam's move into the designated Kurdish safe area in northern Iraq (.) Britain gave America its unequivocal backing . . .	*Head and shoulders shot of newsreader, News at Ten logo replaced by still image of cruise missile over Iraqi flag, word 'Attack' appears at bottom of image*

Perhaps the most immediately apparent feature of these newscasts' introductions is the similarities they share with regard to their respective modes of address. Both privilege as their leading 'news headline' US President Clinton's decision to launch cruise missiles against targets in Iraq, and then rely upon video footage of these (or similar) missiles being fired from a warship to locate the 'news event' in the now-here. No footage is provided of the missiles detonating; instead, the explosions (without the concomitant loss of life) will be represented at a later point in the newscasts through computer-animated graphics. The contours of the preferred definition of the situation are also readily discernible from the outset, as both newscasts instantly grant discursive ascendancy to the words of the US President. More specifically, they each seek to ratify a news frame which affirms the legitimacy of the military action as defined within the terms of the official rationale.

For the BBC newscast, Clinton's claim to be making the Iraqi President 'pay a price for his brutality' is prioritized, as is his contention that the action is to 'check' the 'clear and present danger Iraq poses to its neighbours'. In the case of the ITN newscast, it is Clinton's explanation that 'reckless acts have consequences' which is authorized, along with the attendant assertions regarding the need to 'make Saddam Hussein pay for his brutality'. Crucially, both newscasts are in this way discursively anchoring the official claim that the action was a necessary 'response' to a threat posed by 'Saddam', and hence it constitutes a *defensive*, as opposed to *offensive*, 'strike'. Neither newscast, at least in its first minute, explicitly frames the official rationale as being contestable, as requiring evidence beyond these truth claims to sustain its inflection of reality. Instead, the conflict is immediately personalized as being between 'Us' (good) and 'Them' (evil) (cf. van Dijk, this volume). This is a world where protectors (Clinton, 'America', 'the Pentagon', and Britain, which 'gave America its unequivocal backing') endeavour to 'check' or 'counter' the dangers posed by an aggressive enemy Other (Saddam Hussein, Iraq, Baghdad) to 'the Gulf', 'the west's oil supplies', Iraq's 'neighbours', 'America's interests' and the 'Kurdish safe area in northern Iraq'. The discursive space for a counter-definition of the situation, such as one which contends that the US 'strike' might actually incite an Iraqi 'retaliation', is thus effectively posited outside the boundaries of the preferred interpretation on offer.

Here it is also important not to overlook the larger performative task of these opening sequences for the newscast. That is to say, attention also needs to be directed to their dramatic role in attracting and maintaining the interest of the viewer and, moreover, the sense of reassurance they offer through their very repetition from one weekday to the next (a sharp contrast is provided by the headline of a news bulletin which suddenly 'interrupts' regular programming; see Doane, 1990). News headlines seek to incorporate the 'extraordinary' into the 'ordinary'; the strangeness of the social world (and hence its potential newsworthiness) is to be mediated within the terms of the familiar. A news event can only 'make sense' to the viewer if she or he is able to situate it in relation to a range of pre-existing 'maps of meaning' (Hall et al., 1978) or forms of cultural knowledge about the nature of society.

The framework of interpretation set down by the news headline thus not only tends to nominate precisely 'what is at issue' and how its significance is to be defined, it also must reaffirm the viewer's sense of what is consequential, or at least relevant, in the context of their daily lives. The language utilized in these opening sequences, both verbal and visual, may therefore be analysed as one way in which the newscast indicates the normative limits of the sense of newsworthiness it attributes to its audience. Clearly, then, once a mode of enquiry elects to seize upon the embeddedness of the newscast in the 'now' and 'here' by prioritizing for critique precisely those elements which are usually ignored in analyses of this type, new aspects of the political struggle over the social relations of signification will be brought to the fore for further exploration.

Decoding televisual news

In seeking to better understand the moment of 'decoding', cultural studies researchers have recognized the necessity of investigating the actual ways in which people relate to televisual news. The varied social uses to which televisual news is put have been examined in association with the (usually unspoken) rules by which the very 'normality' of everyday life is defined and reproduced.

The scheduling of newscasts over the course of the day, for example, presupposes a representative domestic pattern within the household (current sub-genres being variations of 'breakfast news', 'lunchtime news', 'early evening news' or 'suppertime news', the 'evening news', 'late-night news', and so forth). This inscription of television's institutional basis in its programming protocols is also revealed in the strategies employed to build and hold an audience throughout the day. Richard Paterson's (1990: 31–2) discussion of the scheduler's lexicon identifies several of the key formulations in play, including: 'inheritance factor' (a programme which follows a particularly popular one is likely to inherit a proportion of that audience); 'pre-echo' (people tuning into a programme often watch the end of the preceding one, and thus may be encouraged to watch it in future); and 'hammocking' or 'tent-poling' (a less popular programme is placed between two popular ones in order to benefit from inheritance and pre-echo), amongst others. Newscasts thus provide the scheduler with a means to facilitate the structuration of programming flow, namely by serving as points of transition in the routines of daily life and between different genres of entertainment (see also Allan, 1997b; Dahlgren and Sparks, 1992; Williams, 1986).

Morse (1986: 74–5) illustrates some of the potential implications of these dynamics for those people who work both inside and outside of the household when she writes:

> Morning and prime time news occur at key thresholds in the day between work and leisure. Morning news precedes the transit from the privacy of the home, where one kind of reality prevails, to the realm of work, a reality with entirely different roles, hierarchies and rules. Morning news can be used as an alarm and pacing device to speed the viewer/auditor into the rhythms of the work world; the news, however lightly attended, may also orient her/him in social reality. . . . In contrast, the evening news has a more hierarchical 'work' structure in its anchor-reporter relations, and the set, dress and demeanour of the news personalities are from the world of work and its imposed roles. . . . The evening news is a mixed form . . . which aids the transition between one reality and another – between the attentiveness demanded by the world of work and the relaxation promoted by the TV fare of prime time drama and entertainment and the exhaustion of work.

A number of these themes are echoed in Hjarvard's (1994) account of how news programmes perform a ritual function: by tying together the different elements of the schedule, news 'provides variation as well as continuity'. The privileged status of the news as a 'reality-oriented genre' tends to be exploited by schedulers: 'the openness of the news structure creates the impression that the earlier reported events continue in a parallel time, but "behind" the screen while we watch other programmes' (1994: 314). This is an illusion, he argues, 'since social reality is not made up by a limited number of events, but by an infinite number of social interactions', and yet it is an illusion which has arisen because 'the reports of events have already been initiated as *continuous stories*' (1994: 314). As cultural studies research on audiences or 'interpretive communities' has recurrently pointed out, individual viewers invest considerable amounts of energy into, and regularly negotiate significant pleasure from, what they are watching in ways which by their very *normality* are challenging to interpret in cultural terms. The integration of televisual news into everyday routines is clearly informed by this sense of normality; it is a casual, habitual, often intimate part of domestic life. In Ellis's (1992: 160) words, television belongs 'to the normal backdrop of expectations and mundane pleasures'. The televisual institution, he argues, is a 'scanning apparatus', one that 'offers to present the world beyond the familiar and the familial, but to present them in a familiar and familial guise' (1992: 163).

Cultural studies attempts to document arguments of this type in relation to televisual news discourse have drawn upon the research strategies of ethnography to considerable advantage. Evidence drawn from these ethnographic accounts often suggests that how people watch televisual news is much less determined by the actual programming than it is conditioned by the social relations of its consumption. In tracing the contours of the social contexts of viewing within everyday domestic life in the household, a range of studies have highlighted the need to explicate the gendered nature of both televisual technology and the practices by which it is negotiated.

In an early study, entitled 'Housewives and the Mass Media', Dorothy Hobson (1980) examines how a range of factors inform a sexual division of household labour which, in turn, conditions a gender-specificity with regard to programming preferences. Her female interviewees (young working-class mothers of small children) revealed a tendency to demarcate televisual news into a 'masculine' domain. In Hobson's (1980: 109) words:

> There is an *active* choice of programmes which are understood to constitute the 'woman's world', coupled with a complete *rejection* of programmes which are presenting the 'man's world' [predominantly news, current affairs, 'scientific' and documentary programmes].

However, there is also an acceptance that the 'real' or 'man's world' is important, and the 'right' of their husbands to watch these programmes is respected: but it is not a world with which the women in this study wanted to concern themselves. In fact, the 'world', in terms of what is constructed as of 'news' value, is seen as both alien and hostile to the values of women.

The social world, as represented in news discourse, is generally seen by the women in this study to be 'depressing' and 'boring'. Still, Hobson (1980: 111) points out that 'the importance of accepted "news values" is recognised, and although their own world is seen as more interesting and relevant to them, it is also seen as secondary in rank to the "real" or "masculine" world' (see also Feuer, 1986; Gillespie, 1995; Gray, 1992).

Morley (1986), in his study entitled *Family Television: Cultural Power and Domestic Leisure*, reaffirms the general trajectory of Hobson's findings. Employing a qualitative, interview-based research strategy, Morley collected material from eighteen inner London familial ('white', primarily working- and lower middle-class) households. Overall, Morley is able to suggest that once a distinction is made between 'viewing' and 'viewing attentively and with enjoyment', it is possible to discern a marked gendering of people's engagement with televisual news. Regarding programme type preference, Morley (1986: 162–3) writes:

> My respondents displayed a notable consistency in this area, whereby masculinity was primarily identified with a strong preference for 'factual' programmes . . . and femininity identified with a preference for fictional programmes. . . . Moreover the exceptions to this rule (where the wife prefers 'factual programmes', etc.) are themselves systematic. This occurs only where the wife, by virtue of educational background, is in the dominant position in terms of cultural capital.

By accentuating this sense of the lived nature of the televisual news experience, Morley demonstrates why this medium needs to be located as an integral part of everyday life in the household and as such acknowledged as one of several sites of contestation. Televisual news, as his work and that of Hobson illustrates, can be the object of a micropolitics of domestic power, the material nature of which may be shaped by the hierarchical dictates of familial ideology.

This 'turn to ethnography' within cultural studies continues to facilitate the development of new research agendas for investigating the decoding of televisual news. That said, however, most of the more recent work has been directed to other genres, most notably 'soap opera' (which does exhibit a number of similar narrative conventions: see Fiske, 1987). One important exception is the work of Klaus Bruhn Jensen (1986, 1990, 1994), who has sought to examine the processes of meaning production in empirical terms by focusing on the 'oppositional decoding' of televisual news content by various groups in the USA.[7] In taking issue with the claim that the very process of watching televisual news may be properly conceived of as a political, even oppositional activity in and by itself, Jensen (1990: 58) argues that counter-hegemonic decodings are not in themselves a concrete materialization of political power. Instead, he maintains, the 'wider ramifications of opposition at the textual level depend on the social and political uses to which the opposition may be put in contexts beyond the relative privacy of media reception'. It follows that in addition to questioning whether or not the 'preferred meanings' of the newscast are accepted by the viewer, attention needs to turn to consider the designated social uses of this genre of discourse (and how they have evolved over time), on the one hand, and the changing forms of its actual relevance to the viewer, on the other hand.

Briefly, Jensen (1990) identifies four general types of 'uses' which the viewers in his study ascribed to televisual news in terms of its significance for their daily lives.

1 Televisual news has *contextual uses*: that is, the (usually gendered) roles and routines of ongoing activities in the household, especially with regard to domestic labour, are often partially structured by news viewing. The daily rhythms associated with news times, he argues, have become *naturalized*: 'There are no arguments [amongst the respondents], for example, that the evening news might be scheduled differently, fitting news to everyday life rather than vice versa' (1990: 64).

2 There are *informational uses* of televisual news for the viewer, particularly in their roles as 'consumer, employee, and, above

all, as citizen and voter'. Here he discerns a tension in the interview material from his respondents between 'the active and public uses which are associated with the news genre in a political perspective and . . . its more limited practical relevance for audiences in terms of "keeping up" with issues for the purpose of conversation or voting in political elections' (1990: 68). One respondent, identified as a 'printer', is quoted by Jensen (1990: 67) as making a typical statement about the opportunity for political participation:

> Well, I can vote. As far as taking any further, I don't know. I guess the opportunity will have to arise. Being, you know, I feel I'm just the average person out here . . .

3 The implications of this tension for the social definition of news are even more pronounced with respect to what Jensen calls the *legitimating uses* of televisual news. His interview material indicates that the political relevance of news to the viewer may be characterized in terms of the twin concepts of control and distance: 'The news may give its audience a sense of control over events in the world which would otherwise appear as distant . . . it is the *feeling* of control which is crucial, even if "you can't do anything about it"' (1990: 68, 69). To the degree that televisual news is seen by the viewer to offer a 'generalised sense of community', then, it is equally likely to be considered to be an adequate forum for the articulation of public issues (see also Allan, 1997a; Corner, 1995; Hartley, 1996).

4 Finally, Jensen pinpoints the *diversional uses* of televisual news as discussed by his respondents, namely the variety of its visual pleasures for the viewer. The designated social uses for news, whilst generally defined by the respondents as distinct from those of entertainment, nevertheless share with them several important features. In particular, the 'holding power' of the visual narrative is deemed to be significant. The respondents attached salience not only to the visuals of the news events, which were seen as communicating 'a sense of experiential immediacy' (words such as 'pleasing', 'enjoyable', 'easy', 'vivid' and 'exciting' are used by the respondents), but also to the actual performance of the news. In the case of newsreaders, for exam-

ple, both journalistic competence and personal appeal are stressed, whilst other respondents emphasized the appeal of 'nice, trivial information'.

These four types of 'uses', then, suggest to Jensen (1990: 73–4) that:

> The reception of television news may, accordingly, be seen as an agent of *hegemony* which serves to reassert the limits of the political imagination. . . . [E]ven though the social production of meaning can be seen as a process in which the prevailing definition of reality may be challenged and revised, the outcome of that process is overdetermined by the historical and institutional frameworks of communication. The polysemy of media texts is only a political potential, and the oppositional decoding of media is not yet a manifestation of political power. . . . [P]eople make their own sense of the media, but that sense is bounded by the social definitions of genres [such as news].

It is to the issue of how best to advance new research strategies to explore further the extent to which televisual news discourse operates to 'reassert the limits of the political imagination' that this chapter now turns.

5 Conclusion

The importance of cultural studies research is being increasingly recognized by language analysts working in such diverse areas as sociolinguistics, conversational analysis, pragmatics and, perhaps most markedly, critical discourse analysis. As I have attempted to show in this chapter, cultural studies provides a new vantage point from which we may proceed to engage in a radical rethinking of the ideological embeddedness of media discourse in relations of power and resistance. By seeking to render problematic an array of conceptual and methodological assumptions which tend to underpin more conventional approaches to the dynamics of meaning production, cultural studies re-centres for critique a range of questions that otherwise tend to be displaced as being 'outside' the realm of language analysis proper.

At the same time, of course, it would be advantageous for cultural studies researchers to look beyond semiotics to consider what these other, more linguistic-centred approaches can contribute. The finely detailed insights into the mechanisms of ideology being generated in areas such as critical discourse analysis, for example, have much to offer a cultural studies approach which cannot attend to the same degree of linguistic specificity. Perhaps now is the moment to consider a closer alignment of these two modes of enquiry where warranted by the discursive dynamics under investigation. An effort to enhance the connections between these approaches may have positive strategic advantages as well, given that they share a commitment to an interventionary form of analysis directed toward the advancement of a progressive cultural politics.

Over the course of its discussion, this chapter has endeavoured to highlight several such points of connection so as to help to secure, in turn, a basis for future collaborative efforts. It is with this aim in mind that I wish to suggest that investigations into televisual news may advantageously extend the theoretical trajectory outlined here in a number of substantive ways. Specifically, I would argue that the concept of hegemony needs to be further elaborated so as to account more rigorously for the complex ways in which the news media, as key terrains of the ongoing political struggle over the right to define the 'reality' of public issues, operate to mediate the risks, threats and dangers engendered across the society they purport to describe.

This aim could be realized, in part, by focusing our analyses more directly on the indeterminacies or contradictions (the exceptions to the conventionalized rules) implicated in televisual news discourse's preferred appropriations of 'the world out there'. Here I am suggesting, especially in light of the ethnographic research on news audiences assessed above, that we need to be much more sensitive to the contingent nature of the representational strategies being used in news discourse. Attempts to demonstrate how these strategies are organized to disallow or 'rule out' alternative inflections of reality should, at the same time, seek to identify the extent to which the same strategies are being challenged, even transgressed, over time. Given that the *naturalization* of any truth claim is always a matter of degree, it is crucial that analyses recognize the more subtle devices by which 'common sense' has to be continuously revalidated as part of the reportorial performance, and thereby avoid a reliance upon rigid, zero-sum formulations of hegemony to sustain their theses.

Such an approach may enable us to identify much more precisely the nature of the processes by which this form of media discourse structures the public articulation of truth. Following Williams (1974: 130), who contends that the 'reality of determination is the setting of limits and the exertion of pressures, within which variable social practices are profoundly affected but never necessarily controlled', I would agree with those who argue that a much greater conceptual emphasis needs to be placed on how televisual news conditions what counts as 'truth' in a given instance, and who has the right to define that truth. At the same time, though, equal attention needs to be given to discerning the openings for different interpretive communities to potentially recast the terms by which 'truth' is defined in relation to their lived experiences of injustice and inequalities (once again, after Williams, determination is not a single force, but rather an exertion of continuous, but often unpredictable, pressures). Such a shift in focus would mean that research questions posed within a narrowly framed 'domination–opposition' dynamic could be clarified through a much more fundamental interrogation of the very precepts informing the fluid configuration of facticity in the first place.

Televisual news discourse could thus be deconstructed not only through a critique of its projection of journalistic distance and 'impartiality', but also by resisting its movement toward closure around 'common-sense' criteria of inclusion and exclusion. It follows that in addition to asking *whose* common sense is being defined by the newscast as *factual*, we need to ask: by what representational strategies is the viewer being invited to 'fill in the gaps', or being encouraged to make the *appropriate, rational* inferences, in order to reaffirm journalistic procedures for 'handling' contrary facts which are otherwise discrepant to the news frame? In my view, once this 'setting of limits' on the narrativization of meaning has been denaturalized to the point that the politics of its *naturalness* are rendered explicit, analyses may proceed to identify in televisual news the slippages, fissures and silences which together are always threatening to undermine its discursive authority. In other words, this type of research may be able to contribute to the empowerment of those counter-hegemonic voices seeking to contest the truth politics of televisual news discourse, not least by helping to first disrupt and then expand the ideological parameters of 'the obvious facts of the matter'.

NOTES

I wish to thank the editors of this volume, as well as Barbara Adam, Gill Branston, Cynthia Carter and Tom O'Malley, for their helpful comments on an earlier draft of this essay.

1 Four additional points are important here. First, while there is certainly no one 'approach' that is representative of cultural studies research on news discourse, I shall use the term here as a form of analytical shorthand to stand in for an array of contending approaches that rely upon some configuration of 'cultural studies' in their engagement with a particular news problematic. Second, it is important to recognize that even at that time there was much disagreement within the CCCS regarding what should constitute cultural studies, and what its 'true origins' actually were (here several of the essays collected in Morley and Chen (1996) offer insights into these developments; regrettably, however, there is little mention of the work around news discourse). Third, the notion of 'discourse' in much of this early work is loosely derived either from Barthes (1967, 1973) or from Vološinov (1973), but it would later undergo much more rigorous scrutiny in the subsequent debates around Foucault's provocative formulations. Finally, for a consideration of various re-inflections of cultural studies in different national contexts, particularly in North America and Australia respectively, see Blundell, Shepherd and Taylor (1993); Brantlinger (1990); Davies (1995); Grossberg Nelson and Treichler (1992); McGuigan (1992); and Storey (1996).

2 Echoes of this study's findings reverberate throughout Reeves and Campbell's (1994) examination of televisual news coverage of the so-called 'cocaine epidemic' in the USA. Regarding the processing of 'drug stories', they argue that 'reporters seek out "appropriate" enforcement, medical, and academic experts who typically provide enough conflict to sustain the news narrative. Police, doctors, and social scientists contribute their *expert* voices to the pool of knowledge that the reporter then arranges and (re)presents. These news characters are from the land of specialised knowledge. And the language of this realm is frequently

"jargonese", which often has to be decoded and translated into "common sense" by the reporter' (1994: 56).

3 Hall's intervention took the form of a 1973 Stencilled Occasional Paper, entitled 'Encoding and Decoding in the Television Discourse', published by what was then the Centre for Contemporary Cultural Studies at the University of Birmingham. An edited extract of that paper, entitled 'Encoding/Decoding', appeared as Hall (1980) and it is this version which has been so widely cited.

4 Over the years, a number of different case studies have been launched within cultural studies in order to try to interrogate the precepts underpinning the rather abstract neatness of these decoding positionalities. For recent overviews of this work, see Ang (1996), Moores (1993) and Nightingale (1996).

5 'Ideological hegemony in the news media', as Fishman (1980: 140) writes, 'can occur without the direct intervention of publishers or editors, without the existence of informal news policies into which reporters are socialised, and without secret programs in news organisations to recruit reporters sharing a particular point of view. The ideological character of news follows from journalists' routine reliance on raw materials which are already ideological.'

6 This discussion of the first minute of these two newscasts could clearly be extended in a number of interesting ways. In addition to those features briefly highlighted here, greater attention could be given to the means by which ideological processes are being embedded in relations of transitivity, nominalization, modality, and so forth. Moreover, and in following the encoding–decoding agenda, researchers could also investigate the institutional relations which inform the production of the opening sequences and headlines, as well as the extent to which audiences actually negotiate this mode of address within the parameters intended by the newsworkers. Examples, except where stated otherwise, are drawn from six different newscasts (BBC: 1.00 p.m., 6.00 p.m. and 9.00 p.m.; ITN 12.30 p.m., 5.40 p.m., 10.00 p.m.) broadcast in the week of 10 July 1996.

7 Regarding the research methodology, Jensen (1990: 59) writes: 'A total of twelve news programmes and twenty-four interviews were recorded in a metropolitan area of the north-eastern United States during three randomly selected weeks in the autumn of 1983. On a given night, a particular news programme was recorded, and on the following day the recording was shown to two respondents individually, who subsequently were interviewed individually.'

Chapter 5

Political Discourse in the Media: An Analytical Framework

Norman Fairclough

My main objective in this chapter is to set out an analytical framework for researching political discourse in the contemporary mass media. Political discourse is seen as an 'order of discourse' (the term is explained shortly) which is continuously changing within wider processes of social and cultural change affecting the media themselves and other social domains which are linked to them. The proposed analytical framework is an application to a particular field of a version of 'critical discourse analysis', and I therefore begin the chapter with a summary account of it. I shall then set out the analytical framework, and illustrate it with an analysis of extracts from an edition of the BBC Radio 4 news and current affairs programme *Today*.

My starting point for this chapter is a critical comment of Bourdieu's about discourse analysis:

> it would be superficial (at best) to try to analyse political discourses or ideologies by focusing on the utterances as such, without reference to the constitution of the political field and the relations between this field and the broader space of social positions and processes. This kind of 'internal analysis' is commonplace . . . as exemplified by . . .

attempts to apply some form of semiotics or 'discourse analysis' to political speeches. . . . all such attempts . . . take for granted but fail to take account of the sociohistorical conditions within which the object of analysis is produced, constructed and received. (Quoted in Thompson, 1991: 28–9)

While I think that 'internal analysis' in the sense of close textual analysis is essential if we are really to develop an understanding of political discourse, Bourdieu is right to insist that internal analysis of political discourses or texts which does not place them with respect to the political field and its wider social frame is of limited value. I propose to partially meet this criticism by arguing that analysis of media political discourse (and indeed of any sort of discourse) should have a duality of focus: on communicative events, and on the order of discourse. It should aim to simultaneously illuminate particular communicative events, and the constitution and transformation of the political order of discourse. By the political order of discourse, I mean the structured configuration of genres and discourses which constitutes political discourse, the system – albeit an open and shifting one – which defines and delimits political discourse, at a given point in time. Bourdieu's criticism of discourse analysis is well grounded: much discourse analysis is analysis of communicative events which does not attempt to map them on to orders of discourse. Yet an adequate analysis of communicative events as forms of social practice – an adequate discourse analysis of communicative events – does need to locate them within fields of social practice and in relation to the social and cultural forces and processes which shape and transform those fields. Orders of discourse are fields of practice seen in specifically discursive terms. I am suggesting that we can do discourse analysis in a way which moves to meet Bourdieu's criticism, although I am not suggesting that this is the whole answer: discourse analysis also needs to be properly integrated with other forms of social analysis.

1 Critical Discourse Analysis

I have space here only to give a summary account of main features of the version of critical discourse analysis (henceforth CDA) which

I work with that are particularly relevant to the issue at hand (for more detailed descriptions, see Fairclough, 1992, 1995a, and 1995b). This version of CDA is characterized by the combination of two commitments: an interdisciplinary commitment, and a critical commitment. The interdisciplinary commitment is to constitute CDA as a resource for the investigation of changing discursive practices, and thereby enable it to contribute to a major contemporary research theme in social science: the analysis of ongoing social and cultural change, often construed in terms of major shifts within or shifts away from modernity (towards 'late modernity' or 'postmodernity'). The critical commitment is to understanding from a specifically discoursal and linguistic perspective how people's lives are determined and limited by the social formations we are blessed or cursed with; to foregrounding the contingent nature of given practices, and the possibilities for changing them. These two commitments come together, for instance, in the study of contemporary processes of marketization of discourse – the tendency to restructure the discursive practices of, for example, public service domains such as education on the model of the discursive practices of the market (entailing, for instance, a proliferation of forms of advertising discourse).

This version of CDA is conceived as mapping three different sorts of analysis on to one another in an attempt at integrated statements which link social and cultural practices to properties of texts. The three sorts of analysis are:

- analysis of texts (spoken, written, or involving a combination of semiotic modalities, e.g. televisual texts);
- analysis of discourse practices of text production, distribution and consumption;
- analysis of social and cultural practices which frame discourse practices and texts.

A key feature of this version of CDA is that the link between texts and society/culture is seen as mediated by discourse practices. Since this mediating form of analysis is conceived of in a way that is distinctive, a little more needs to be said about it.

The analysis of discourse practice is probably best thought of as actually a complex of different sorts of analysis, including more discursive aspects of institutional processes (e.g. practices of producing TV news programmes), as well as sociocognitive aspects of discourse processing. But my focus here and more generally is on intertextuality: on how in the production and interpretation (as part of what I called above 'consumption') of a text people draw upon other texts and text types which are culturally available to them. This cultural resource for text production and consumption is conceptualized in terms of a concept borrowed but also adapted from Foucault (1984) – 'order of discourse'. The claim is that texts have a dual orientation to 'systems' in a broad sense: there are language systems, and there are orders of discourse. The text–system relationship in both cases is dialectical: texts draw upon but also constitute (and reconstitute) systems. An order of discourse is a structured configuration of genres and discourses (and maybe other elements, such as voices, registers, styles) associated with a given social domain – for example, the order of discourse of a school. In describing such an order of discourse, one identifies its constituent discursive practices (e.g. various sorts of classroom talk and writing, playground talk, staffroom talk, centrally produced documentation, etc.), and crucially the relationships and boundaries between them. The concern, however, is not just with the internal economy of various separate orders of discourse. It is with relationships of tension and flow across as well as within various local orders of discourse in an (open) system that we might call the 'societal order of discourse'. For instance, two pervasive tendencies affecting contemporary orders of discourse are what I have called 'conversationalization of discourse' – the colonization of public orders of discourse by the conversational practices of the order of discourse of everyday life (the 'lifeworld'); and 'marketization of discourse' as defined above (Fairclough, 1995b).

The framework combines the concepts of 'heteroglossia' and hegemony: it stresses the diversity and proliferation of discursive practices and generative processes in which they are creatively rearticulated; but it sees these processes as limited by hegemonic relations and structures, and as a terrain of hegemonic struggle.

The framework also foregrounds the texture of texts: it is addressed both to correcting the socially impoverished nature of much analysis of language within linguistics, and the textually impoverished nature of much analysis of discourse in social science: hence the focus on what close analysis of texture can contribute to social and cultural analysis of discourse.

2   Contemporary Politics and Political Discourse

There is a general perception that politics is currently changing, in transition. For many, it is a crisis of politics. Some people see it as the political being squeezed out of contemporary social life. Others see it more as a partial relocation of the political, from the empty shells of the political system, towards what some call 'subpolitics', the politics of new forms of grassroots social movement like animal rights groups or roads protesters in European countries (Beck, 1994). My longer-term aim in current work is to bring a specifically discourse analytical perspective to bear on this debate. My questions are these: how is the contemporary order of political discourse structured, and what are the major tendencies of change?

One major problem in such a project is delimiting the political. Where does politics end? It is not just the analyst's problem, it is a structural problem of social life. I find it helpful here to use a characterization of politics as an interaction of different societal systems, suggested by Held (1987): in his terms, the interaction of the political system (meaning the system of official professional politics – the political parties, Parliament, and so forth), the social system and the economy. The nature of politics in different times and places is a matter of how these systems differently interact. This means that the limits of the political are constantly at issue: what is the relationship between the state and civil society? how politicized is domestic life? and so forth. There is a discourse analytical reading of this: the shifting nature of politics can be characterized and explored in terms of shifting relationships between – shifting articulations of – orders of discourse. Thus contemporary political discourse articulates together the orders of discourse of the political system (conventional, official politics), of the media, of science and technology, of grassroots sociopolitical movements, of ordinary private life, and so forth – but in an unstable and shifting configuration. Questions here are: what, at a given point in time, is the space taken up by political discourse in terms of relationships between orders of discourse, and what are the main points of tension, the main flows, the main directions of movement?

Also helpful here is Bourdieu's (1991) suggestion that the political discourse of professional politicians is doubly determined. It is, so to speak, 'internally' determined by its position within the rarefied field of professional politics, the political structures as such. And it is, so to speak, 'externally' determined by its relationship to fields outside politics – particularly to the lives of the people politicians 'represent'. Strangely, though, Bourdieu does not foreground the mass media. Mediatized politics is an important part of contemporary politics. One would think that the media were an obvious place to look to see processes of 'external' determination of professional political discourse.

In the terms of the CDA framework I have introduced, power enters the picture here as power struggle to achieve hegemony in two ways:

(a) 'internally' within the order of discourse of the political system in the articulation of different discursive practices;
(b) 'externally' in the articulation of different systems and different orders of discourse. The internal struggle for hegemony is a struggle between political parties and political tendencies.

An example is the struggle to establish the hegemony of Thatcherite political discourse in Britain first within the Conservative Party, then within the political system as a whole, and ultimately beyond it – so 'internal' struggle turns into 'external' struggle. The external struggle for hegemony is a struggle between professional politicians and other social agents in fields which intersect with the political system – for example, between politicians and journalists in the mass media, and between politicians and grassroots activists in social movements such as the environmentalist and ecological movements. In focusing on 'struggle', I do not wish to suggest a struggle of each against all: accommodations and alliances are also an important part of the picture (see below).

3   Political Discourse in the Media

Agents

A way into the articulated structure of mediatized politics is to identify the main categories of agents that figure in mass media politics. Professional politicians are one, of course. Journalists are another. They have a prominent political role in their own right; they do not just 'mediate' others. Another category is 'experts' of various sorts – political analysts, academic political scientists, pundits. Another is people who are politicians, but in a non-traditional sense: representatives of various new social movements, such as ecologists or animal rights activists. Another is economic agents – employers, trade unionists. And another is 'ordinary people', who have for instance started to play a bigger part in political conversation and debate in audience discussion programmes, like the *Oprah Winfrey Show* in the USA or *Kilroy* in Britain. All of these categories of agent are potential protagonists and antagonists in struggles for hegemony in the media, or potentially in alliances and accommodations. The categories of agent that I have identified are very general. They have their own internal complexity. Politicians, for instance, belong to different parties and tendencies. And there is the question of how social class, gender and cultural membership cut across, inflect and diversify these categories. Also, there are important movements between these categories of agent. For instance, at a certain point some grassroots environmentalist political activists shifted into the official political system to form Green parties, whereas others stayed outside the system.

The articulation of these categories of agent in mediatized political discourse points to the articulation of different social systems, as suggested by Held, and an articulation of different orders of discourse. So mediatized political discourse as an order of discourse is constituted by a mixing of elements of the orders of discourse of the political system – the lifeworld (ordinary life), sociopolitical movements, various domains of academic and scientific expertise, and so forth – with journalistic discourse. One issue is how well the hybridity of mediatized political discourse represents the hybridity of politics – whether, for example, the media give undue prominence to the official political system, whether that is true of some sections of the media, or some types of programme within the broadcast media, more than others, and so forth. It is important to focus not only upon the shifting discursive practices of politics but also the shifting representations of those practices, which are an important aspect of the practices and an important factor in struggles over the direction of their articulatory movement. In addition to struggle between agents and orders of discourse, we need to look out for confluences and alliances. Derrida has warned of the powerful emergent confluence between political discourse, academic discourse and media discourse. Indeed, one of the issues is whether to see predominantly struggle or complicity between agents in media discourse, and to decide how real or how superficial apparent struggle is, to decide who the real protagonists and antagonists are.

There are strong associations between different categories of agent and different discourses established in the orders of discourse which are articulated together in mediatized politics. To an extent, the different categories of agent 'bring their discourses with them' from other orders of discourse. But the matching of agents to discourses is not simple. Professional politicians change their political discourses in response to the shifting structure of the political field. 'Blairism' is in some ways like 'Thatcherism', for instance. But it is more than this. Different categories of agent appropriate each other's discourses in complex ways. For example, ordinary people may appropriate professional political discourses and expert discourses to varying degrees, and politicians certainly now systematically appropriate the lifeworld discourse of ordinary people, as indeed do experts. And professional politicians extensively appropriate the discourses of 'subpolitics', for instance those of the environmentalist movements. Indeed, there is a dual movement: a 'subpoliticization' of official politics, but also an official 'politicization' of subpolitics, so that, to take the case of green discourses, we find them within the environmentalist and ecological social movements, in the Green parties and in the 'mainstream' parties. Their recontextualization entails transformation – green discourses do not simply remain invariable across these sites (Bernstein, 1990). What we might call 'ownership' of discourses, like access to discourses, is a significant aspect of hegemonic struggles over orders of discourse.

Genres

To operate successfully in the media, agents from other domains need to command the discourses and the genres of the media. One of the problems for politicians in the new mediatized politics is learning a new form of cultural capital: how to operate, for instance, within media genres such as not only the political interview but also phone-in programmes, chat shows, and even domains of 'covert politics',[1] such as women's magazine programmes. Media genres involve a complex admixture of genres from other domains – such as genres of political debate and political speaking from the political system – which are recontextualized (and in the process may be significantly transformed) within the media. The genres of broadcasting often have a complex hybrid or heterogeneous character. For instance, Livingstone and Lunt (1994) suggest that audience discussion programmes like the *Oprah Winfrey Show* evolve a heterogeneous genre which combines three established genres only one of which is 'political' – debate, romance, therapy. A corollary of this generic diversity is that the categories of agent that figure in such programmes are plurally constructed. To quote Livingstone and Lunt (1994: 56):

> The generic ambiguity is clearly seen in the role of the host: is he or she the chair of a debate, the adored hero of a talk show, a referee, a conciliator, a judge, the compere of a game show, a therapist, the host of a dinner party conversation, a manager or a spokesperson? At times, the host plays any one of these roles, thus altering the roles of other participants and listeners.

As the last sentence of this quotation suggests, the heterogeneity of genres implies a shift in audience address and a change in the cultural capital of audiences, and raises questions about audience reception which also need to be part of researching mediatized political discourse. Indeed, the issue is wider than that. Discourse analysis cannot simply focus upon the texts and talk of mediatized politics; it needs also to analyse the practices of political discourse both on the side of production, and on the side of reception/consumption. On the side of production, one might for instance trace the development and projection of political programmes as processes which systematically chain together various types of political talk and text into 'intertextual chains' (Fairclough, 1992, 1995a) – private and public discussion and debate, drafting and editing of documents, news conferences, political interviews, and so forth.

A fruitful perspective may be to see the genres of mediatized politics as devices for articulating together the adjacent orders of discourse which define the space of political discourse. It is thus perhaps better to talk about 'generic complexes' (see the Introduction to Fairclough, 1995b) of mediatized politics, given that they can incorporate a number of genres. A generic complex articulates orders of discourse (genres, discourses) together in particular ways, and effects particular positionings of agents in relation to them. For instance, contemporary political interview might be looked at as a device for articulating together the orders of discourse of the political system, the media and the ordinary lifeworld of the audience. Political interviews typically mix their genres and their discourses. In complex ways, politicians characteristically shift into conversational genre, and draw upon lifeworld discourses, in finding ways to address mass audiences who are listening or watching in mainly domestic environments. A particular articulation of genres and discourses within a generic complex is a particular effect of power corresponding to a particular state of hegemonic relations. It is also a potential focus for resistance and struggle. To take an example, not all professional politicians are willing to go along with more aggressive and contestatory styles of political interview which fit in with media priorities to make programmes more entertaining by subordinating political discussion to gladiatorial contest.

4   Example: The *Today* Programme

The approach to political discourse set out above is formulated in terms of a large-scale programme of research on the contemporary order of political discourse. No single example can therefore really do justice to it. The illustration which follows is intended just to give a sense of some of the potential of the approach. I have chosen an edition (Saturday 13 July 1996) of the BBC Radio 4 *Today* programme which is broadcast six days per week between 6.30 a.m. and 8.40 a.m. (7 a.m.–9 a.m. on Saturdays). I suggested at the beginning of this chapter that a response within discourse analysis to the critical comments of Bourdieu would be to maintain a duality of focus, on the order of discourse and on the communicative event. I wish to do that with this example. More specifically, I would like to address in turn two questions which respectively reflect these two focuses:

• how does the *Today* programme contribute to articulating the political order of discourse?
• how are the resources of the order of discourse interactively used here?

The first of the questions draws attention to the different ways in which different programmes on radio and television (and also different newspapers) not only manifest a political order of discourse which transcends them, but also actively contribute to its constitution and transformation. A programme like *Today* assembles a distinctive set of political agents, discourses and genres and combines them in a distinctive way: how similar to and how different from other programmes and outlets needs to be established. It may constitute a more or less influential intervention to push the political order of discourse in a particular direction. Since I am focusing on just one edition of *Today*, my aim here is simply to get a preliminary sense of its particular contribution to the articulation of the political order of discourse.

The news item which dominated the programme was a crisis in Northern Ireland: the aftermath of the decision by the Chief Constable of the Royal Ulster Constabulary to allow the unionist Orange Order to march through a nationalist area in Portadown, Northern Ireland. The decision led to vigorous and sometimes violent protests from the nationalist community against what was perceived as British Government capitulation to the unionists, and there was a perception that the whole peace process in Northern Ireland was at risk.[2] I shall focus on this item. It is interspersed in the programme with other items. For example, the programme begins with a news bulletin which covers Northern Ireland along with other issues, followed by two interviews appertaining to Northern Ireland, but then two unconnected reports (on a dispute between clergy at an English cathedral, and on a landless peasants' movement in Brazil), a review of readers' letters (some about Northern Ireland), a sports report, a weather forecast, and a news summary (which again is partly about Northern Ireland). In total, there are six interviews relating to the Northern Ireland crisis in the programme, and the crisis is also covered in two news bulletins and two news summaries, readers' letters, a report on the day's press, as well as in the religious spot *Thought for the Day*.

The main agents assembled by the programme are Northern Ireland political leaders (Gerry Adams of nationalist Sinn Fein, David Trimble of the Ulster Unionists and John Hulme of the Social Democratic Labour Party); the British Northern Ireland Secretary (Sir Patrick Mayhew); the Prime Minister of the Irish Republic (John Bruton); a former Chief Constable of the Royal Ulster Constabulary (Sir John Herman); a former professor at a university in Northern Ireland who is now a Minister in the South African government; the Irish Catholic leader (Cardinal Daley) and an Anglican Bishop (Bill Westwood), who does *Thought for the Day*. All of them speak for themselves, though some are interviewed at length whereas others are represented only through brief recorded excerpts. Ordinary people (though from the British mainland, not from Ireland) also have a presence in the programme but only in the highly mediated form of selected extracts from their letters which are read by the two presenters, John Humphrys and Sue McGregor. One of the objectives of the analysis is to identify absences, and it is notable in this case that the voices of ordinary people in Northern Ireland are not included.

One striking feature of the programme is the extent to which it is anchored in the presenters: there are relatively few reports from journalists or correspondents; most of the features in the programme are interviews involving one of the presenters. Even journalists and correspondents are in some cases interviewed by the presenters rather than giving their own reports. The main exception to this constant mediating presence of the presenters is the news bulletins and summaries which are read by another journalist, though even in this case one of the presenters gives the news head-lines before the news bulletin is read. There is a sharp contrast in communicative style between the news and the rest of the pro-gramme. The following is part of a news summary:

> Anglo-Irish relations are under severe strain after the Irish Prime Minister John Bruton attacked the Government's hand-ling of the Orange Order march through Portadown. He said the decision to allow the marchers through a Catholic area was a serious mistake which had damaged the peace process. His remarks have been condemned as offensive by the Northern Ireland Secretary Sir Patrick Mayhew. There's been further violence in the nationalist areas across Northern Ireland over-night. Police say hundreds of petrol bombs were thrown at them. They responded by firing large numbers of plastic bul-lets. Shots were fired at a police station in western Belfast.

Generically, this is a (monological) narrative of events, many of them verbal events. This is written language which is read out (which is why I have transcribed it as written sentences). It is a series of categorical statements – declarative sentences, unmodalized – which authoritatively claim knowledge of events. The discourses drawn upon are public discourses. This is evident in the vocabulary, which is drawn from discourses of official politics and diplomacy (e.g. *under severe strain, the peace process*) and official police discourse (e.g. the categorization of nationalist reaction as *violence* and of police reaction to it as *responding*). Categorization in news (another example here is the categorization of certain areas as *nationalist* rather than, say, *Catholic*) is carefully calculated in rela-tion to the range of discourses within the field of politics, and is itself a potential focus of political struggle. The public nature of the discourse is also evident in the grammar – in the density of nominalizations (in just the first two sentences: *Anglo-Irish relations, the Government's handling of the Orange Order march, the Orange Order march, the decision to allow the marchers through, a serious mistake, the peace process*) and in agentless passive clauses (*hundreds of petrol bombs were thrown at them, shots were fired at a police station in west Belfast*). Both of these grammatical features background the actions and agency of people.

In contrast with the news, the rest of the *Today* programme is dominated by dialogue (and especially interview) between the presenters and most of the agents referred to above. The different agents bring a variety of discourses into the dialogue: political, diplomatic, legal, administrative, religious. The presenters have a crucial and distinctive role in articulating different discourses together: in their interaction with interviewees, they give voice to discourses brought to the dialogue by other agents. But the discourse which is predominant in the talk of the presenters is one which they bring to the dialogue themselves (apart from its marginal presence in readers' letters, which are in any case voiced – selectively quoted from – by the presenters themselves): it is a lifeworld discourse, the presenters' version of the discourse of ordinary people in ordinary life. I suggest that this is the crux of the *Today* programme's intervention to shape the way the political discourse is articulated: the programme centres the discourse of ordinary life, confronting the various discourses within the political order of discourse with the presenters' lifeworld discourse. *Today* projects a version of the order of political discourse in which all other discourses are evaluated against this lifeworld discourse.

The following extract from an interview between John Humphrys and the leader of the Ulster Unionist Party, David Trimble, illustrates this (a dot in parentheses indicates a pause of less than a second; square brackets indicate overlapping talk; a colon indicates prolongation of the immediately preceding sound):

BBC Radio 4, *Today* programme, 13 July 1996

Trimble: had the (.) Orange Order not reacted in the way that it did and had it not given leadership in the way that it did the consequences for the whole community in Northern Ireland would have been much much worse

Humphrys: had the Orange Order withdrawn from Dumcree Drumcree had it said alright we will not go ahead with this march becau- peace is more important than a march none of this would have happened

Trimble: no that's quite wrong that's completely and utterly wrong because had the Orange Order acted in the way that you said (.) or suggested (.) then the situation would have been much worse ⌈now
Humphrys: ⌊why
Trimble: well this is what (.) I'm sorry to say (.) neither Mr Alderdyce (.) nor the Northern Ireland Office appreciated (.)

they didn't appreciate the strength of feeling that existed throughout the community in Northern Ireland (.) and had the Orange Order collapsed in the way you suggested (.) then there would have been (.) spontaneous e: (.) outbursts in Northern Ireland there would have been a flood of support for the paramilitaries and the loyalist paramil- the loyal- the loyalist truce would have collapsed

Humphrys: well what you're telling me is the ⌈Ul-
Trimble: ⌊(unclear)
serious disorder
Humphrys: what you're telling me is that the Unionist leadership cannot control its members

Humphrys' first contribution is discoursally heterogeneous. His first clause (*had the Orange Order withdrawn from Dumcree Drumcree*) echoes Trimble's discourse of political argumentation, repeating both the formal hypothetical syntactic construction and the expression *the Orange Order*. But his second combines the same syntactic construction with a shift into direct speech (*alright we will not go ahead with this march . . .*) which effects a shift from a discourse of the political system into the lifeworld discourse (also evoked by *none of this would have happened*). In the case of *peace is more important than a march*, on the other hand, Humphrys is perhaps confronting Trimble with an echo of the discourse of political agents critical of the Unionists (cf. Greatbatch, this volume). Humphrys' closing contribution is a challenging reformulation of what Trimble has said which the latter unsurprisingly does not accept. There are a number of others in the interview: *well what you're telling me again in that case is that the mob rules; well is it that or is it one group of people in Northern Ireland reminding another group of people who is top dog.* These reformulations involve again a shift in discourse, a shift to the lifeworld discourse in the latter two examples, a shift to the discourse of anti-Unionist political agents in the case of the example in the extract above.

Humphrys' other turn, when he interrupts Trimble with the question *why?*, points to the need to elaborate the analytical framework I am using. The word is articulated with a rise + fall intonation contour which reaches a high pitch level. It is a rather aggressive challenge, not just a question, and it expresses incredulity. What is significant about it is that it works sensually and effectively to evoke a particular voice, a particular personality type, and associated values – what I wish to sum up as a particular ethos (see Fairclough, 1992). It is the ethos of common sense – common-sense values, common-sense attitudes, people who possess common sense. Obviously it goes together with the lifeworld discourse I have been referring to: the presenters' version of the discourse of ordinary life. But whereas the concept of a discourse is centrally ideational/referential and to do with how the world is constructed, the concept of ethos centres upon the identities and values that are evoked by particular communicative styles, including quite subtle aspects of pronunciation and prosody.

Today is not only effecting a particular articulation between discourses which privileges the lifeworld discourse; it is also effecting a parallel articulation between ethoses which privileges common sense. In that Humphrys does the main interviews in this particular programme, the privileged ethos is more specifically a white, male and English common sense. For example, *why?* in the extract above evokes for me a talkative lower-middle-class white Englishman propping up the lounge bar on a Sunday lunchtime. This is, of course, just my personal reaction, but the general point is that discoursal markers of ethos do work sensuously by evoking particular people, places, emotions and sensations. The confronting of the political ethos of David Trimble (or the markedly different one of Gerry Adams) with the ethos of common sense therefore carries an undercurrent of the confrontation of Irishness by Englishness.

In the case of Sir Patrick Mayhew, by contrast, it strikes me that there is a social class dimension to the confrontation:

Mayhew: the Chief Constable has made it clear he was faced (.) with a new situation when there was a risk of 50,000 or many more Unionist e: Orange supporters (.) converging upon Portadown and he was faced with the serious risk of lives being lost and he said it was not worth the risk of losing a (.) life I think (.) that those who are critical now of e: what took place and of the Chief Constable's decision (.) have to be asked and have to answer the question how many lives would it have been satisfactory to have lost acceptable to have lost (.) in order to stand by a decision taken in different circumstances five days ago

Humphrys: so in other words if there are enough of them the rule of law gives way

Mayhew: no the rule of law is applied (.) the ⌈law

Humphrys: ⌊but we didn't see the rule of law (*Mayhew:* no no) the Chief Constable did not want that march to go ahead. (*Mayhew:* no just) he gave in because there were so many of them that's what he said

Mayhew: the Chief Constable applied the same law that he applied on Thursday on the sixth of July and that law requires him (.) to take account of likely (.) serious (.) disorder (.) he applied a consistent test what had changed were the circumstances now I regard it (.) as absolutely wrong and irresponsible (.) that a vast number of people should have been threatening to overwhelm the police lines supported as they would have been (.) by (.) the army I regard that as calculated to cause (.) very serious disorder and (.) serious (.) risk of loss of life that was exactly what the Chief Constable assumed

Humphrys: but they got their way so they can do it again

There is a strong presence of legal discourse in Mayhew's contributions throughout this interview, evident here for instance in *that law requires him to take account of likely serious disorder*. In this case, Mayhew is stating what the law is (in others above, he is making assertions about how the Chief Constable applied the law), and doing so in an authoritative, even pontificating, way. It is a categorical assertion (like many of Mayhew's sentences), and one feature of its authoritative delivery which is indicated in the transcription is the rhythm of the last three words – *likely (.) serious (.) disorder* – (presumably quoted from the law) which is even and slow (note the pauses between the words), giving a weightiness to the words. Claiming a specialist knowledge of the law and a capacity to judge its application is itself a basis for authoritative talk. But Mayhew's authoritativeness also has another basis which is not evident from the transcription: his marked upper-middle-class accent and the easy authority of his delivery overall manifest a social facility which is a feature of upper-middle-class cultural capital and ethos

(Bourdieu, 1984). Humphrys' lifeworld discourse and common-sense ethos undermine the taken-for-granted superiority of this upper-middle-class cultural capital, challenge Mayhew's authoritativeness, and in so doing take on a class force in this context which they do not have elsewhere.

This example is already shifting us from the first to the second of my questions, which I just wish to touch briefly upon – how are the resources of the order of discourse interactively used? In addition to looking at the transcriptions above from a structural perspective in terms of the articulations they effect between discourses, one can look at them from an interactive perspective in terms of how participants use the resources available to interactively manage their social relations. For instance, in the interview with Mayhew, Humphrys is faced with the difficult task of challenging a Minister who has played a questionable role in the emergence of this new crisis in Northern Ireland but who has exceptional cultural and rhetorical resources and authority at his disposal. Perhaps it is because Humphrys sees a danger that Mayhew's authoritative pronouncements will swamp his challenges that he is rather aggressive in repeating them, as in the extract above, interrupting Mayhew to do so and talking over his attempts to retake the floor:

> but we didn't see the rule of law (*Mayhew:* no no) the Chief Constable did not want that march to go ahead. (*Mayhew:* no just) he gave in because there were so many of them that's what he said

The particular style of interview used here, including Humphrys' willingness to argue rather than just ask questions, to object, interrupt, is a matter of genre: interviewers have a repertoire of variants of interview genre available which they can deploy strategically according to interactional circumstances, as well as developing their own preferred interviewing styles. Another strategy here which Humphrys often uses in moments of difficulty is attribution – claiming to be reporting what the Chief Constable said (cf. Greatbatch, this volume). However, the formulation of this reported statement draws upon a lifeworld discourse which the Chief Constable himself would be very unlikely to use – *I gave in because there were so many of them* is quite implausible. Humphrys is using lifeworld discourse (including also deictic features: *we*, *that march*) in a rhetorically effective way here to deal with the interactional problem of challenging Mayhew's account.

To close the discussion of this example, I wish to return to the sharp distinction I noted earlier between news and dialogical elements in the *Today* programme. We might see this distinction in terms of a bifurcation of the institutional voice: news maintains some of the authority and distance traditionally associated with the voice of the BBC, whereas the dialogical elements mark a shift away from authority and distance to a voice which simulates and takes its legitimation from the voices and discourses of ordinary life and their common-sense ethos. This appears to be a democratizing move, but it is at the same time an institutionally controlled democratization: the voices of ordinary people are 'ventriloquized' rather than directly heard. It is also arguably a democratization which is open to manipulation: it lends a democratic legitimacy which can be used.

The *Today* programme manifests a more general tendency affecting contemporary public discourse which I have referred to as the 'conversationalization' of public discourse: that is, the modelling of public discourse on ordinary conversation (Fairclough, 1994). An optimistic reading of this development would see it simply as a facet of cultural democratization. But there are difficulties with such an account: conversationalization is generally imposed from above, ordinary people have little control over it, and the relationship between the simulated versions of conversation which it generates and people's real conversation is problematic.

Conversationalization strikes me as neither simply democratic, nor simply engineered for institutional purposes, but as ambivalent, and a focus of struggle. This points again to the importance of Bourdieu's argument that any particular discursive event should be located within a field of discourse and the social forces which shape it. In the case of political discourse, one needs to know first how political talk in a programme like *Today* stands in relation to other political discourse inside and outside the media – its relationship to the structured order of political discourse – and then how it stands in relation to the whole field and practice of politics and the wider social forces which frame it. Only within such a perspective can one decide what to make of the conversationalized discourse of the *Today* programme.

5 Conclusion

I have given only a very partial illustration of how the proposed analytical framework for mediatized political discourse might be used. The framework is also, I think, of value in exploring the emergence of new practices – new genres, new discourses, through the articulation together in new ways of existing ones. I have discussed such processes elsewhere with respect to transformations of the genre of political interview (Fairclough, 1995b) and with respect to the constitution of a new political discourse, that of Thatcherism (Fairclough, 1989, 1995a).

The value of this approach is that it avoids particular discursive events and texts being treated in isolation from the orders of discourse and the wider social fields and processes they are embedded within. A corresponding difficulty with the approach is that one needs an overall sense of the order of discourse and the social order in analysing individual discursive events and texts. One needs, for instance, a sense of the range of genres and discourses used within the political order of discourse as a horizon against which to assess the genres and discourses drawn upon in a particular discursive event. It is ultimately the objective of a research programme using the framework I have suggested to map the genres and discourses of the order of discourse. But meanwhile, readers using this approach have to rely upon a mixture of their own cultural knowledge and what published accounts there are of political discourse.

I will conclude with a summary of the approach in terms of six questions which one can ask about a particular discursive event (e.g. a newspaper article, or a radio or television programme) within mediatized politics:

1 Who are the political agents involved, and what genres, discourses and ethoses are drawn upon?
2 How are they articulated together?
3 How is this articulation realized in the forms and meanings of the text?
4 How are the resources of the order of discourse drawn upon in the management of interaction?

5 What particular direction does this (type of) discursive event give to the articulation of the political order of discourse?

6 What wider social and cultural processes shape and are shaped by the way this discursive event articulates genres, discourses and ethoses?

Notes

I am grateful to Erzsebet Barat, Carlos Gouveia and Anna Mauranen, Celia Ladeira Mota, and Sari Pietikainen, for their comments on a draft of this paper.

1 A term suggested to me by Anna Mauranen.

2 The unionists are in favour of the continuation of the union (i.e. Northern Ireland being a part of the UK), whereas the nationalists favour the reunification of Ireland.

Chapter 6

Conversation Analysis: Neutralism in British News Interviews

David Greatbatch

1 Introduction

The approach and findings of Conversation Analysis (henceforth CA) have been used to examine several forms of broadcast talk, including news interviews, talk shows and phone-in programmes (Crow, 1986; Clayman, 1988, 1989, 1991, 1992, 1993; Clayman and Whalen, 1988/89; Greatbatch, 1986, 1988, 1992; Heritage, 1985; Heritage, Clayman and Zimmerman, 1988; Heritage and Greatbatch, 1991; Heritage and Roth, 1995; Hutchby, 1991). This research aims to explicate the routine, institutionalized speaking practices associated with particular forms of broadcast talk, and to consider how these practices enable and constrain programme participants as they pursue their various tasks and objectives. In this chapter, I illustrate the perspective of CA through an exemplary study of television and radio news interviews broadcast in the United Kingdom.

Several studies of the news interview have been conducted by researchers using analytical frameworks other than CA (e.g. Bull,

1994; Harris, 1991). However, whereas these investigations code and assess news interview conduct, CA studies focus on the locally produced orderliness of news interview encounters. That is to say, they describe the practices and conventions that speakers use and rely upon in order to 'bring off' their interactions as news interviews. In so doing, these studies illuminate the ways in which the statements of news-makers and commentators are shaped and informed by the conventionalized speaking practices which characterize this form of broadcast talk.

Having outlined the methodological framework of CA, I illustrate the approach by examining the relationship between the conduct of participants in UK news interviews and a central constraint associated with broadcast journalism in the UK, namely that broadcast journalists should maintain balance and impartiality in their coverage of news and current affairs. I conclude by discussing some of the analytic implications of the research, and by suggesting some directions for future research.

2   Conversation Analysis

CA emerged in the 1960s, as part of the research programme of ethnomethodology which developed from a series of seminal studies conducted by Harold Garfinkel (1967). From the 1950s onwards, Garfinkel developed an approach to the study of social life which recognizes the interpretative character of situated human action and which is concerned with explicating the competencies which underlie the production and intelligibility of everyday social actions and activities.

The pioneering research of Sacks and his colleagues, Schegloff and Jefferson, led to the emergence of a substantial corpus of ethnomethodological studies concerned with illuminating the social organization which underlies intelligible spoken interaction. These studies were inspired, in particular, by Sacks' proposal that the analysis of tape recordings of talk-in-interaction provides the possibility of developing a 'naturalistic observation discipline which [can] deal with the details of social action(s) rigorously, empirically, and formally' (Schegloff and Sacks, 1974: 233). The methodological framework developed in these studies came to be known as Conversation Analysis.

CA involves detailed, qualitative analysis of audio and video recordings of naturally occurring social interaction. CA research does not involve the formulation and empirical testing of *a priori* hypotheses; rather, it uses inductive search procedures to identify regularities in verbal and/or non-verbal interaction. The objective is to explicate the practices and reasoning which speakers use and rely upon in producing their own behaviour and interpreting and dealing with the behaviour of others. The central resource out of which analysis emerges are the moment-to-moment understandings of their circumstances that parties unavoidably display as they interact with each other.

In locating and analysing recurring patterns of action and interaction, CA researchers repeatedly replay their audio or video recordings of naturally occurring interaction, carefully transcribing the events. The transcripts capture not only what is said, but also a variety of details of speech production, such as overlapping talk, pauses within and between utterances, stress, pitch and volume. They may also track visual conduct such as gaze direction and gesture. These transcripts facilitate the fine-grained analysis of the recordings, enabling researchers to reveal and analyse tacit, 'seen but unnoticed' aspects of human conduct which would otherwise be unavailable for systematic study. Moreover, extracts from the transcripts are included in research reports as exemplars of interactional phenomena under investigation.

Although CA began from the study of ordinary conversations, it has increasingly been used to explicate the competencies underlying social activities within a range of other forms of interaction, including medical consultations, broadcast interviews, calls for emergency assistance, business meetings, divorce mediation sessions, small claims courts, and psychiatric intake interviews (see, for example, Atkinson and Heritage, 1984; Button and Lee, 1986; Boden and Zimmerman, 1992; Drew and Heritage, 1992). It has also been extended to encompass visual as well as vocal conduct (e.g. Goodwin, 1981; Heath, 1986). Thus, despite its name, CA represents a generic approach to the study of social interaction. (For introductions to CA, see Goodwin and Heritage, 1990; Heath and Luff, 1993; Heritage, 1989; Zimmerman, 1988; Greatbatch, Heath, Luff and Campion, 1995.)

CA research on the news interview has focused on various aspects of news interview interaction in the UK and the USA. These include the allocation of opportunities to speak (Greatbatch, 1988; Heritage and Greatbatch, 1991), the design of interviewer utterances and interviewee responses (Greatbatch, 1986; Clayman, 1988, 1992, 1993; Heritage and Roth, 1995; Schegloff, 1988/1989), topic introduction and change (Greatbatch, 1986), openings and closings (Clayman, 1989, 1991) and disagreement between interviewees (Greatbatch, 1992). These studies describe recurrent patterns of interaction and the normative orientations and conventions which underpin them. They explicate how various features embody and exhibit the institutionality of an interaction in general, and its character as a news interview in particular. This involves detailed consideration not only of cases which exhibit conformity with news interview conventions, but also those which involve departures from them (Clayman and Whalen, 1988/89; Schegloff, 1988/89; Heritage and Greatbatch, 1991).

CA research has, then, illuminated the relationship between the interactional practices used in news interviews and the tasks and constraints associated with this form of broadcast journalism (cf. the approach taken by Fairclough, this volume). Below, I illustrate this through a consideration of several aspects of conduct in contemporary news interviews in the UK. In so doing, I draw on previous research by Steven Clayman, John Heritage and myself (Clayman, 1988, 1992; Heritage, 1985; Heritage and Greatbatch, 1991; Heritage, Clayman and Zimmerman, 1988; Greatbatch, 1988). The data are audio and video recordings of television and radio interviews broadcast by the BBC in the UK. These are part of a larger corpus of recordings collected since the late 1970s from a variety of sources.

3   Neutrality and the British News Interview

The news interview has been an important component of broadcast journalism in the UK since the mid-1950s. Its basic function is, of course, the communication of information or opinion from public figures, experts or other persons in the news for the benefit of the news audience. The task of the news interviewer (henceforth IR) is to elicit information and opinion from them and, in some circumstances, to probe or test the views they express.

However, in managing these tasks, IRs must attend to a constraint that bears on all broadcast journalists in the UK. This is the legal requirement that they should maintain impartiality and balance in their coverage of news and current affairs and should refrain from editorial comment on matters of public policy. This requirement is laid down in the charters, licences and Broadcasting Act which set the terms of reference for television and radio broadcasting organizations, and there are penalties for infringement. In the context of the news interview (in which professional journalists are regarded as representatives of the news organizations that employ them), these obligations effectively translate into the requirement that IRs should (1) refrain from the direct assertion of opinions on their own or their employers' behalf, and (2) refrain from overt affiliation with, or disaffiliation from, those expressed by interviewees (henceforth IEs) (Heritage and Greatbatch, 1991). Recognizing that IRs' neutralistic utterances often embody assumptions that are either supportive of or hostile to the positions of IEs and cannot be regarded as neutral, CA researchers refer to this stance 'as embodying a position of "formal neutrality" or, more simply, as a "neutralistic stance"' (Heritage and Greatbatch, 1991: 107).

It is important to be clear about how the term 'neutralistic' is being used here. The term describes a manner or style of interviewing; it refers to patterns of IR conduct which can escape formal charges of bias – whether in the interview context itself or beyond. As such, it does not involve judgements about the substantive neutrality or bias which may be held to inhere in IR conduct (Heritage and Greatbatch, 1991; Clayman, 1992). The maintenance of a neutralistic stance by IRs does not, then, guarantee that their conduct will be viewed as neutral in a substantive sense. IRs may obviously be accused of bias even though they have avoided the direct expression of opinion. For example, the use of aggressive or hostile lines of questioning may be taken as reflecting bias on the part of an IR (Clayman and Whalen, 1988/89). Or relatedly, accusations of bias may be based on apparent discrepancies between the ways in which different categories of IE are interviewed (Hall, 1973b; Schlesinger, Murdock and Elliot, 1983; Jucker, 1986). None the less, the maintenance of a neutralistic stance provides IRs with a first line of defence against such charges.

4   The Maintenance of Interviewer Neutralism

IRs characteristically display an orientation to the constraint that they should maintain a neutralistic stance by producing utterances that are at least minimally recognizable as 'questions' and/or distancing themselves from evaluative statements by attributing them to third parties (who may or may not be named) (Heritage, 1985; Greatbatch, 1988; Clayman, 1988, 1992). IRs also avoid responses which are characteristically produced by 'questioners' in private conversation, as well as other forms of broadcast talk (Greatbatch, 1988; Heritage and Greatbatch, 1991), but which could be taken as indications of agreement or disagreement with what an IE has said. Thus there is an almost complete absence of acknowledgment tokens ('mm hm', 'huh huh', 'yes' etc.), news receipt objects ('oh', 'really', 'did you' etc.) and assessments (Heritage, 1985). By these means, IRs present themselves as soliciting the opinions of others, rather than expressing their own views: that is, they advance a neutralistic stance.

However, as Clayman notes, 'neutralism' does not inhere solely in the conduct of individuals, in this case news IRs (Clayman, 1988, 1992; and see also Heritage and Greatbatch, 1991; Greatbatch and Dingwall, forthcoming). Other participants may challenge or undermine the neutralistic stance advanced by an individual by constituting them as advocates of either personal or institutional positions. The ability of an individual to occupy a neutralistic position in talk-in-interaction is thus dependent upon the collaboration of other participants.

IEs usually collaborate in the maintenance of the neutralistic stance advanced by IRs. They do not generally treat IR utterances as expressing or indexing personal standpoints, regardless of their private opinions about the IRs' motivations. Instead, IEs treat IR utterances as soliciting their viewpoint on the issues raised. This is illustrated by the following case which is taken from an interview between Sir Robin Day and Arthur Scargill, then president of the National Union of Mineworkers, broadcast on 13 March 1979. At the time of the interview, Scargill and Mick McGahey, the Scottish mineworkers' leader, were rivals for the presidency of the NUM. Transcription conventions are set out in the appendix to this chapter.

(1)   BBC Radio 4: *World at One*
IR: .hhh er What's the difference between your marxism and
      Mister McGahey's communism.
AS: er The difference is that it's the press that constantly call
      me a ma:rxist when I do not, (.) and never have (.) er er
      given that description of myself.
      [.hh I-
IR: [But I've heard . . .

In responding to the IR's question, Scargill rejects its presupposition
that he is a marxist. However, he does so without directly challenging the neutralistic stance of the IR. First, he explicitly frames his
response as an answer to the IR's question by repeating its frame
('the difference is'). Second, he treats the presupposition as involving an error of fact (ascribed to 'the press'), not as the expression of
the IR's opinion. During the course of the answer, the IR underlines
his role as a 'neutralistic' elicitor of opinion by withholding response tokens which could be taken as agreement or disagreement
with what the IE is saying.

In Extract 2, we find a similar process after an IR produces a free-
standing evaluative statement which directly counters what the IE
has said in response to an earlier question. This case is drawn from
a BBC interview with Neil Kinnock, then leader of the Labour Party.
It begins just after Kinnock has asserted that a recent Labour Party
policy review is consistent with traditional socialist values.

(2)   BBC Television: *Newsnight*
1   Kin: . . . What you gain of course is a ma:jor (.) taproot .hh
           of socialism.
2   IR: The argument goes of course that (.) this sort of social-
           ism which you
3   descri:be is de<u>fined</u> by Missus Thatcher the fact that
           you've .hhh
4   given <u>up</u> (.) old nationalization you've given up (.) .h
           the sort of
5   taxa:tion which you would have employed ten years
           ago you've
6   given up unilateral nuclear disarmament. She has
           defined the way
7   you have changed.

8   *Kin*: Anyone would (.) who thought that ten years could
     pass (0.5) in: <u>any</u>
9   (.) point of history and not make any <u>dif</u>ference to the
          ter<u>rain</u> .hhh eh
10   (.) in which you have to fight and the appeal that you
          have to make
11   would be: an absolute (.) fool. I suppose I could re<u>but</u>
          the claim by
12   quoting (.) I don't know (0.2) Trotsky. I:t was not from
          our own
13   genius that we made the revolution but from: the
          inheritance
14   bequeathed to us by capitalism. .hhh And <u>that</u> was an
15   acknowledgement a pragmatic acknowledgement of
          reality just as we
16   know now. .hhh But the <u>pas</u>sage of time (0.3) the
          <u>change</u> in the
17   economy (0.1) .h the <u>fact</u> that <u>ten</u> years have gone on:
          (0.2) .h <u>means</u>
18   that (.) it is <u>now</u> (.) in the early <u>nine</u>ties that we have to
          re<u>late</u> to (0.1)
19   <u>n:ot</u> to the late seventies or even (.) .h the nineteen
          fo:rties.

At lines 2–7, the IR produces an assertion which directly challenges
Kinnock's view that the Labour Party's policy review is in accord
with socialist values by proposing that the review has been 'defined' by the agenda and policies of Margaret Thatcher's Conservative administration. However, he does not do this on his own
behalf; rather he describes it as an argument that is made (although
he does not attribute the argument to anyone in particular). As such,
the IR does not go on the record with a personal endorsement of the
counter-assertion and thereby avoids direct disagreement with the
IE (Clayman, 1988, 1992). Correspondingly, Kinnock does not treat
the utterance as expressing the IR's own opinion. Instead he treats
the assertion anonymously ('I suppose I could rebut the claim
by . . .'). As he does so, moreover, the IR remains silent, thereby
withholding response tokens which might compromise his institutionalized role.

In each of these cases, IRs produce utterances which embody contentious propositions with which the IE may be expected to disagree. However, they are careful not to present them as overt expressions of their own or their employers' opinions. The propositions are respectively formulated as a 'factual' presupposition of a question and as the view of unnamed third parties. Correspondingly, the IEs do not challenge or comment on the presuppositions or character of the IRs' utterances. They treat the IRs' utterances as interactionally neutralistic; as designed to solicit their opinions, rather than to express those of the IRs themselves (Clayman, 1988, 1992; Greatbatch, 1988; Heritage, 1985; Heritage and Greatbatch, 1991). As such, they collaborate in the constitution of IRs as neutralistic 'questioners'.

5 Departures from Neutralistic Interviewing

The collaborative maintenance of the IR's neutralistic stance is not inevitable. To begin with, IRs may openly constitute themselves as advocates of particular standpoints. Examples of this are extremely rare and are largely restricted to interviews with the representatives of groups or nations that are widely perceived in the West to be criminal, terrorist or anti-democratic. The following example from a radio interview with a Soviet journalist, broadcast on 24 January 1980, provides a rare example of an IR openly and unilaterally abandoning a neutralistic stance.

The journalist had written a letter to *The Times* objecting to attempts by the United States government to organize a boycott of the forthcoming Olympic Games in Moscow in protest at the Soviet Union's recent invasion of Afghanistan. The IR, Sir Robin Day, points to an apparent contradiction in the IE's position after the latter argues that the call for a boycott is illegitimate because the Olympics should be above politics. If the IE believes this, then why is he against the Olympic Games being held in South Africa? The IE responds by suggesting that the South African case concerns the denial of human rights to the black majority, whereas the Soviet situation is a political matter. The IR responds with a hostile question which challenges the IE's right to talk about human rights given that the Soviet Union has exiled a leading dissident, Andrei Sakharov.

(3)   BBC Radio 4: *World at One*
  1 IR: What right have you got to talk about human rights when your (.)
  2   country has just er .h taken away the liberty of Andrei Sakharov er
  3   .hh for his er .hh opinio:ns.
  4   (.)
  5 SB: Well it's not for his opinions. Bu::t .h for e::r u- what (.) you .hhh er
  6   may er ( )- er what we say here in the Soviet Union for .hhh usi:ng (.)
  7   er the Soviet people to become ( )- (to influence of er hostile ad-
  8   er- er - er- hostile actions) and interferences into the Soviet .hhh
  9   [(   )]
 10 IR: [But how could y-] how could you talk about human rights when
 11   Doctor Sakharov has been banished .hhh without (.) tria::l (.) .hh er
 12   and without as far as we can see any form of just (.) process.
 13 SB: Well e can say about an- er uhm any of the administra-tive actions
 14   taken by the British government
 15   [in   Ulste   or   North]ern Ireland or in other=
 16 IR: [Well I'm talking about the-]
 17 SB: =parts. But this has [had nothing to do with] the human=
 18 IR: [Well if you'd like tu-]
 19 SB: =rights of sportsmen.=
 20 IR: =If you'd like [to] give- if you'd like to give me an=
 21 SB: [of-]
 22 IR: =exam[ple I'll deal with it.]
 23 SB: [They are infringed] by the: uhm by this threat to boycott

24   Olympic Ga:[mes.
25 *IR*:   [But why- why is Doctor Sakharov . . .

At lines 5–9 the IE, Begloff, takes issue with the IR's proposition that Sakharov has been exiled because of his opinions. He begins by disagreeing with the proposition ('Well it's not for his opinions') and then provides an alternative reason for Sakharov's imprisonment. However, despite the hostility of the IR's 'question', the IE does not directly undermine the neutralistic stance which the IR has thus far sought to maintain in the interview. Subsequently, however, the IR himself departs from this stance.

Notice, first, that in his response (at lines 5–9), the IE uses the collective pronoun 'we' ('. . . but what we say here in the Soviet Union'), rather than a third person reference such as 'what they say' or 'what the government say(s)'. As such, he explicitly constitutes himself as a 'spokesperson' for the Soviet nation as opposed to, for example, an independent political commentator. The IR subsequently adopts a similar stance. Thus, although the IR produces a question-formatted utterance, he explicitly aligns (through the use of 'we') with the proposition that Sakharov has been banished 'without as far as we can see any form of just (.) process' (lines 10–12). Here, then, the IR departs from a neutralistic stance by speaking on behalf of 'we' in the 'West'. Moreover, the IR continues to act in this vein after the IE attempts to draw a comparison between the case of Sakharov and the actions of the British government in Northern Ireland (lines 13–24). Instead of merely asking the IE to substantiate this claim, he invites him to provide an example and announces his willingness to deal with it. The IR thus abandons a neutralistic interviewing style, adopting instead the role of advocate. The situation is transformed from a neutralistic interview with a Soviet journalist into a 'debate' between spokespersons representing different political perspectives.[1]

In cases such as this, IRs step outside the normal bounds of acceptability by constituting themselves as the representatives of particular groups or nations. This results in the interview being transformed into a radically different event than is the norm; one in which the actions, views or intentions of IEs and/or the organizations or nations that they represent are treated as 'beyond the pale'.[2] Here broadcasters become advocates, speaking on behalf of 'democracy', 'decency', 'basic human rights' and the like. Such cases define the boundaries of neutralism in news interview conduct and emphasize the caution exercised by IRs when dealing with mainstream political figures, even in ostensibly hostile interviews.

However, the collaborative constitution of IRs as neutralistic is more commonly undermined as a result of the actions of IEs. Such departures are normally brief (even when IEs openly characterize IRs as having expressed a point of view on their own behalf) (Heritage and Greatbatch, 1991). On the one hand, IRs defend their neutralism by, for example, distancing themselves from contested propositions or presuppositions or, alternatively, reasserting their factual status. On the other hand, IEs quickly revert to the tacit rules of the 'interview game' by once again collaborating in the constitution of the IR as an elicitor, as opposed to an advocate of opinion (Heritage and Greatbatch, 1991).

However, IEs sometimes do mount sustained attacks on the conduct of IRs. The following example is from an interview with the leader of the Liberal Democratic Party, Paddy Ashdown. The interview was conducted on BBC Television's news and current affairs programme *Newsnight* on 7 December 1993, shortly after the Liberal Democratic Party in the London Borough of Tower Hamlets was accused of circulating racist literature in order to enhance its prospects in local elections. The extract opens with the IR asking Ashdown to respond to the proposition that the Liberal Democratic Party is 'immature . . . irresponsible . . . undisciplined . . . unserious' (lines 1–5).

(4)   BBC Television: *Newsnight*

```
1  IR:   S:o (0.2) you have loose cannon:s. (0.2) on your deck
          jus:t (.)
2         as you rightly say a:ll parties have. .hh But if we
          generously put
3         this do:wn to (0.1) over exuberance. (0.2) tch .hh (0.1)
          doesn't
4         that suggest that your party is still: (0.2) immatur:e.
          (0.3)
5         irresponsible (.) undisciplin:ed h (0.2) unserious.
6  Ash:   Well, (0.2) prove tha:t.
7         (0.6)
```

8   *Ash*: You made th'proposition, (0.2) propose it to me.=

9   *IR*:   =Well, (0.1) I'm saying t'you: that h (e)this (.) e:h(w)-
      is what

10   appe:ars that the: allegations in:- in[: uh (ha ha ha)

11   *Ash*:   [So you have one
      council:

12   [which question ( )-

13   *IR*:   [No, (.) hang on, there are also allegations in: uh- eh-
      uh- by

14   Emma Nicholson of <dirty tricks, .hh there is-=but
      this leads t'

15   th'more>[se:rious cha:rge. if I may[put it like this.
      [.h that you=

16   *Ash*:   [But-   [But Ja:mes,
      [whatever

17   *IR*:   =are- maybe you are opportu:ne- that you are
      opportunists.]

18   *Ash*: you- ( ) (never) made a very serious cha:rge. Perhaps
      you let-]

19   (.)

20   *Ash*: Perhaps you- (.) Well- (0.1) again:, (.) .h before you:
      recy:cl:e.

21   (0.2) conservative (0.1) propaga:nda. (0.2) as fact, (0.2)
      justify

22   it.

23   (.)

24   *IR*:   .hhh I am putting th'char:[ges Mister Ashdo:wn.

25   *Ash*:   [But you see you ca:n't, that's

26   th ['point.

27   *IR*:   [I- oh a:bsolutely you can: because .hh it i:s- it is:
      u:h not

28   just conservative propaganda nor is labour
      propaganda=it is .hh

29   (.) it is (.) wi:dely belie:ved. h .h that [you::- (.) that you

30   *Ash*:   [huh huh.

31   (0.2)

32   *IR*:   tailor (0.2) your politica[l (pote). you massa:ge (0.2)
      your:

33   *Ash*:   [C'n-

34   *IR*:   m̲essage.=
35   *Ash*: =But Jame[s-
36   *IR*:   [That you- .h That [you are (to:rie:s)
37   *Ash*:   [James-
38   (0.2)
39   *IR*:   ([   )   [(that you) ( ) labour and l̲abour[( ).
40   *Ash*: [James, [you've made-   [you've
            made a
41   very s̲e:rious (Tower) ( ). (0.1) We're d̲ealing with
            that. .hh g̲ive
42   justification.   .h̲h   Were   you   th̲e:re?   (0.2)   at
            Christchurch (0.1)
43   When I made it qu̲:ite clear t'people, .h that the al-
            ternative
44   to VAT, (0.2) in order t'c- o̲:vercome our economic
            problems
45   may w̲ell be raising income tax? (.) an' a̲:sked them
            t'v̲ote f'r it?
46   *IR*:   (.hh[hh.)
47   *Ash*: [N̲inety percent put up their ha̲:nds, .hh you c̲an-
            not sa̲:y on
48   th'o̲ne ha:nd that we've got th'cl̲earest an'y̲ou claim
            most
49   unp̲opular policies in E̲urope. .hh and say that we
            t̲ailor our
50   p̲olicie:s. W̲e're the only pa̲:rty at th'last el̲ection. .h̲hh
            who
51   put forward v̲ery clearly th'n̲eed t'have .hh an e̲nergy
            ma̲:rket
52   sy̲stem that would enc̲ourage efficiency, th't̲ories
            campaigned u̲p
53   and down th'country against it .hh and put some-
            thing in place
54   a̲:fterwards.=

The IE does not treat the IR's question as a neutral elicitor of opinion. Rather, he responds by treating the IR as having made an
assertion that he can be challenged to 'prove' ('Well prove that')
and, subsequently, asserting that the IR has made a proposition
('You made the proposition (0.2) propose it to me'). Although the IR

defends the proposition, he reacts to the threat to his neutralism by moving to distance himself from it (lines 9–10). However, before he can name the authors of the allegations to which he refers, the IE interrupts to complain that the allegations centre on the activities of only a single council, Tower Hamlets. The implication here is clearly that this is insufficient grounds on which to base the proposition that has been put to him by the IR. The IR counters by suggesting that the allegations made against the Liberal Democratic Party extend beyond the case of Tower Hamlets. In support of this he references the allegations of 'dirty tricks' which have been made against his party by Conservative MP Emma Nicholson (lines 9–15). He then suggests that this leads to the still more serious charge that the Liberal Democratic Party may be opportunists (lines 14–15, 17). Although the IR's conduct is consistent with the adoption of a neutralistic stance, the IE responds by upgrading his attack on the IR's conduct. He states that the IR has made (not merely reported) a very serious charge (line 18), and then accuses the IR of having recycled Conservative Party propaganda (lines 20–21).

This is followed by an exchange during which the IR counters continued IE criticism by justifying his actions on the grounds that he is putting to Ashdown charges that have been widely raised, and which are neither Tory nor Labour propaganda (lines 24–39). Again, then, the IR continues to defend the introduction of the proposition to which Ashdown has objected on the basis of the views expressed by third parties. In doing this, he not only defends his conduct, whilst exerting pressure on the IE to deal with the issue; he also attempts to distance himself from the 'allegations' to which he is asking Ashdown to respond. At no point, then, does the IR personally affiliate with the proposition to which the IE so strongly objects. As such, even in the heat of a sustained attack on his conduct, his conduct remains largely, if not wholly, consistent with the advancement of a neutralistic stance. However, Ashdown declines to collaborate in the restoration of the IR's neutralism. He repeatedly treats the IR as having 'taken a position' by asking him to 'prove' his proposition (lines 6 and 8), by asserting that the IR 'has made a very serious charge' (line 18), by accusing him of recycling Tory propaganda (lines 20–21), and, even after the IR has repeatedly sought to distance himself from the charges through third-party attribution, by again treating the proposition as one for which the IR is personally accountable (lines 40–45). Lastly, although he does finally respond to the propositions raised by the IR (42ff), he directly formulates his statements as in opposition to the IR (lines 47–49), rather than to the other parties mentioned by the IR.

In sum, an orientation to IR neutrality is a pervasive feature of news interviews in the UK. It infuses the conduct of both IRs and IEs, informing the ways in which they solicit and proffer information and opinion. IRs avoid the expression of opinionated statements on their own behalf and refrain from open affiliation with, or disaffiliation from, IE responses. IEs normally collaborate in the preservation of the IRs' neutralistic stance. As a general rule, they treat IR conduct, regardless of how presuppositionally weighted against their positions it might be, as part of the cut and thrust of the modern interview. IRs are not treated as advocates of personal or institutional positions, although IEs may well on occasion believe them to be so. In contributing to the maintenance of neutralistic interviewing, IEs exhibit a considerable degree of restraint, legitimizing the conduct of IRs on a moment-to-moment basis and thereby enabling IRs to present themselves as eliciting, testing and probing the views of others without expressing opinions on their own behalf. But this co-operation is not guaranteed. IEs may respond to IR utterances in ways which, to varying degrees, challenge or doubt their neutralism; that is, they may treat IRs as having taken a position. Such threats to IR neutralism are usually relatively brief, with IRs moving to repair the situation and IEs collaborating in the restoration of 'business as usual'. However, as the Ashdown example illustrates, extended attacks on IR neutralism do occur and, indeed, represent a potent weapon in the armoury of experienced and accomplished public figures.

6   The Limits of Neutralism within the News Interview

Attacks on IR neutralism are commonly associated with IR questions which display an expectation in favour of answers that are the opposite to the stated or known positions of IEs. Thus, for example, in extract (4) above, the IR uses a form of question which strongly conveys an 'expectation or preference for a particular type of response'. Specifically, he uses a question frame which projects acceptance by the IE of the proposition that follows it, a proposition with which the IE, as leader of the Liberal Democratic Party, can be expected to strongly disagree.

The use of question forms such as this in conjunction with highly contentious propositions lies at the limits of IR neutralism in the contemporary UK interview. It is here that the co-operation between IR and IE which underpins ostensibly combative interviews often breaks down, with IEs treating IRs as 'taking a position'. In the light of this, it is perhaps not surprising that when using these types of question, IRs often take care to attribute the contentious propositions to third parties, with the use of third-party attribution acting *inter alia* as an additional shield against attacks on their neutralism. In the following example, John Redwood, a Conservative Minister who subsequently resigned from the Cabinet in order to challenge John Major for the leadership of the Conservative Party, is being questioned about his opposition to the adoption by the UK of European Union employment regulations.

(5)   BBC Television: *Newsnight*
IR: Isn't it a fact that the rather <u>neg</u>ative approach that you
       seem to take (0.1) uh and I:'d and I'm using words charac-
       terized by Mister Heseltine Mister Heath and o[thers .hhh
       uh is in=
Red: [Mm
IR: =fact damaging (0.3) your chances of contributin[g to
       the=
Red: [No
IR: =<u>fu</u>ture of the community.
Red: What I've been saying tonight is not negative at a:ll I don't
       take a negative view of the community I think there's a lot
       to be gai:ned by Britain being an <u>ac</u>tive member of Europe
       (0.2) and <u>be</u>ing an active member of Europe means argu-
       ing these very points and trying to point <u>out</u> to our (.)
       com<u>mun</u>ity partners (0.2) that <u>cer</u>tain types of social <u>regu</u>-
       lation and inter<u>ven</u>tion (.) could <u>wreck</u> (.) .h the dream of
       a more prosperous more open Europe (.) which is the one
       that we suppo:rt.

Here the IR begins a question which clearly projects an expectation or preference for acceptance of the proposition that is to follow ('Isn't it a fact that . . .'). As the proposition emerges it becomes clear that it is one which will characterize the IE's position in terms that he is unlikely to accept. However, instead of straightforwardly continuing through to completion, the IR interrupts himself in the midst of the emerging proposition in order to attribute it to a number of the IE's colleagues in the Conservative Party ('Mister Heseltine Mister Heath and others'). In so doing, he produces a question which strongly projects acceptance of a proposition that is counter to the IE's stated position, but, in contrast to the case above, he distances himself from the proposition. Subsequently, the IE rejects the proposition and in so doing treats the question as a neutralistic object.[3]

7   The Relative Vulnerability of Free-Standing Assertions By Interviewers

A number of IRs quite often produce evaluative statements without either interrogative components or third-party attribution. What is more, these utterances often involve provocative propositions which are counter to the expected, known and/or stated views of IEs. Interestingly, however, these utterances generally escape treatment as non-neutralistic by IEs.

One reason for this may be that these statements are often designed in ways which provide IEs with more room for manoeuvre than do, for example, questions which project 'preferred' responses. Consider the following example, which is taken from a BBC radio interview with the Labour Party's election campaign manager, Brian Wilson. The interview concerns the dismissal of Baroness Turner from the Labour Party's front bench over her defence of a political lobbying company, Ian Greer Associates, of which she is a director. The company stands accused of paying Conservative MPs to ask parliamentary questions. Although she had made no secret of her involvement with the company, the Labour Party took no action against her until she spoke out to reject the allegations against the company. However, Labour Party spokespersons, in attempting to retain the political advantage, have tried to emphasize the difference between their 'swift action' and what they describe as the reluctance of the Conservative Party to act decisively against members of their party.

(6) BBC Radio 4: *AM*
1 *IR*: .hh No question of impropriety: and y̲e̲t̲ you decided
         she had to go.=
2   Now the f̲act is .hhh she spoke out but y̲ou had
         kno::wn (.) in the
3   Labour Party you'd known for a very long time in-
         d̲eed .h that she
4   was a non-executive member of Ian Greer's company.
         She'd never
5   made any secret of the fact?
6 *BW*: Oh absolutely not.=No. It's- it's in the r̲egister of
         interests a well
7   known f̲a:ct a legitimate business and er:: and er she
         had an
8   association with it.
9 *IR*: [So we're back to the question of why you got rid of
         her?
10 *BW*: [(There's ab- abs- absolutely nothing wrong with
         that).

After the IE has confirmed that Baroness Turner was not herself guilty of any impropriety, the IR begins by contrasting the absence of any wrong-doing with the fact that the Labour Party has removed her from office (line 1). He then goes on to state that although she spoke out on this occasion, her association with the company was well known to the Party (lines 2–5). This raises the question of the timing of the action against her: namely, why was she not removed from office earlier. The suggestion here is that the Party's standards are not as clear-cut as is being suggested. Notice, however, that this is implied, not asserted. That the 'accusation' is done in an indirect fashion means that the IR's utterance does not directly solicit a response to it. In responding, the IE takes advantage of this by addressing the relationship between Baroness Turner and Ian Greer Associates as described by the IR (lines 6–8 and 10). This enables him to stress an aspect of the case which is positive in so far as his party is concerned (namely, that there is no suggestion that a party member failed to fulfil their parliamentary duties), whilst avoiding any reference to the underlying negative implications of the IR's utterance.

The indirectness associated with utterances such as the one in this example, then, provides IEs with considerable room for manoeuvre. By contrast, questions which project preferred or expected responses that run counter to IE positions establish a much more interactionally hostile context for IEs to communicate their perspectives. It is for this reason, perhaps, that, despite their being grammatically formatted as interrogatives, the latter are more vulnerable to attack by IEs.

8 Concluding Remarks

In this chapter we have explored the relationship between the interactional organization of news interviews and the requirement that broadcast journalists maintain impartiality and balance in their coverage of news and current affairs. In so doing, we have not attempted to assess the neutrality of broadcast journalists in their interviews with politicians and other public figures. Instead, using the approach and findings of CA, we have considered 'neutrality' as a members' phenomenon: a constraint that participants in news interviews demonstrably orient to as their interactions unfold. Specifically, we have explicated some of the ways in which IRs advance a neutralistic stance and in which IEs either ratify or challenge this stance.

The research reported here raises a number of important issues for future research. First, the limits of neutralism are obviously not fixed. On the one hand, definitions of neutralistic interviewing can change over time according to the varying degrees of freedom allowed to broadcasters in different eras and by different broadcasting organizations. On the other hand, some IRs may be more willing than others to test the boundaries of neutralism, whilst some IEs may be more prone than others to challenge the neutralistic stance advanced by IRs. An understanding of how neutralism is differentially defined and challenged both within the interview and beyond is critical to understanding the ways in which news and opinion is generated and shaped in news interviews.

Another important topic for future research is the comparative analysis of interviewing in different countries. Preliminary work in this area has begun to identify important differences between interviewing in the UK, USA and Australia (Heritage et al., forthcoming). Interviews in the USA, for example, are often less formal than those in the UK. Relatedly, Australian interviews regularly appear to involve styles of questioning that would lie beyond the boundaries of the permissible in either the USA or the UK. Cross-cultural comparative studies should thus reveal the implications of politicians and others communicating their opinions in interviews in which broadcast journalists advance and defend a neutralistic stance, as opposed to contexts in which journalists do not display the same degree of expressive caution.

More generally, the approach we have illustrated provides a distinctive means of explicating the details of all forms of broadcast talk which, like the news interview, are, at least in part, 'spontaneous'. As noted in the introduction, a start has already been made in this direction in studies of talk shows. Consequently, CA research in the field of media discourse is beginning to reveal the ways in which participation in broadcast programmes is shaped and constrained by interactional practices which are related to the tasks, constraints and conventions associated with different forms of broadcast talk.

It is perhaps worth mentioning that, in addition to illuminating the social interactional organization of the output of the broadcast media, CA could also be used to study its production and consumption. Returning to the theme of our exemplary analysis, for example, CA studies of neutralism could be extended beyond the news interview and other forms of broadcast talk in order to examine the ways in which 'neutrality' and 'neutralism' feature both as a constraint and as a resource in the interaction and work of broadcasters, programme participants, news production personnel and those who watch or listen to broadcast programmes – such as politicians, ordinary members of the public, pressure groups and, perhaps, social scientists. In treating the assessment of the neutrality of broadcast journalists as an empirical phenomenon to be investigated, rather than as an objective of social scientific analysis, CA studies of the production and consumption of broadcast news and current affairs programmes would address such questions as the following: In what ways do people assess or otherwise mention the 'neutrality' of IRs in the course of their everyday encounters? Which aspects of IR conduct do they refer to? In what contexts? For which purposes? In order to undertake such research, however, it would be necessary to secure access to the sites in which such interactions take place and to obtain consent to record them. The difficulty in doing this is, perhaps, reflected in the absence of research of this type. Studies of 'output' are, by contrast, relatively easy to undertake since data can be easily collected by recording television and radio programmes.

NOTES

1   See Clayman and Whalen (1988/89) for a detailed consideration of an encounter in the USA between Dan Rather and President George Bush, which was widely perceived to have followed a similar course.

2   See Schlesinger et al. (1983) for a consideration of the ways in which the representatives of 'terrorist' organizations receive similar treatment.

3   Clayman (1992) details a range of the, often subtle, ways in which IRs attribute positions to third parties during the production of questions in television news interviews in the USA.

APPENDIX: TRANSCRIPTION SYMBOLS

Speakers are identified to the left of the talk: IR is the interviewer; IEs are identified by abbreviation of their name. The transcription symbols are drawn from the transcription notation developed by Gail Jefferson. For details of this notation, see Atkinson and Heritage (1984) and Button and Lee (1986).

[	A left bracket indicates the point at which overlapping talk begins.
]	A right bracket indicates the point at which overlapping talk ends.
=	Equals signs are used to indicate that the utterances of different speakers are 'latched'. They are also used to link continuous talk by a single speaker that has been distributed across non-adjacent lines due to another speaker's overlapping utterance.

(0.5)	Numbers in parentheses indicate the length of silences in tenths of a second.
(.)	A dot in parentheses indicates a gap of less than two tenths of a second.
<u>Word</u>	Underlining indicates some form of stress via pitch and/or amplitude.
Wo::rd	Colons indicate prolongation of the immediately preceding sound.
. , ?	Periods, commas and question marks are used to indicate falling, non-terminal and rising intonation respectively.
(Word)	Parenthesized words indicate that the transcriber was not sure of what was said.
( )	Empty parentheses indicate that the transcriber was unable to hear what was said.
(( ))	Double parentheses contain transcriber's comments and/or descriptions.
.hhh	h's preceded by a period represent inhalations.
hhhh	h's without a preceding period represent aspirations.

Chapter 7

Front Pages: (The Critical) Analysis of Newspaper Layout

Gunther Kress and Theo van Leeuwen

1 Multimodality

All texts are multimodal. Language always has to be realized through, and comes in the company of, other semiotic modes. When we speak, we articulate our message not just with words, but through a complex interplay of speech-sound, of rhythm, of intonation; accompanied by facial expression, gesture and posture. When we write, our message is expressed not only linguistically, but also through a visual arrangement of marks on a page. Any form of text analysis which ignores this will not be able to account for all the meanings expressed in texts.

Nevertheless, there has long been an insistence on the monomodal, especially in the most 'serious', the most highly valued kinds of speech and writing. Television newsreaders minimize facial expression and gesture, and in the early days of BBC television they were not even shown, since 'illustration would destroy balance' (Inglis, 1983: 211). Many academic papers, important documents and 'high' literature worked, and to some extent still work, with words alone, in densely printed pages, with a minimum of visual illustration, and without much overt attention to layout and presentation.

This situation is now being reversed. There is a trend in which, increasingly, the written text is no longer structured by linguistic means, through verbal connectors and verbal cohesive devices (e.g. 'in what follows', 'as was pointed out above', 'as my final point') but visually, through layout, through the spatial arrangement of blocks of text, of pictures and other graphic elements on the page. The wordprocessor has accelerated this trend. Everywhere writing now involves close attention to typeface choices and layout. Newspapers, magazines, company reports, school textbooks and many other kinds of texts are no longer just written, but 'designed', and multimodally articulated.

The semiotic modes in such texts can interrelate in different ways. Writing may remain dominant, with the visual fulfilling a 'prosodic' role of highlighting important points and emphasizing structural connections. But it may also diminish in importance, with the message articulated primarily in the visual mode, and the words serving as commentary and elaboration. Visually and verbally expressed meaning may be each other's double and express the same meanings, or they may complement and extend each other, or even clash and contradict.

Given these changes in writing practices, it is essential that we develop modes of text analysis which can adequately describe the interplay between the verbal and the visual, and adequately analyse visually expressed meanings. Hence, in this chapter, we hope to go some way towards achieving these aims by presenting a descriptive framework we are currently developing for the analysis of layout. The framework builds on our previous work in this area (Kress and van Leeuwen, 1996), and, in this chapter, we extend and further refine it in various ways.

Throughout the chapter, we use newspaper front pages as our examples, and in the final section we present a full analysis of some of these pages, to show the relevance of our approach for critical studies of the press and its function in contemporary society. That is, within our broad social semiotic framework, we treat front pages as (complex) signs, which invite and require an initial reading as one sign. This initial reading is then followed by a more detailed, specific reading, which draws its initial orientation from the first reading of the large sign.

2   Signifying Systems in Layout

We consider that layout simultaneously involves three signifying systems, all serving to structure the text, to bring the various elements of the page (e.g. photographs, headlines, blocks of text) together into a coherent and meaningful whole.

Information value

Our work assumes that the placement of elements in a layout endows these elements with the specific information values that are attached to the various zones of the visual space. A given element does not have the same value and meaning when it is placed on the right or on the left, in the upper or in the lower section of the page, in the centre or in the margins. Each of these zones accords specific values to the elements placed within it. We discuss these values in section 3.

Salience

The elements of a layout attract the reader's attention to different degrees, and through a wide variety of means: placement in the foreground or background, relative size, contrasts in tonal value or colour, differences in sharpness, and so on. We discuss this in section 4.

Framing

Framing devices, such as framelines or white space between elements, can simultaneously both disconnect the elements of a layout from each other, signifying that they are to be read as, in some sense, separate and independent, perhaps even contrasting items of information, and at the same time, framing devices establish what elements, namely those within the frame, are to be read together. Connective devices, such as vectors between elements or repetition of shapes and colour, have the effect of expressing that the elements thus connected are to be read as belonging together in some sense, as continuous or complementary, for instance. We discuss this in section 5. In addition, in section 6 we focus on the 'reading path', the trajectory established on a page (though not necessarily followed) by the reader in reading or scanning the text.

These signifying systems operate simultaneously and are independently variable. In fact, they apply not just to layout, but also to the composition of single pictures, and there too they have an integrating function, bringing the elements of the picture together into a coherent and meaningful whole. In this chapter, however, we concentrate on page layout.

3   Information Value

Given and New

We posit that when a layout opposes left and right, placing one kind of element on the left, and another, perhaps contrasting element, on the right, the elements on the left are presented as Given, and the elements on the right as New. For something to be Given means that it is presented as something the reader already knows, as a familiar and agreed departure point for the message. For something to be New means that it is presented as something which is not yet known to the reader, hence as the crucial point of the message, the issue to which the reader must pay special attention. The New is therefore in principle presented as problematic, contestable, the information at issue, while the Given is presented as common-sense and self-evident. This makes both Given and New problematic, though in quite distinct ways: challenging the Given is to challenge what has been presented as established; challenging the New is to challenge issues not presented as established.

The *Daily Mirror* page (figure 7.1) features on the left an article about a woman stabbed to death by her boyfriend, and on the right an article about the movie star Michelle Pfeiffer adopting a baby, as a single mother. Given, then, is the bad news: an instance of discord between lovers, with dramatic results. This is what we are exposed to day after day in press reports about everyday 'private' relationships: infidelity, break-ups, abuse. New is the good news, a story about a new (and therefore potentially problematic, not yet quite accepted) kind of relationship, that between the single mother and her child, here endorsed by the authority of the movie star as role model. Within the article, Pfeiffer's glamorous image is Given, the story of her adoption of a baby New.

Figure 7.2 shows a front page from the Austrian tabloid *Täglich Alles*. The top section of the page features on the left a short editorial about a politician embroiled in scandal, and on the right a photo of the actor Jürgen Prochnow, who, in a movie to be screened on television that night, plays a journalist uncovering a scandal. Here, too, we have, between Given and New, a thematic link ('scandal'), an opposition between the Given-ness of the bad news and New-ness of the good news, of the redemption of evil, and an opposition between the world of politics and the world of showbusiness in which it is the latter that the reader must turn to for the good news, for the redemption of traumatic or disturbing events.

Such structures are ideological in the sense that they may not correspond to what is the case either for the producer or for the consumer of the layout. The important point is that the information is presented *as though* it had that status or value for the reader, and that readers have to read it within that structure initially, even if they then produce a reading which rejects it.

These structures are ideological in another sense. Both in the *Daily Mirror* example and in the *Täglich Alles* example, particular states of affairs are at least implicitly suggested as established common sense. In the *Täglich Alles* example, there is a further set of meanings at issue, namely around the categories of public and private – the public affair and the public commentary of the editorial vs. the private person of the actor (though he is, of course, brought into the public domain here); the mediation between the 'facts' of the political scandal, and the 'fictive' resolution in the

Figure 7.1   Front page of the *Daily Mirror*

Alles *täglich*

Nr. 1018 UNABHÄNGIGE TAGESZEITUNG S 5,–
Samstag, 28. Jänner 1995. Wien 21, Ignaz-Köck-Straße 17. Tel. 29 160-0

ALLES für WIEN

*Jürgen Prochnow als
Lucona-Aufdecker*

In den meisten Filmen spielt er den Bösewicht – im Streifen „Der Fall Lucona" darf Jürgen Prochnow endlich einmal auch der „Gute" sein: nämlich der Journalist, der den Skandal um das versenkte Schiff aufdeckt (ORF 1, 22.15 Uhr). Interview Seite 46

Alles in Butter...

Wichtigster Aspekt der Affäre ist's nicht, aber es irritiert doch: Da sagt „Aufdecker" Worm, er habe bereits am Montag Marizzi und Kraft über das Tonband, das ihm zugespielt wurde, informiert. Die beiden wußten also, was da blüht. Man sollte denken, daß sie nun bis zur Veröffentlichung, im eigenen wie der Partei Interesse, auf Schadensbegrenzung aus waren, daß sie zumindest die Partei informierten. Wie's aussieht, taten sie nicht

einmal das. Nach zwei Tagen Galgenfrist hatte Kraft seine Erinnerungslücke parat, Marizzi gab an, in ihm sei „das Interesse" erwacht, Sherlock Holmes spielte er. Politiker, die in zwei Tagen nur Ausreden von Taferlklaßler-Niveau gebären und hilflos zuwarten, disqualifizieren sich wohl schon aus diesem Grund. Oder soll man annehmen, daß SP/VP eh seit Montag informiert waren und beschlossen, verdutzte Unwissende zu mimen?

nöstlinger

Killerkommando erschoß
Österreicher in Malaysia

Bericht Seite 12

Wir wissen nicht, wo sie sind.

1995 wieder Zeckenschutz-Impfaktion!
Geimpft – geschützt!

Figure 7.2 Front page of *Täglich Alles*

movie; between the public concern of the reader as citizen, and the private pleasure of the reader as viewer. The Given–New structure exists in spoken language too, of course. There it may be realized by intonation (Halliday, 1985: 274ff). This does not imply, in our view, that the visual Given–New structure is modelled on the linguistic Given–New structure (or on the fact that English and German are read from left to right). It points to the existence of functions which can be realized in different semiotic modes (albeit in different ways – by a 'before–after' structure in spoken language, and by a 'left–right' structure in visual communication). We expect such structures to be culturally specific, and not necessarily applicable, in this form of realization, to cultures in which, for instance, writing is from top to bottom or from right to left. But there are also structures which do not have a clear linguistic parallel (for instance, the structures described in the next three sections) just as there are linguistic structures for which no visual parallel exists.

Real and Ideal

In our framework, when a layout polarizes top and bottom, placing different, perhaps contrasting elements in the upper and lower sections of the page, the elements placed at the top are presented as the Ideal and those placed at the bottom as the Real. For something to be Ideal means that it is presented as the idealized or generalized essence of the information, and therefore also as having ideologically one kind of salience. The Real is then opposed to this, in that it presents more specific information (e.g. details) and/or more 'down to earth' information (e.g. photographs as documentary evidence, or maps, or statistics) and/or more practical information (e.g. practical consequences, directions for action, etc.).

The opposition between Ideal and Real often structures text–image relations. If the upper part of a page is occupied by text and the lower part by one or more pictures (or maps or charts or diagrams), the text will play, ideologically, the role implied in our gloss of 'Ideal' and the pictures the role implied in our gloss of 'Real'. Each is important in its own right, as abstraction or generalization as model perhaps on the one hand, and as specification, exemplification, evidence, practical consequence and so on, on the other. If the roles are reversed, so that one or more pictures occupy the top section, then the Ideal is communicated visually and the text serves to comment or elaborate.

It should be noted that our use of the term 'Ideal' does not necessarily represent a (positive) value judgement. It is possible that in a particular community or culture the values of 'Ideal' or 'Real' are ranked in a hierarchical relation. It is said of the English that they value the practical, the empirical, the pragmatic. Clearly, for the reader/viewer with those values the 'grounded' statement may have higher value. Other cultures may by contrast value the more general, abstract, theoretical; readers/viewers with those values will read the pages in the light of their habitual valuations. Nor are these habits entirely monolithic: a text or an event may address me and place me into an 'inspirational' mode – a religious occasion, a party rally, and so on, so that my otherwise pragmatic orientation is suspended for the duration of the event.

This can be seen in figure 7.3, a *Guardian* front page from March 1993. A salient image of the burial of the 3-year-old victim of an IRA bombing is presented as the Ideal. It visually formulates the essence of the day's events and solicits condemnation of the bombing by virtue of its emotive impact. The bottom half of the page elaborates on this event and places it among the other events of the day. But the top section of the page is itself also divided into an Ideal and Real, with the masthead comprising the essence of the newspaper's content and role as 'guardian', and the photo constituting the day's specific instantiation of its fulfilment of that role.

In figure 7.2, the top section of the page focuses on the paper's role in covering everything (*Alles*), providing independent (*unabhängig*) comment, and uncovering scandals on behalf of the public. The bottom section contains a news headline (signifying the more factual 'report'), and two items of practical interest to the reader: an appeal for vaccination against ticks, and a pointer for finding the classified ads. Advertisements and other items of practical interest are usually found in this position, just as, within advertisements themselves, it is here that one finds the address and telephone number of the advertiser, or the tear-out coupon one can send to obtain further information or to order the product.

Figure 7.3 Front page of the *Guardian*

Centre and Margin

Visual composition may also be structured along the dimensions of Centre and Margin. In contemporary Western layouts this is relatively less common. Most layouts polarize Given and New and/or Ideal and Real. But when teaching on a media design course in Singapore, we found that it plays an important role in the visual imagination of young Asian designers. Perhaps it is the greater emphasis on hierarchy, harmony and continuity in Confucian thinking that makes centring such a fundamental organizational principle in their culture. Much of the work produced by these students had strong, dominant centres, surrounded or flanked by relatively unpolarized elements. In the West too, centralizing designs are found more frequently in certain domains: the religiously inspired paintings of the Virgin and Child, or of the Adoration of the Magi, stand as ancestors to visual representation in which objects of desire or of reverence are given a central place.

When a layout makes significant use of the Centre, placing one element in the middle and the other elements around it, we will refer to the central element as the Centre and to the elements that flank it as Margins. For something to be presented as Centre means that it is presented as the nucleus of the information to which all the other elements are in some sense subservient. The Margins then are these ancillary, dependent elements. In many cases the Margins are identical or at least very similar to each other in some criterial respect, so that there is no sense of polarization, no sense of division between Given and New and/or Ideal and Real. We will reserve the term 'Margin' for this kind of symmetrical structure. In other cases, Centre and Margin combine with Given and New and/or Ideal and Real.

This is the case with figure 7.4, a 'Business' section front page from the *Sydney Morning Herald*. The central picture is a cartoon based on Van Doesburg's *The Cardplayers*: two men playing a game of monopoly. News articles are arranged around it, in concentric layers. But there is some evidence of polarization also: the column of expert comment is New, hence presented as the crucial element of the page.

Figure 7.4 Front page of Business Section of the *Sydney Morning Herald*

It follows from our discussion in this and the previous two sections that the dimensions of visual space constitute the figure of the Cross, a fundamental spatial symbol in Western culture (see figure 7.5). Just how marginal the Margins are will depend on the size, and, more generally, the salience of the Centre. But even when the Centre is empty, it will continue to exist *in absentia*, as the invisible (or denied) pivot around which everything else turns. The relative infrequency of centred compositions in contemporary Western representation perhaps signifies, in the words of Yeats, that 'the centre does not hold' any longer in many sectors of contemporary society.

The triptych

One common mode of combining Given and New with Centre and Margin is the triptych. In many medieval triptychs, there is no sense of Given and New. The Centre shows a key religious theme, such as the Crucifixion or the Virgin and Child, and the side panels show

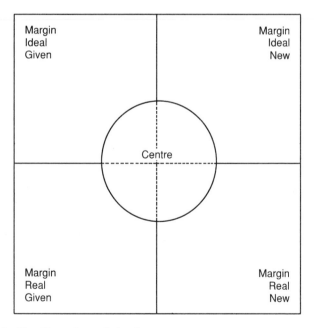

Figure 7.5   The dimensions of visual space

saints or donors, kneeling down in admiration. The composition is symmetrical rather than polarized, although the left was regarded as a slightly less honorific position. In the sixteenth century altarpieces became more narrative and showed, for instance, the birth of Christ or the road to Golgotha on the left panel, the Crucifixion in the Centre, and the Resurrection on the right panel. This could involve some polarization, albeit subordinated to a temporal order, with the left, for instance, as the 'bad' side (e.g. the transgression of Adam), the right as the 'good' side (e.g. the ascent of the blessed) and the middle panel representing Christ's role as Mediator and Saviour (e.g. the Crucifixion).

The triptychs in the layout of modern newspapers and magazines are generally polarized, with a Given on the left, a New on the right, and with the central element as Mediator, bridging and linking the two extremes. This is illustrated in figure 7.6, a triptych from *The Observer*. It forms the Ideal of an article about major building projects for the year 2000. Given is the photo of Crystal Palace, which to readers in the UK is a familiar example of past styles of

Figure 7.6   Triptych from *The Observer*

public building. New is a detail from the Sackler Building in the Royal Academy, presented as an example of good contemporary building. The Mediator is formed by the architect's drawings which will transform the Given into the New.

4   Salience

The fundamental function of layout is textual. Layout places the various meaningful elements into the whole, and provides ordering and coherence among them. So far, we have discussed how it determines 'where things go', and how the positioning of the elements on the page endows them with specific information values in relation to each other. But layout also involves assigning degrees of salience to the elements of the page. Regardless of where they are placed, salience can create a hierarchy of importance among the elements, selecting some as more important and more worthy of (immediate) attention than others. The Given may be made more salient than the New, for instance, or the New more salient than the Given, or both may be equally salient.

We judge salience on the basis of visual cues. Readers are able to judge the 'weight' of the various elements of the layout, and the greater the weight of an element, the greater its salience. This salience is not objectively measurable but results from a complex trading-off relationship between a number of factors: size; sharpness of focus, or, more generally, amount of detail and texture shown; tonal contrast (areas of high tonal contrast, for instance borders between black and white, have high salience); colour contrasts (for instance, the contrast between highly saturated and 'soft' colours, or the contrast between red and blue); placement in the visual field (elements not only become 'heavier' as they are moved towards the top, but also appear 'heavier' the further they are moved towards the left, due to an asymmetry in the visual field); perspective (foreground objects are more salient than background objects, and elements that overlap other elements are more salient than the elements they overlap). There are also quite specific cultural factors, such as the appearance of a human figure or a potent cultural symbol.

In other words, the reading and consequent assessment of salience is a complex process. We do not wish to make a particular judgement here about the relative importance of psychological and physiological as against cultural and social factors. Without doubt both are present and both significant; and as always, particular cultures provide particular trainings for readers/viewers. For instance, in literate 'Western' cultures, some readers/viewers (probably older and middle-class) may find written text more significant; other reader/viewers may find the visual more attractive. Assessments of the salience of elements on the same page would therefore differ between readers: not anarchically, but on the basis of cultural histories.

Being able to judge the visual weight of the elements of a layout is being able to judge how they 'balance'. The weight they put in the scales derives from one or more of the factors just mentioned. Taken together, the elements create a balancing centre, the point, one might say, from which, if one conceived of the elements as parts of a mobile, that mobile would have to be suspended. Regardless of whether this point is in the actual centre of the composition or off-centre, it often becomes the space of the central message, and this attests to the 'power of the centre' (Arnheim, 1982) to which we have alluded already, and which exerts itself even when the Centre is an empty space. It follows that balance and therefore layout is a truly bodily aspect of the text, an interface between our biological and our semiotic selves. Without balance, co-ordination in space is not possible. Balance forms an indispensable matrix for the production and reception of spatially organized messages, and for this reason it also plays a key role in producing the aesthetic pleasure in layout, and hence our affective relation towards it. Via this affective process the effects and functions of a message are deepened, and it is in such aspects that ideology, affect, and subjectivity become inextricably mixed.

But salience not only has an aesthetic function; it also plays a vital role in structuring the message. In figure 7.1, for instance, it is the picture of Michelle Pfeiffer which has the greatest salience, due to its size, the bright colour of her dress (red), and the salience of her look at the viewer. Her sexual allure in the end overrides the story of her adopting a baby, or is at least as important as the contrast between the 'bad news' and 'good news' items which flank it. This contrasts with figure 7.7, where, despite strong similarities in overall layout and Given–New structure (two 'European' stories), it is the headline which is most salient, due to its size and to the strong tonal contrast with the black background.

Figure 7.7   Front page of the *Sun*

5   Framing Devices: Connecting and Disconnecting Items

The elements of a layout may either be disconnected, marked off from each other, or connected, joined together. Connection and disconnection are a matter of degree. Elements may be strongly or weakly framed, and the stronger the framing, the more the elements in different frames are presented as separate units of information. The context can then colour in the more precise nature of this separation. Elements may also be strongly or weakly connected, and the stronger the connection, the more they are presented as one unit of information, as belonging together.

Disconnection can be realized in many different ways, for instance by framelines (the thickness or colour of which can then indicate the strength of the framing), by discontinuities of colour or shape, or simply by empty space between the elements. Connection can be realized by the repetition of formal features of the connected elements, shapes or colours for instance, as in figure 7.1. Here, blue is the colour of the background of the Michelle Pfeiffer photo and the two frames on top ('Mirror Gives Shoe Scandal The Boot' and 'Which Famous Fan Owns This Motor?'), of the small photos in the article on the left, and of the frame around the 'Catwoman Star Buys Baby' article. Connection can also be realized by vectors, formed either by features of depicted objects, e.g. the head tilt and eyeline of the British Prime Minister, John Major, in figure 7.7 (a frontal shot in a rectangular frame would have produced much less connection), or by the tilting of layout elements, as in the 'pinboard' layout in figure 7.8.

Newspaper pages generally, and tabloid pages especially, tend to use strong framing (e.g. see figures 7.3 and 7.7 for the difference between a 'quality newspaper' and a tabloid). Yet, on closer inspection there are many subtle continuities, especially in the use of colour, and these almost subliminally hint at the thematic continuities between what at first sight appear to be discrete items.

Elf „Punkt-Wuffis" tummeln sich derzeit bei Familie Griessmayer in Wien auf dem Wohnzimmerteppich und halten Mutter „Inka" (4) auf Trab. Die reinrassigen Dalmatiner-Welpen, neun Weibchen und zwei „Spitzbuben", suchen jetzt ein Zuhause. Wer eines der entzückenden Tiere haben möchte: 0222/98 29 818

Späte Ehrungen für Politiker-Legenden

Späte Ehren für Bruno Kreisky und Rosa Jochmann: Die Namen der beiden verstorbenen Politiker-Legenden werden auf öffentlichen Plätzen verewigt. Der Gemeindebau Hernalser Hauptstraße 230 wird nach dem Altbundeskanzler „Bruno-Kreisky-Hof" heißen, der Park in der Weintraubengasse 23 (Leopoldstadt) wird künftig den Namen der großen Wegbereiterin der österreichischen Sozialdemokratie tragen.

Nahversorger im Container

Im neuen Stadtteil am Marchfeldkanal gibt es noch keine Nahversorger. Bis es soweit ist, bietet die Firma LOWA einen provisorischen Supermarkt in acht Containern an.

WIEN-STENOGRAMM

● **Kinderspital**
„Das Preyersche Kinderspital muß auf jeden Fall erhalten bleiben", meint Gemeinderat Georg Fuchs zu den von Gesundheitsministerin Christa Krammer geplanten Spitalsschließungen. „Sonst sind sieben Bezirke medizinisch unterversorgt."

● **Kilimandscharo-Dias**
„Ein Floridsdorfer am Kilimandscharo" ist der Titel einer Diaschau, die Johann Orth am 2. Februar im Bezirksmuseum Floridsdorf abhält (19.30 Uhr). Orth hat sich mit der Besteigung des höchsten Berges Afrikas einen Jugendtraum erfüllt.

● **Sicherheit im Bezirk**
Am Donnerstag findet in der Bank Austria in der Josefstädter Straße 64 die Veranstaltung „Sicherheit in der Josefstadt" statt (18.30 Uhr). Polizeipräsident Günther Bögl und prominente Politiker diskutieren das Thema mit den Bürgern.

● **Kabeltausch**
In der Sieveringer Straße (Döbling) wird ab Mittwoch ein Stromkabel ausgetauscht. Autofahrer müssen mit kurzfristigen Behinderungen rechnen.

● **Neuer Vorstand**
Univ.-Doz. Dr. Ingrid Schindler ist neuer Abteilungsvorstand für Anästhesie und Intensivmedizin im Krankenhaus Floridsdorf.

● **Preise für 1995**
Die Stadt Wien vergibt auch heuer wieder Preise für hervorragende Leistungen in Kunst, Wissenschaft und Volksbildung. Bewerbungen bis Ende Februar an die Kulturabteilung, 1082 Wien, Friedrich-Schmidt-Platz 5.

● **Sparen in der Schule**
„VP-Schulsprecher Walter Strobl zeigt für die Proteste der Lehrer Verständnis. Sein Sparvorschlag: „Mehr Autonomie und weniger teure Verwaltung."

Happy Birthday!
Eartha Kitt, amerikanische Sängerin und Schauspielerin, feiert heute ihren 67. Geburtstag. Die Tochter eines schwarzen Landarbeiters erlangte mit ihrer erotischen Stimme und den raubkatzenartigen Bewegungen Weltruhm.

Eartha Kitt, 67

Das Goebel vom Ei
Alexander Goebel, glatz- und eierköpfige Ulknudel aus deutschen Landen, präsentiert heute noch einmal seine Erfolgsshow „Das Goebel vom Ei" – exklusiv für die österreichische Firma „Druckdenker-GmbH" und deren Freunde im Wiener „Marriott"-Hotel.

Wie aus dem Ei gepellt: Goebel

Teure Claudia
Claudia Schiffer, deutsches Top-Model und Sexsymbol, kassiert pro Arbeitstag nicht weniger als 420.000 S. Kein schlechtes Monatsgehalt! Ihre amerikanische Kollegin Cindy Crawford verdient „nur" 210.000 S am Tag.

Scharfrichter
Alexander Bernard, Wiener Sänger und Schauspieler, spielt ab 27. Jänner in dem Stück „Josef Lang, k. u. k. Scharfrichter" im alten Jugendstiltheater auf der Baumgartner Höhe.

In luftiger Höhe: Franco Andolfo

Franco Andolfo, österreichischer Schlagerstar, erlebte den „Höhepunkt" seiner Karriere, als er in 5.000 Meter Höhe ein Konzert für allerlei heimische Promis gab – in einer „AUA"-Maschine auf dem Weg nach New York, wo gestern nacht der traditionelle New Yorker „Wiener Opernball" im „Waldorf Astoria"-Hotel über die Bühne ging. Eröffnet wurde das Society-Spektakel von Wiens Kulturstadträtin Dr. Ursula Pasterk.

„IN": Sizilianische Blutorangen: geniale Frucht für Säfte, aber auch im Strudel oder Kuchen hervorragend „OUT": Blutrache

13

DONNERSTAG, 26.1.1995

6 Framing: Reading Paths

In densely printed pages of text, we suggest that reading is linear and strictly coded. Such pages are read, at least at a first reading, the way they are designed to be read: from left to right and from top to bottom, line by line. Any other form of reading (skipping, looking at the last page to see how the plot will be resolved or what the conclusion will be) is regarded as a form of cheating and may produce a faint sense of guilt in the reader. Other kinds of pages, such as traditional comic strips, are also designed to be read in this way.

Newspaper front pages are read differently, and can be read in more than one way. Their reading path is less strictly coded, less fully prescribed. They are *scanned* before they are read, and this scanning process sets up connections between the different elements, relating them to each other in terms of their relative importance, and in terms of the information values we have discussed. Thus the page as a whole is visually grasped before any article is read, if, indeed, any article *is* read. In some cases (cf. the headline in figure 7.2) the article does not even appear on the front page, so that the page becomes a kind of summary, signalling both the relation between the paper and its readers and the relation between these two and the events and issues represented on the page, and in the newspaper as a whole.

In scanning the page, the reader will follow a certain reading path. In some cases this reading path will be encoded in the design of the page. The layout of pages can set up particular reading paths, particular hierarchies of the movement of the hypothetical reader within and across its different elements. Such reading paths begin with the most salient element, from there move on to the next most salient element, and so on. We would assume, for instance, that the picture of Michelle Pfeiffer in figure 7.1 is noticed before any of the text is read, and that the 'Catwoman Star Buys Baby' headline is scanned before the article on the left. And whether the reader 'reads' only the pictures and headlines or also part or all of the text, a complementarity, a to-and-fro between text and image, and between the various elements of the page generally, is guaranteed.

Analysing reading paths with students, we found that some are easy to agree on, others harder, others impossible. This was not, we think, due to a lack of analytical ability on our part or on the part of our students, but to the issues of cultural differences between reader/viewers which we have raised above and to the structure of the pages themselves. Pages encode reading paths to different degrees. Some, though no longer densely printed pages, still take readers by the hand, and attempt to guide them firmly through the text, or at least through the key elements of the text. This is the case, for instance, in many magazines and contemporary school textbooks. On other pages we cannot detect any reading path that is more plausible than any other, and this is the case with many newspaper pages. Such pages seem to offer their readers a choice of reading path, and leave it up to them how to traverse the textual space. To use the currently fashionable term, they were already 'interactive' before interactive multimedia had been invented, and they would appear to be becoming increasingly so.

This is not a trivial phenomenon but is an instance, we believe, of a more general trend away from certain forms of textual order, certain forms of textual coherence: for instance, a relative decline of the importance of sequentially ordered text (e.g. 'narrative') and a move towards 'textual resources', whether as a database, or as the 'resource-books' now common in schools.

Nevertheless, the way the elements of such pages are arranged is not random. It is not random that a picture of an attractive movie star should be placed in the centre of a *Daily Mirror* front page, or a picture of the mishaps that can befall 'ordinary people' in the centre of many of the front pages of the popular Austrian tabloid *Neue Kronenzeitung* (figure 7.9), or that a picture of an important political event should become the Ideal in a *Guardian* front page (figure 7.10). The values of Given and New, Ideal and Real, and Centre and Margin are not dependent on an order of reading. Layout selects the elements that *can* be read, and presents them according to a certain spatial logic, the logic of Centre and Margin, for instance, or of Given and New, but it leaves it up to the reader how to sequence and connect them. Readers thus perceive, consciously or otherwise, the non-linear, spatial structure of the page, *and* are involved in the active, 'linear' process of traversing that structure, of 'navigation'.

Figure 7.9 Front page of *Neue Kronenzeitung*

Structures differ from paper to paper. The *Daily Mirror* and the *Sun*, with their unambiguous Given–New structures, habituate their readers to a daily dose of the reproduction and reaffirmation of a seemingly unchanging set of norms and values. However, other

Figure 7.10　Front page of the *Guardian*

newspapers have quite different structures, and as a result may produce quite different habits of reading and hence quite different orientations to the world.

7 The Framework Applied

The distinctions we have introduced so far are summarized in figure 7.11. The double-headed arrows stand for graded contrasts ('more or less' rather than 'either/or') and the curly brackets for simultaneous choices (e.g. 'a polarized layout can have *both* a Given/New *and* Ideal/Real structure'). The superscript 'I' means 'if' and the superscript 'T' means 'then' (hence, e.g. 'if there is no horizontal polarization, then there must be vertical polarization' – the opposite follows from this).

Guardian *and* Sun *layouts*

Putting a number of *Guardian* front pages from the period March–April 1993 side by side (see e.g. figure 7.3 and figure 7.10) immediately reveals a regular pattern, even though every front page has a slightly different layout. Overall, the pages have a predominantly vertical structure. They prioritize and idealize one story, and then ground this story in the Real of a plethora of other newsworthy events.

The Ideal comprises the masthead, symbol of the paper's identity and mission, and an article which deals with a major national and international public event, an event from the world of the politics of nation states and global institutions. It is dominated by a large and salient photograph whose 'universal' connotations contribute to an interpretation and evaluation of the event and play on the emotions of the viewer: Presidents Clinton and Yeltsin, surrounded by sun-dappled spring foliage, with Clinton as Given and active, Yeltsin as New, and listening with bowed head; UN soldiers in Bosnia rescuing women and children; mourners for 3-year-old IRA bomb victim.

A grey bar, thicker than any other bar on the page, separates this Ideal from the Real, which comprises a jumble of national and

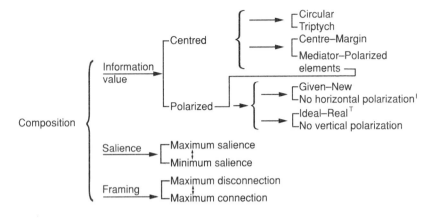

Centred	An element (the Centre) is placed in the centre of the composition.
Polarized	There is no element in the centre of the composition.
Triptych	The non-central elements in a centred composition are placed either on the right and left or above and below the Centre.
Circular	The non-central elements in a centred composition are placed both above and below and to the sides of the Centre, and further elements may be placed in between these polarized positions.
Margin	The non-central elements in a centred composition are identical or near-identical, so creating symmetry in the composition.
Mediator	The Centre of a polarized centred composition forms a bridge between Given and New and/or Ideal and Real, so reconciling polarized elements to each other in some way.
Given	The left element in a polarized composition or the left polarized element in a centred composition. This element is not identical or near-identical to the corresponding right element.
New	The right element in a polarized composition or the right polarized element in a centred composition. This element is not identical or near-identical to the corresponding left element.
Ideal	The top element in a polarized composition or the top polarized element in a centred composition. This element is not identical or near-identical to the corresponding bottom element.
Real	The bottom element in a polarized composition or the bottom polarized element in a centred composition. This element is not identical or near-identical to the corresponding top element.
Salience	The degree to which an element draws attention to itself, due to its size, its place in the foreground or its overlapping of other elements, its colour, its tonal values, its sharpness or definition, and other features.
Disconnection	The degree to which an element is visually separated from other elements through framelines, pictorial framing devices, empty space between elements, discontinuities of colour and shape, and other features.
Connection	The degree to which an element is visually joined to another element, through the absence of framing devices, through vectors and through continuities or similarities of colour, visual shape, etc.

Figure 7.11   Realizations

international events, all, again, from the world of public events. They are presented without any clear pattern, distinct only by virtue of their relative salience, as realized by the size of the articles, and the size and boldness of their headlines. The Real also contains an advertisement, and though it may seem small and insignificant, its position is nevertheless important. New and Real, it is the position of the pragmatic imperative. In advertisements, it is here that one finds the information necessary to obtain the product. In school textbooks it is here that one finds the questions and the assignments – in other words, the things the pupil must *do*. And on these pages it is here that the reader is addressed as a consumer, and that the underlying economic reality of the press is revealed.

Comparing *Sun* front pages from the same period (see figure 7.7) is equally revealing. Here the overall structure is horizontal. The *Sun* selects one event as a Given, and then relates it to another, much more salient event, which is presented as New, as the most controversial and dramatic event of the day, and the event to which the reader should pay most attention.

The Given event is a good deal less salient and comparatively undramatic. It generally bears some relation to the everyday concerns of ordinary people: celebrating a victory with champagne; Euro MPs banning the English 'banger'; the author of *A Year in Provence* selling his house. This event then forms a backdrop for, and a contrast to, the New event, which is invariably dramatic and sensational. Its internal vertical structure idealizes its dramatic values in a screamer headline and enhances its salience through a comparatively salient colour photo. The nature of these New events varies. Political events, events from the world of showbusiness and events befalling ordinary people seem indiscriminately mixed, and all interpreted in terms of the same dramatic values (cf. 'A Knife In Major's Heart'). The precise link between Given and New also varies. Sometimes there is a thematic link, as in the case of the two 'European' stories. Sometimes 'good news' and 'bad news' are contrasted. But there are always two events, brought together in a Given–New relation, and made distinct by a much stronger framing than can be found on the front pages of the *Guardian*.

The seemingly indiscriminate mixing of kinds of events leads us to ask about further, less immediately visible regularities. One such regularity seems to concern, as we mentioned in relation to *Täglich*

Alles, the boundaries of the public and the private, and their mediation/regulation by the newspaper. 'A Knife In Major's Heart' is an example precisely of this: an event of the public sphere – involving the Prime Minister of a nation and members of the governing party – is portrayed via the use of metaphor as a physical event befalling a private person. The other point worth drawing attention to here is the contrast between the *Guardian*'s vertical orientation and the meanings of that (Real vs. Ideal, and its various instantiations: written language vs. image; pragmatic vs. abstracted; local vs. global) and the *Sun*'s horizontal orientation and its meaning (Given vs. New, and its various instantiations). This is a distinction which aligns the *Guardian* much more with the *Daily Telegraph* than with, say, the *Daily Mirror*, despite the clear political differences between the first two, and the greater political affinities between the first and the third.

Table 7.1 summarizes these observations.

Neue Kronenzeitung *and* Täglich Alles

The *Neue Kronenzeitung* is Austria's largest tabloid, and easily as controversial as is the *Sun* in the UK, though for different, more explicitly political reasons. As with the British papers, its layout displays a regular pattern (cf. figure 7.9).

The pages constitute vertical triptychs, with a large photo acting as Mediator between a bold headline and a collection of three or four miscellaneous items. The headline is the Ideal. Sometimes it relates to the same story as the central photograph, sometimes to a separate story ('New Arms Purchase Scandal'; 'Hash Parties In Graz Barracks'). But it is always sensational. The paper signifies the public domain as ridden by corruption and scandal, and presents itself as essentially and 'ideally' a 'scandal sheet'.

The Real contains a variety of items: short items of political, human interest or sports news; advertisements; short poems (the one shown is a rhyme about taxation, its last lines 'No chance to save, you have to pay tax . . . Effort does not bring rewards'). These categories are therefore presented as relatively interchangeable. They all appear in the same boxes, like the items in a supermarket advertisement. But the advertisements are less salient, because,

Table 7.1   Comparison of the *Guardian* and the *Sun* front pages

Guardian	*Sun*
National and international public events	Political, showbusiness and human interest events are mixed and all interpreted as private dreams
Large variety of events	Only two events selected
An Ideal–Real structure idealizes, interprets and evaluates one event	A Given–New structure presents one event as relatively unexceptional and the other as dramatic and sensational
One advertisement positioned as New and Real	No advertisements
Comparatively weak framing: the events must be seen as similar	Comparatively strong framing: the events must be seen as contrasting
The Ideal is most salient	The New is most salient
Dominant classifications: 'public domain'/NEWS	Dominant classifications: 'private domain'/NEWS
Dominant semiotic orientation: Ideal/Real	Dominant semiotic orientation: Given/New

unlike the other items, they are printed in sober black and white, rather than against a coloured background, and in a coloured frame.

Bridging the Ideal and the Real, and most salient on the page as a whole, is a composite element. On the left, as Given, is the masthead, in salient red; on the right is a photo which often portrays ordinary people involved in dramatic events (car crashes, fires). These photos therefore have elements in common with the Ideal (drama) as well as with the Real (ordinary people). But they may also show happy events (two children dressed for their confirmation) or be drawn from the world of showbusiness, as in the case of the publicity photo of the stars of the new James Bond film (caption: 'The deadliest weapon in the new James Bond film is a lady'). The significance of the central space, however, remains the same: it is these photos which are presented as most crucially instantiating the Given of the identity and mission of the *Kronenzeitung*, and which form a bridge between the headlines and the Real world of the reader, in which small human interest events and issues mix with the role of the consumer.

Täglich Alles (see figure 7.2) is the main competitor of the *Kronenzeitung*. Here the structure is again vertical. The Ideal combines a short editorial and a photo which generally shows a celebrity from the world of showbusiness or sport, who will appear on television that night, or is interviewed in the paper: Brooke Shields ('Brooke Shields has plenty of reason to smile: her friend, the tennis star Andre Agassi goes from strength to strength at the Australian open'); tennis stars Arantxa Sanchez and Mary Pierce ('Don't let this picture deceive you . . . they are going to fight a relentless battle'); an Austrian radio personality whose horoscope is discussed in the paper.

The short, populist editorials deal with public events: terrorism ('murderous madness'); the Auschwitz commemorations ('People need to forget . . . it is too painful to remember how inhuman people can be to each other'); the habit of politicians to speak denigratingly of 'the little man' ('A pity we have not found suitable new terms, now that the vocabulary of the class struggle has been abolished'). They appear as the Real of the masthead, and so exemplify the paper's identity and mission, and realize it as the explicit affirmation of a set of norms and values. *Täglich Alles* differs here from the other papers we have discussed, which do not feature opinion on their front pages.

These editorials, however, are a Given for the most salient elements of the pages, the photographs: it is in sport, the movies, the media, that these values now find their most crucial expression and address us directly, through the look of the stars and role models, or so the layout of *Täglich Alles* suggests.

The Real is sharply disconnected from this Ideal: the top section of these pages is all colour, with the masthead in bright blue, the editorial printed on strong yellow, with a red headline, and the photo printed in strong colour. The bottom section is predominantly in black and white, with the exception of the '*Unsere Haltung*' ('Our View') box, which is bright red. It is itself also divided into an Ideal and a Real, with the Ideal a bold headline, centring on some scandal (the hash-smoking soldiers; the arms purchase scandal) and the Real a set of three or four miscellaneous items: short items of political, human interest and sports news; an announcement of the paper's TV guide supplement; advertisements; and the 'Our View' block ('Critical of the powerful, helpful to the weak, committed to the facts'). *Täglich Alles* thus compresses the essentials of the layout of the *Kronenzeitung* in its Real and adds a new Ideal which combines prominently placed opinion and a strong shift in the direction of the symbolic world of showbusiness and sport (and colour). We summarize these observations in table 7.2.

Table 7.2   Comparison of *Neue Kronenzeitung* and *Täglich Alles*

Neue Kronenzeitung	*Täglich Alles*
Treats (by mixing them) public and private events, and politics and showbusiness, as 'the same'	Treats (by mixing them) public and private events, and politics and showbusiness, as 'the same'
Sport is included, but not saliently	Sport can be saliently included
Combines one main scandal story and a selection of miscellaneous items	Combines one main scandal story and a selection of miscellaneous items
A vertical triptych structure idealizes the scandal and, in a large photo, links it to the Real world of a mixture of advertisements and miscellaneous items	An Ideal–Real structure prioritizes opinion and sports/showbusiness, and constructs the latter as the New of the former. The Real combines the scandal (Ideal) and a mixture of advertisements and miscellaneous items
Advertisements are interchangeable with other items but not very salient	Advertisements are interchangeable with other items and equally salient
The Mediator is most salient and forms the New of the masthead	The Ideal is most salient, and, within it, the New
Medium framing	Strong framing between the Ideal and the Real, and, within the Ideal, between Given and New

8   Conclusions

In the previous sections we have applied our descriptive framework to the front pages of two UK and two Austrian newspapers. Our analysis indicates that:

1   Newspaper front pages orient their readers to the world. They may, for instance, present the reader with a world of public events (the *Guardian*) or with a world in which the boundaries between public and private events have become blurred, and in which the symbolic worlds of sport and showbusiness have to some extent taken over from the world of the politics of nation states (the *Sun*; the *Neue Kronenzeitung*; *Täglich Alles*). They may orient their readers to a structure of Ideal/Real (general/particular, global/local, etc.) or to a structure of Given/New (what is assumed/what is startling).

2   Newspaper front pages position genres such as opinion, report and advertisement in relation to each other, and provide them with different degrees of salience and framing, and thereby endow them with particular valuations.

3   Newspaper front pages construct relations between different events in the news, for instance by positioning some as Ideal and others as Real, or some as Given and others as New.

4   Different newspapers do all these things in different ways and to different degrees, which relate to the nature of their readership and to the wider (national) cultural context.

5   Front page layout is subject to change. We have looked at two months' issues of the *Sun* from 1993. Figure 7.12 shows an issue from June 1995, which has a quite different layout, although there are also some continuities. The timings of and reasons for changes would be well worth investigating. But as a general point we can say that front pages as signs are subject to the same social, cultural, ideological factors in their making and in their reading as are all signs. History as change is therefore normal.

With these few examples we have not, of course, given an exhaustive analysis. We nevertheless hope that we have been able to provide some pointers and ideas for a further exploration of this

Figure 7.12   Front page of the *Sun* from June 1995

field, and some support for our assertion that layout analysis has an important role in the critical study of newspaper language.

To us, this last requirement seems entirely uncontentious. The novelty of our approach nevertheless arouses at times kinds of critique which we find surprising. We proceed from the assumption that the visual as a mode of representation and communication displays regularities which are discoverable. If it did not, communication would not happen, unless the visual is an entirely transparent medium of expression. Noticeable and entirely regular cultural differences rule that possibility out as an implausible one.

The major challenges to our approach take the form: 'How do you know?' That is, they are challenges to the epistemological status of our claims. For instance, how can we know that, in 'Western' visual semiosis, left and right, top and bottom have the values we attribute to them, or, more fundamentally, have any value at all? We regard these as legitimate challenges, and of exactly the same kind which can be raised in relation to linguistic structures. How do we know that there is a difference in meaning between *Bill married Mary*, and *Mary married Bill*? How do we know not only that agency has shifted from one participant to the other, but also that if I utter *Mary married Bill*, I am saying something about my presuppositions concerning gender relations: that is, I am saying things of a wider cultural and social provenance? How do I know that there is a difference between *Mary and Bill married* and *Bill and Mary married*, so that when I hear one or the other of them uttered, I make (and am entitled to make) inferences about the closer relationship of the speaker with one or the other of these two people: in other words, I make legitimate inferences about the *interest* of the utterer in this described event?

In our view, these and other questions apply equally to all semiotic systems. The greater familiarity with the linguistic (some 3,000 to 4,000 years of detailed sustained study in the 'West') has, to a large extent, made these issues less visible or even invisible in relation to language. We regard our efforts here as a beginning, an attempt to put this issue on the map in the broadest terms, and an attempt to begin to assemble items for a new agenda of research. The unquestionable increase in the use of the visual mode from the 1970s on makes this unavoidable in relation to many enterprises – media studies, education, information science, psychology, and others. But this development will also, inevitably, have effects on 'language itself', in what we believe will be quite fundamental ways. It is an issue that can no longer be avoided.

NOTE

Nik Coupland acted as respondent to an oral presentation of the first version of this chapter. His meticulous, empathetic critique proved most helpful to us in our redrafting and we wish to record our thanks to him. No blame should attach to him, however, for errors of any kind.

Chapter 8

Signs and Wonders: Interpreting the Economy through Television

Kay Richardson

1 Introduction

The analysis of media discourse can be approached in many different ways, as is shown by the variety of approaches reflected in the contributions to this volume. The present chapter focuses upon the role of the *audience* in mass media communication, not in order to displace these textual studies, but in order to investigate a little more closely how we might seek to relate textual and reception analysis. The substantive focus of the enquiry is upon representations of the economy through television: a news domain which has been very little studied to date, and one which presents a challenge to both broadcasters and viewers.[1]

2 Textual Analysis and Reception Analysis

Textual analysis is very commonly concerned with questions of *representation* in media discourse and often with the object of determining the ideological character of representations, whilst still allowing psychoanalytic theories, Marxist theories, structuralist theories, postmodernist theories to inflect their analytic accounts in their different ways (Allen, 1992 offers a wide range of different approaches in accessible form). Sometimes the analytic focus is directed more towards the interactional character of media discourse (as in Scannell, 1991; Livingstone and Lunt, 1994). Sociolinguists such as Bell (1991) have been more concerned with the textual structures by means of which media discourse achieves its distinctiveness, recognizing the variability to be found across media and genres.

The standpoint of reception analysis as this has developed since the early 1980s is one which takes issue with 'textualism': that is to say, it takes issue with the assumption that meaning is always and only a product of the text alone. In reception analysis, the claim is that meaning is negotiated between a text and its readers (viewers, listeners . . .). Hence, since media readers are plural, readings are likewise plural. The assumption of textual determinacy is rejected.

Of course, textual analysis increasingly does appreciate the possibility of divergent interpretations (Kress, 1994), thus legitimizing a 'division of labour' for academic work on media discourse. And the empirical results of 'reception analysis' do not necessarily invalidate textual analysis. Different responses to characters such as 'JR Ewing' in *Dallas*, different judgements of his moral worth, are compatible with the same understandings of that character's relations with other characters in the diegesis (see Ang, 1985). As far as research is concerned, the result is that there is still a question mark over the potential for divergence at 'lower levels' of interpretation – 'before' JR Ewing is *evaluated* as a fine example of a capitalist entrepreneur, he is (presumably) *understood* in terms of his relations with other characters in the diegesis. However, it is not so much in connection with popular TV fiction as with TV material of a more *propositional* character (news, current affairs, documentary) where the question of variable meanings seems most worth asking. It is the project of such broadcasting to influence its viewers and listeners by causing them to modify their understandings in the light of its propositional information. These issues are usefully discussed in Corner (1991).

In this context we can begin to appreciate why researchers such as Hoijer (1993) have begun to argue for a return to questions of *comprehension* within the field of reception studies. Hoijer makes the point that an existing literature in this area is all but ignored within currently influential approaches to the study of reception. We can view these influential approaches, notwithstanding their differences, as belonging to a 'cultural studies' tradition.² It is not difficult to explain the neglect Hoijer identifies. The cultural studies tradition inherited a different agenda: one in which comprehension took second place to questions of ideological influence, or alternatively, in which the emphasis was upon the 'meaning' of viewing as a situated social practice, rather than the meaning of texts. The experimentalism of comprehension studies, and their undertheorized and psychologistic conception of the audience, are regarded with suspicion within this framework. As well, there is considerable resistance to research with an unproblematic notion of media *content*, which pays insufficient attention to communicative form and which can be regarded as ignoring or denying the openness of the text to different interpretations.

Hoijer's paper does not mention the research of linguists such as Bell, Wodak and van Dijk, some of which has been likewise concerned with comprehension, and has likewise been ignored within the cultural studies tradition (see Bell, 1991 chapter 11; van Dijk, 1988b chapter 4; Wodak, 1987). This research has itself undergone a movement away from the limitations of the earlier comprehension studies. As yet, however, there has been very little work, apart from Hoijer's own, which attempts to reconceptualize the study of comprehension from within the perspective of reception research, as this is now understood in media studies. But it is now possible to think about what this reconceptualization might involve. There *is* a place in reception research for the study of comprehension: this should be a suitably enriched view of the nature of textual meaning, of the viewers' own meaning systems, and of the processes of textual interpretation, in which 'comprehension' is only one part.

The present chapter is intended as a contribution to the 'public information' project within audience studies, and one which takes the role of *the text*, and textual analysis, in that project very seriously. As Corner (1991) argues, it is not desirable to follow the currently fashionable doctrine of textual polysemy to the extent of abolishing all ideas of textual determinacy:

> Whatever the reason for this assumption of general textual 'openness', such a perspective neglects among other things the considerable degree of *determinacy* possessed by texts. This determinacy is simply a result of their using, among other things, systems of signification based on widespread social/national acceptance, and having relatively low levels of ambiguity . . . it clearly remains true, as the new interpretative perspective is keen to point out, that 'meaning' does not inhere within texts, and is far better seen as a property of interpretative production (and therefore as inherently 'unstable') even where the most uncomplicated and familiar of routine significations are concerned (e.g. NO ENTRY, 'Hello David'). But the effect of determinate *signification* upon this production is something which the use of the term 'polysemy' has not always recognised, and, at its worst, has dismissed. (Corner, 1991: 274–5)

Textual determinacy has its limits, for we know that there are levels of meaning which are not underwritten by fully shared codes and coding orientations. But 'low level' textual determinacy is fully compatible with the principle of textual 'constructivism': the notion that viewers, readers and listeners are *active* in the processes of meaning construction. It is even compatible with that part of textual constructivism which puts emphasis upon the contribution of viewers' own frameworks of knowledge and understanding. The point here is that there are some very widely shared frameworks of understanding, and viewers can internalize complex articulations of frameworks. They can, for example, 'hear' in media texts, beliefs and values which they are familiar with but do not share, do not hold as their own beliefs and values. This is what happens when left-wing and liberal viewers watch a text which appears to sustain a right-wing view of the unemployed as work-shy scroungers (Richardson and Corner, 1986). What they do *not* do is ascribe their own values to the text. They hear it as reactionary, and they contest this: they do not try to hear it as radical.

Textual determinacy is not incompatible with the empirical discovery of large-scale interpretative variation throughout the mass audience. Reception studies is committed to the study of this variation, but it is theoretically inadequate to view all interpretative differences as evidence of viewers' 'creativity'. Analytic differentiation is essential. Some variation will be describable in terms of distance from the offered meaning, including 'simple' misunderstanding and incomplete readings. An early attempt to articulate something along these lines was Hall's so-called 'encoding–decoding' model, originally published in 1973 (cf. Allan's chapter in this volume). This was later criticized by Lewis (Wren-Lewis, 1983), among others, for being too determinist. The approach adopted in this chapter is certainly influenced by Hall's account: however, it is not a direct adaptation of that model, for two reasons. Firstly, Hall's principal concern was not, as in the present case, with audience comprehension and understanding, but with the limits of mass media power to reproduce dominant ideology. Secondly, we need to get away from some of the conceptual confusions which have been the legacy of the encoding–decoding model. There has been a tendency to treat the model as a theory of different ways of reading a *text*: hegemonic reading, oppositional reading, negotiated reading. This is a misguided interpretation. It is much better to treat it as an account of different ways of reading or understanding *reality* (i.e. what the text is about) and of the extent to which the text is compatible or incompatible with that understanding. Some variation will be describable in terms of differential appropriation of ambiguous or polysemic possibilities (no doubt some taken meanings *are* textually underdetermined), and some will be describable, not at the level of comprehension/understanding, but as variation in 'uptake' or response to the text.

3   The Economy on Television

The considerations above are ones which apply quite generally to reception research with a 'public knowledge' agenda. Within that agenda, the specific news domain of 'the economy' has distinctive features of its own. Our approach both to television economic reporting and to viewer interpretation is informed by a recognition of 'the economy' as essentially a systemic notion (see Emmison, 1983, for a historical account of the term as indicating a sphere of national polity). That is to say, as an entity, 'the economy' is dispersed across a range of interrelated processes, states and indicators (e.g. interest rates, unemployment levels, exchange rates, balance of payments, public sector borrowing, inflation). But the configuration of this dispersal is subject to change in various ways. Different factors can be included or excluded as parts of the system, the relationship assumed to be desirable between parts (the economy 'in balance') can vary, and the priority accorded to given parts can alter too.

Economic news is most often led by a reported change in one or more components of the economy. Such change requires connections to be made in order that some overall assessment of shifts in the systemic condition can be offered. This assessment, articulated within the requirements of news immediacy, is essentially one of the *short term* (indeed, the 'picture' it offers is sometimes referred to as a 'snapshot'). However, it gets news value from its relation to *longer-term* expectations, which in turn are set by the reporting of broad trends. During the period over which our study was conducted, news of shifts in the British national economy were set against the larger trend of a 'recovery' whose 'fragility' was widely recognized. The primary significance of an item therefore often lay in the degree to which reported change served to confirm or to put in question the trend towards recovery. Within the broad terms of 'progress' it was also possible to extract news value from *variations in pace*, and the vocabulary of the news over this period shows a rich variety of possible modes of movement (e.g. from faltering, inching and lumbering through to accelerating and racing). When the point was reached at which the fact of 'recovery' was beyond doubt among economists, then 'sustainable recovery' became the new expectational framework for the according of news value.

It has since been joined by 'the feelgood factor'. Unlike the two previous news thresholds, 'the feelgood factor' is an *explicitly subjective* measure of how the economy is performing, although objective improvements may be dependent upon it being established. 'The feelgood factor' turns on the public experiencing economic upturn, in part, perhaps, on their belief that there is a trend 'coming their way'. It is a moot point as to whether, within the present definitions, arrival of the 'feelgood factor' is a necessary preliminary to the attainment of 'sustainable recovery' or vice versa:

'But there'll be few celebrations, few cries of joy while the feelgood
factor remains so elusive' (economic story sign-off, *News at Ten*, 12
October 1994)

4   Researching Television and the Economy

An ongoing study at Liverpool of TV and the economy is attempting to explore what the TV news makes of 'the economy' in Britain
and how, in turn, TV news discourse on economic matters is understood by the viewers. Six viewing groups participated in a pilot
study: science students, Labour and Conservative Party members,
university security staff, local government officers, and participants
from the local Unemployed Resource Centre. These volunteers
watched extracts from the news programmes of the two major
channels, including some Budget Day coverage and some later
material. These channels were the BBC and ITV. The latter is the
main commercial, terrestrial channel on British television, and
shows the ITN news. On Budget Day, the incumbent Government,
in the person of the Chancellor of the Exchequer, gives an official
assessment of the state of the economy and the policy measures to
be introduced in the light of that assessment. Budget Day speeches
always attract a lot of media coverage. At the time of the broadcast
the Chancellor of the Exchequer was Norman Lamont. The inter-
view/screenings were conducted in the School of Politics and Communication Studies at the University of Liverpool within six weeks
of the original broadcasts.

The small-scale nature of this project of course raises many questions for further research respecting the specificity of the viewing/
knowing experience for different sections of the public. I would not
wish to claim that the viewers who participated in the study were
'representative' either of the viewing public in general or of the
interest groups from which they were drawn. I would wish to claim
that in spreading the net over this particular set of participants,
clustered by groups to ensure a 'spread' of response constituencies,
we did all that could be expected in a pilot study to draw out
reactions along 'fault lines' of attitude/opinion (those of political
affiliation and of relation to the world of paid employment) which

seemed likely to be of significance in relation to this particular topic. But the dangers of oversimplification are real enough and the usual caveats about relying too much upon small samples apply.

5 Texts

For the purposes of the present chapter, I wish to focus upon one particular economic news item from the tape which we used in the pilot study. My discussion will be more intensive than is usually the case in studies of this kind: it is very 'narrow' in focus, yet deliberately so, as the purpose is to demonstrate the possibility of relating text to interpretation at the most detailed levels of linguistic form. A full transcription is provided below.

The selected item of news coverage is about a rise in 'growth rates' in the national economy. This rise in growth rates gets its news value from a narrative which is pushed back as far as the 1930s. This is a move which undoubtedly enhances the dramatic qualities of the story. Most viewers were not alive in the 1930s, and know of it as 'the Depression' with a cluster of meanings to do with the experience of poverty and unemployment. It also signifies, here, 'a long time': a scale-enhancing device of a type common in news discourse, and one which is repeated in other terms elsewhere in the text:

> Britain's worst recession since the thirties is now over, according to the government.

> From the middle of 1990 to the end of last year, total production in the economy stagnated and fell in what proved to be the longest recession in half a century. But in the first three months of 1993, output jumped by 0.6 per cent.

> At an annual rate, growth in the first three months of the year was two and a half per cent. Only just back up to the annual rate of growth in the UK in the last 40 years.

The chronology of the story divides time into four successive sections: the depression of the 1930s, followed by a long period

BBC 9.00 News, 26 April 1993

Michael Buerk,
presenter
Voice-over Leyland
workers

The Government's declared the recession over. The latest figures show the economy growing again for the first time in two and a half years.
[headlines for other stories edited out]

Michael Buerk
Studio, to camera

Good evening. Britain's worst recession since the thirties is now over, according to the Government. Official figures show the gross domestic product – that's the total value of goods and services produced after ruling out erratic oil production – rose by 0.6 per cent in the first three months of this year. Until then, production had been flat or falling for more than two and a half years. The Chancellor said there were now clear signs of recovery across a broad front. During the recession, unemployment doubled and sixty thousand companies went bust.

Gerry Baker,
economics
correspondent
Voice-over Leyland
Daf footage
[launch]

At the Leyland Daf plant in Birmingham this morning they had plenty to celebrate. The news of the economy's return to growth coincided with the completion of the management buy-out there, that will save a thousand jobs.

Leyland Daf
chairman
Speaking on film at
launch

Today we are reborn. A brand new company. Tomorrow, just watch us go.

Gerry Baker
Voice-over Leyland
Daf footage
[workers

The van maker's employees will be able to work with renewed enthusiasm now that the recovery is finally under way. From the middle of 1990 to the end of last year, total

assembling vans] *Voice-over growth* *bar chart*	production in the economy stagnated and fell in what proved to be the longest recession in half a century. But in the first months of 1993, output jumped by 0.6 per cent. Although this kind of growth hasn't been seen for three years, manufacturers remain cautious.
Geoff White, *Pressac* *Holdings* *[interview]*	We're seeing different signs of recovery in the various markets we operate in. Certainly I think sentiment has improved. But I think we're seeing a batch of indicators, and at this stage we are looking forward to recovery but not confident that it is really there and really sustainable.
Gerry Baker *Voice-over different* *production scene*	The caution is understandable. At an annual rate, growth in the first three months of the year was two and a half per cent. Only just back up to the annual rate of growth in the UK in the last 40 years.
Professor David *Currie, London* *Business School* *[interview]*	We're not yet making up lost ground. We need to get growth above two and a half per cent up to 3 per cent or 4 per cent, to make up the ground we lost in the recession and to bring unemployment clearly in a downward direction.
Gerry Baker *Studio: on camera*	It's now clear that the economy spent most of last year bumping along the bottom after two years of decline. At the start of this year, a series of economic figures pointed somewhat inconclusively to a revival in economic prospects. Now today's GDP figure provides the chapter and verse that Britain is gradually moving out of recession. But before a complete recovery can be declared, even faster growth must be achieved, and maintained. And with a daunting trade deficit and huge government borrowing, that won't prove easy.

Michael Buerk *Studio: on camera*	The Chancellor says it's now up to manufacturers to take advantage of the changed economic conditions and create a sustainable recovery. But Labour has warned against complacency, and says Britain's productive base has been so damaged by the recession, new measures are needed to ensure lasting growth.
Robin Oakley, *political editor* *Voice-over footage* *from Lamont's* *meeting.* *Exterior shot* *from Union Jack* *to building: then* *interior*	Britain's export flag will be flying ever more vigorously as a result of the recovery heralded in today's GDP figures, the Government hopes. Today at a European Bank for Reconstruction and Development meeting in London the Chancellor argued that sales to Europe will flourish, even though some EU partners are starting their recessions as Britain begins to pull out of hers. Mr Lamont was distinctly bullish.
Norman Lamont *Studio [interview]*	Recession, in the sense of output actually falling, probably ended quite some time ago. But we've now got a recovery that I believe will be firmly based. We have low inflation. We have the lowest interest rates in Europe. Productivity has been rising so that our exports are very competitively priced. There is no reason at all, provided companies keep control of their costs, there is no reason at all why this recovery should not be sustained.
Gordon Brown, *Shadow* *Chancellor* *Studio [interview]*	The key question is whether we have the productive capacity to succeed in the world markets of the future. And for that to happen we have to have levels of investment in skills and in industry that are on a par with our competitors. And unfortunately there is as yet no sign that government ministers recognize that instead of complacency and self-congratulation we need to set in place the industry and skills policy.

without notable problems, followed by the recession of the 1990s and culminating with the return to growth in January, February and March 1993. The structure of the piece is fairly straightforward. It begins in the studio with Michael Buerk as the news presenter, who produces both the headline at the top of the programme as a whole, and the lead at the top of the item itself. What follows is offered in two sections: an economic section and a political section. Buerk hands over to the economics correspondent, who goes into more detail, using the Leyland Daf footage as a hook for a sub-theme on business confidence: this is further elaborated by accessing the voice of manufacturing industry (the Pressac Holdings executive): the more general perspective is developed with the voice of academic business expertise (the university professor). The economics correspondent's contribution moves from facts about the economic present to speculation about the future, and this focus on the future, via a short sequence back in the studio, forms a link between the economic and the political sections. During the latter both the (Conservative) Government and (Labour) Opposition have their say.

6 Reception

Using this item, in conjunction with the audience data, I will discuss the viewers' 'discourse of interpretation' under three headings. Firstly, I will talk about what viewers *recall* from this material, focusing upon how they appropriate remembered information to their own perspectives. Secondly, I will provide some evidence for viewers' *attention to textual form* in this situation. This will also include some specific discussion of *variant* comprehensions, and how these relate to the textual form. And thirdly, I will address the question of *comprehension and understanding*: that is to say, I will talk about the role of prior understanding in the construction of comprehended meaning, and the function of the text in allowing respondents to elaborate their understanding of the economy.

Recall and thematic memory

Traditionally, research on comprehension proceeds through tests of what viewers and readers recall from their exposure to news texts.

Comprehension and recall are, of course, not the same thing: a proposition comprehended at the time may fall out of active memory, so that the recipient needs reminding of what she has seen. However, recall testing does provide one useful way into the investigation of comprehension. It is also relatively easy to operationalize under experimental conditions. There is a good case, though, for methodologies which are 'ethnodiscursive' rather than experimental in character, designed to elicit data in the form of *talk*, allowing the respondents to discuss the texts in their own terms. This provides a different type of access to the details of recall.

The pilot study reported here did not set out to *test* the viewers' recall of the material screened. Nevertheless, they inevitably did invoke propositions and images – 'meanings' of a general or of a specific character – from the text. There was substantial convergence in the details of what viewers recalled. As far as the verbal discourse is concerned, all groups recalled this BBC item in global terms as being about the end of the recession. From the visual track, most groups mentioned either the 'growth rate' graphic, or the Chancellor of the Exchequer's interview, or both.

Undoubtedly people's memory for detail is selective. It is also *thematic*: details are recalled when and as they fit in with general interpretations which are being developed. This means that the same proposition can be recalled by different groups and yet be appropriated in very different ways by those groups. A notable example of this concerns the way that two groups recall from the BBC item the proposition that 60,000 companies went bust during the recession. The security staff are reminded of this proposition when talking about the imagery of 'happy workers' during the Leyland Daf sequence. Their point about the Leyland workers is that this firm is a single company, and hence not reliable as a piece of evidence for the end of the recession. For the security staff, the statistics on company failure provide support for a sceptical view of that sequence:

> *Speaker A*:   They could have showed plenty of industries were – are – still running down, but they chose a little bit of good news like that, and you're not partic . . . That's like a biased opinion isn't it?

Speaker B: Cos they did actually say there was . . . was it
sixty thousand, sixty-five thousand businesses gone bust,
you know?

The other group to recall this detail is the Conservative group. Like
the security staff, they want to question the BBC's impartiality
(though to prove a left-wing rather than a right-wing bias), but they
do not connect the information on business failure with the Leyland
Daf sequence. For them the issue is how to interpret the significance
of such a statistic:

I mean, one thing we keep hearing about is that how many
small businesses have gone into liquidation – record numbers
– but people seldom point out that in fact there's more people
who've opened more businesses for that to happen. If those
small businesses had not opened in the first place there
wouldn't be that number to in fact go down.

The security staff do not question that the management buy-out at
Leyland Daf is good news; the Conservative viewers do not question that there have been record numbers of company liquidations,
nor that this is a bad thing.

In the next section I will talk about the role of textual form in
guiding interpretations. In anticipation of that discussion, it is
worth pointing out that reception research of this kind can encounter some surprises in the data. It would be wrong to expect total
convergence in what viewers remember. It is surprising when small
details are recalled which are given very little prominence in the
text. In such cases, viewers' own frameworks of understanding, pre-
existing the encounter with the text, enable them to 'hear' things
which other viewers would miss without considerable prompting.
This is idiosyncratic recall: only one viewer in our study recalled
that the ITN recovery story (four days earlier) had mentioned a
survey of business confidence:

When they say 'recovery' though, I think the most important
thing they said was the confidence that business had. I thought
that was the most important thing. That's sort of the usual
implication of recovery, cos like, like you say, you can't get the

up to date figures, so you have to go on some form of indication, which is like how much confidence there is.
(*Interviewer*: Did you think that was important then?)
I thought that was the important part of the . . . They said, was it a four-year high of the business confidence?

His recall is correct, down to the very phrasing of the measurement as 'four-year high':

Registered job vacancies were up. Also up were house sales and production figures to their highest in March for 19 years, and business confidence. That's at a four-year high, according to a survey by the British Chambers of Commerce.

This statistic was not given much of a chance, textually speaking. It is one amongst four positive indicators, all of which are incidental support for the key indicator as featured in the news lead: the improvement in the unemployment figures. There is no supporting visualization, and it occurs just before a shift of format from studio presentation to filmed report. And yet, despite its low prominence, there is this one viewer who is able to pull it out of its context and elevate it to the status of 'the most important thing they said'.

Comprehension and the text

Economic reality is not a 'given' which the news discourse seeks simply to pass on to the viewers. The 'reality' itself is of a complex and contested kind. 'The economy' as an entity is real enough, since so much economic activity is oriented towards it or interpreted in terms of it. But it is an abstract entity. Its properties are not, therefore, directly manifest but show themselves through 'indicators': interest rates; investment rates; cost of living indices; inflation rates; unemployment rates, and so on. These are the outward, manifest signs of a deeper underlying reality, and they have to be interpreted before they tell us anything about that reality.

Sometimes the indicators of economic change are directly contestable. Unemployment figures are a case in point: there is a well-established reflex of contestation in Britain to the official unemployment figures which are issued by the Government each month. The government figures do not give the full picture of the true extent of unemployment in Britain. The unemployed viewers who participated in our study had a lot to say along these lines, some provoked by the ITN 'recovery' story which used a fall in unemployment rates as its news lead.

It's totally convincing as a programme, but if you actually know about it, you know, they're just telling lies, basically – in the sense that, OK, the figures dropped, but why have the figures dropped? Because people are not signing on or they're in part-time work, or they're going on a scheme which they've been forced on to, you know. That's the reason.

This is a critical reading: the text is convincing, but he is not convinced. Such a response presupposes a split view of the audience: a minority who have resources like his own, and can therefore distinguish truth from falsehood, and a majority without such resources. It is important to pay attention to such claimed understanding of what *others'* interpretative resources include and exclude, in determining the extent of the shared knowledge which informs reception. Even where the indicators are not contestable in themselves as figures, the interpretation of the indicators is always contestable. In the case of the growth rate story, the issue is the relationship between the core news fact, and the interpretation of that fact as a sign of 'recovery' in the economy. The BBC partly endorses the Government's 'recovery' interpretation, partly withholds endorsement. This is a very precisely analysable textual equivocation, and turns on how to interpret signs of a 'trend', where trends involve relations between the present and the future, as well as the past. We can begin with the headline and the lead paragraph:

The Government's declared the recession over. The latest figures show the economy growing again for the first time in two and a half years. Good evening. Britain's worst recession since the thirties is now over, according to the Government. Official figures show the gross domestic product – that's the total value of goods and services produced after ruling out erratic oil production – rose by 0.6 per cent in the first three months of this year. Until then, production had been flat or falling for more than two and a half years. The Chancellor said there were now clear signs of recovery across a broad front. During the recession, unemployment doubled and sixty thousand companies went bust.

The core news fact here is a newsworthy change of direction in a key economic indicator: namely, growth rates. Upon that fact is projected an interpretation: the change signifies economic 'recovery'. This interpretation of the rise in growth rates is attributed to the Government, both in the headline and in the intro, though in textually distinctive ways. In the headline, the attribution is via the reporting clause 'The Government's declared . . .' But this attribution is a 'soft' one. The initial sentence is followed by a second one which stands in a relation of *evidentiality* to it. The latter sentence is the evidence for what the first sentence claims to be true. The fact that it is the *Government* making the claim thus recedes into the background.

There is a gesture of attribution in the lead paragraph as well as in the headline. In the case of the lead paragraph, however, the attribution is held over to the end of the sentence: '. . . according to the Government'. What the viewer hears first is the claim itself. This is temporarily accorded the status of a fact, uttered on the authority of the presenter and thus of the programme. And it is a strong claim with high news value. A high-impact initial statement like this is likely to resonate much more strongly with viewers than the subsequent dutiful but weakening attribution, which requires them to rework their understanding of the authority for the proposition. It is moved down the hierarchy of voices: it is the Government, not the BBC, asserting that the recession is over.

It is not only Buerk but also Baker the economics correspondent who endorses the Government's recovery claim. In Baker's discourse, the relation of economic growth and recovery is not one of interpretation, but one of *synonymy*: his second sentence refers to 'the news of the economy's return to growth' whilst in his third sentence (after the Daf chairman's soundbite) he paraphrases this as 'the recovery is finally under way':

> The news of the economy's return to growth coincided with the completion of the management buy-out there [at Leyland Daf] that will save a thousand jobs.

The van maker's employees will be able to work with renewed enthusiasm now that the recovery is finally under way.

Even the more modest formulation by Baker is problematic as a truth claim: through nominalization, time reference disappears and this helps to project the present fact (the January/February/March data) into the future, for which there is no evidence. Eventually, Baker is as explicit as it is possible to be that the recovery has arrived:

> Now today's GDP figure provides the chapter and verse that Britain is gradually moving out of recession.

(The phrasing of this 'beyond doubt' formulation is interesting in its connotations of biblical levels of authority, although one has to wonder about the residual power of such expressions in a secular age.)

The recovery interpretation is nevertheless undermined from within the text, and not just through attribution to the Government. Other voices partly agree and partly disagree with the 'recovery' interpretation in making the issue one of 'sustainable recovery'. Baker undermines himself in his sympathy for the manufacturers' cautiousness. Geoff White of Pressac Holdings says: 'we are looking forward to recovery but not confident that it is really there and really sustainable' and Baker comments: 'The caution is understandable'. Later, he acknowledges, in line with what the business expert says, that 'complete' recovery requires better figures than the ones just announced:

> But before a complete recovery can be declared, even faster growth must be achieved, and maintained. And with a daunting trade deficit and huge government borrowing, that won't prove easy.

Lamont complicates matters by proposing that only *falling* growth rates define recession, rather than falling *and static* growth rates, which was the implication previously:

> Recession, in the sense of output actually falling, probably ended quite some time ago.

A different kind of complication occurs when the programme stops talking in terms of a quarterly growth rate increase of 0.6 per cent and starts projecting that rate as an annual one of two and a half per cent:

> At an annual rate, growth in the first three months of the year was two and a half per cent. Only just back up to the annual rate of growth in the UK in the last 40 years.

For viewers who are uncertain how economic reasoning works, and need interpretative guidance from the text, this is not very helpful. There is *no* inferable single account of what constitutes recovery, and hence no definitive warrant for believing that the recovery has arrived, despite what Gerry Baker says. The 'recovery' interpretation, though it is 'pulled up' from the Government's discourse into the broadcasters' own, is too thoroughly undermined by difficult-to-assess contra-indications: the 'experts' don't quite believe it, and the broadcasters appear to endorse their caution just as initially they appeared to endorse the Government's confidence.

It would not be productive to develop this account of what the text means by 'recovery' any further. There is a real danger of producing textual analysis which is too detailed in its attention to nuances of formulation. The danger is of attributing significance to features that viewers are not attentive to. For the reception study to make sense, it is important to concentrate upon those features which seem likely to have the potential to affect reception.

Comprehension and the viewers

So what do the viewers make of this? News discourse is understood by viewers as sequences of *authored* messages. To comprehend those messages is thus not necessarily to believe them to be true. A viewer 'comprehends', not that the recession has ended, but that they are being told that it has ended, and told on the authority of someone with greater or lesser credibility. Thus much interpretative sophistication is a feature of all the discussions we conducted with respondents, as the following quotations show:

. . . on the ITN one [a story from four days earlier than the BBC one, with unemployment rates as its news lead, not reproduced here] it was quite clear that the whole message of the bulletin was that the recession had actually ended, whereas on the BBC one the report was about 'the Government says the recession has ended . . .' (Conservative viewers)

. . . this time the BBC really did take the Chancellor's line. This sort of assumption that we were in a recovery, which proved to be junk. (Labour viewers)

Speaker A: I mean, how anyone can stand up on the twenty-sixth of March at three o'clock and say 'The recession's now over'. . .

Speaker B: Hurrah!

Speaker C: Er, it seemed to me . . .

Speaker A: . . . is something beyond me.

Speaker D: And how many times have we heard it before?

Speaker B: And both sides tried to do it, like, and they. . . really 'Hurrah! It's all over', like. Nobody actually pinpointed that it isn't.

(Unemployed viewers)

The Conservative speaker here seems to believe that the recovery is a reality which the BBC's discourse, in effect, misreports as no more than Government propaganda, and undermines through its use of other voices. Most other viewers take the line that the recovery is Government discourse, though some think that the BBC endorses the Government's view and some do not. Thus, viewers diverge in their propensity to believe the proposition that the recession is over, with the Conservatives notably more confident than the rest. And they also diverge in their comprehension of it as reportage on the authority of the broadcasters or on that of the Government alone.

We cannot tell from these data whether the Conservative speaker believes in the recovery as a consequence of the text alone (reading 'against the grain' of what he perceives as the broadcasters' strategy of playing down that recovery; privileging the voice of the Government over that of the broadcasters) or whether his belief in the recovery is an element in his own systemic understanding which has been established over the week intervening between the item being broadcast on 26 April and the project screening and interview on 2 May. The effect would be the same in either case. For him, the BBC item is a univocal discourse, one which, in being 'balanced', improperly authorizes sceptical doubts about the reality of the recovery.

Of the other five groups, all but the local government officers hear the BBC announcing the reality of the recovery. Two groups, however, the students and the security staff, also hear the BBC authorizing sceptical doubts about the reality of the recovery. For them, the text seems multivocal in a way that is deviant or unsatisfactory, and not what they expect or desire from TV news:

> I found the word[?] 'recovery' misleading, because they were saying that . . . big headline was 'the recovery has started' and then what they seemed to say part-way through the report was: 'the recovery's not here yet', basically. (Student viewers)

> And the BBC side, I thought, you know, the opening . . . the opening titles were very sensationally announcing that the recession was over, and then they went on to tell us that it wasn't over, you know, using experts to emphasize the fact that it's not over. Whereas, you know, they announced that it is, you know. I thought that was a little bit confusing. (Security staff)

The other two groups, the Labour viewers and the unemployed viewers, do not hear this second, contradictory authorization: they hear a univocal discourse endorsing the Chancellor's view:

> The thing that was so appalling . . . was it was just a Government press release that they repeated *verbatim*. And they only gave two clues to that. The one said that 'according to the Government', and I think the other said 'the Government hopes'. And the rest of it was just quoting the Government line – that we're coming out of recession. (Labour viewers)

> I think it was more like a Party Political Broadcast by the Tory Party. I mean it was put that way, especially the BBC one: Big music, 'oh it's great, everything's over now, no problems'. And then, they give it to Lamont, as if to say 'there's no problems, everything's worked now'. . . (Unemployed viewers)

(Party Political Broadcasts are time slots in broadcast output across all channels allocated to the political parties on the basis of their voting strength. Broadcasting organizations are legally obliged to provide these slots, but editorial control is entirely with the parties.)

Finally, there is one group – the local government officers – which hears a univocal discourse with no view of its own, only an honourably balanced account of conflicting views:

> when the BBC came on, they stressed . . . they balanced it up, didn't they? They said 'this has happened, this has happened, but this is still there and this is still there'. And I thought that was really much more balanced in their approach.

At the risk of oversimplification, these differences between the viewers can be presented as in table 8.1.

Table 8.1   Comparing readings

Group	How it hears the BBC	How it hears the Government	How it hears other voices	Own view
Conservative	Questioning recovery	Announcing recovery		Recovery
Labour	Announcing recovery	Announcing recovery		No recovery
Unemployed	Announcing recovery	Announcing recovery		No recovery
Students	Announcing *and* questioning recovery	Announcing recovery	Questioning recovery	
Security staff	Announcing *and* questioning recovery	Announcing recovery	Questioning recovery	
Local govt officers		Announcing recovery	Questioning recovery	

The differences we have identified between viewers are interesting for what they tell us about the role of textual form in the comprehension process. Textual form is 'read' for signs of authorization. Viewers refer to such formal properties as the use of reporting clauses, and to the terms upon which the voices of interested parties are accessed, as when the security staff say: 'they went on to tell us that it [the recession] wasn't over, using experts to emphasize the fact that it's not over'. In some cases a top-down reading induces a very selective appropriation of such signs of authorization. The following viewer is happy to ignore the contributions of the sceptical manufacturer and business expert in deriving his 'pro-Government' interpretation of the text:

> just jumping up and down with a point six per cent increase, jumping up and down screaming: 'it's over, it's over'. I think it was obviously good news and should have been portrayed as such, but it should have been more guarded. A very small jump like that could be a blip. It's a long road. I think the main thing, it's going to take a long time to get out. I just think it didn't really say anything. It just reported Lamont being … going round telling everybody how wonderful it was. (Labour viewer)

What we cannot confidently say on the basis of this material, though it is an interesting speculation, is that the least politically committed viewers are the ones who register the text's equivocation between endorsing and not endorsing the Government's 'recovery' interpretation. If this is true, we could explain it as a function of paying greater attention to the text than the more politically committed viewers are inclined to do. Clearly, though, it would be imprudent to offer this as a 'finding' of the study reported here on the basis of such slight evidence, though it would be an interesting hypothesis to pursue.

Other examples from the respondents' discussions show further how viewers talk about the form of the text in producing their interpretations:

> But then they cut away and showed us this buy-out thing in this Daf firm. And I thought, well they're trying to convince us

by using the storyline as well that there was some substance to it [the 'recovery' idea]. (Local government officers)

When they showed you the bit about the – what was it? – the jump in the economic out . . . sorry, the manufacturing output – it jumped, like, nought-point-six per cent – and it showed this big . . . it looked like a really significant thing. It reminded me of that . . . have you read a book called: *How To Lie With Statistics?*
(*Interviewer*: Yes)
Darrell Huff. And I thought to myself, that's an example of how to do it, you know. I mean you show it in such a way that it looks huge, but when you get down to it, what does it mean? (Local government officers)

This last example is of interest because it touches upon the *visual* characteristics of television news. This viewer has a *critical* interpretation of a particular visualization: he believes that the size of the bar which represents the last quarter's GDP of 0.6 is misleadingly large on the screen. Unfortunately for his argument, bars representing negative growth in earlier quarters are on exactly the same scale, though of course these appear below rather than above the median line which runs horizontally across the screen. Nevertheless, there is some sense in what he says, suggesting that it is easier for viewers to attend to a 'primary' level of visual codification (how much screen-space does the bar representing 'growth' occupy?) than to secondary recodification via alphanumeric signifiers (what is the scale this graph is based on?).

Comprehension and understanding

There is more to understanding than its propositional base. Cognitive representations take the form of mental maps, schemas, scripts and frames, and draw upon the discourses which are publicly available for sense-making. Meanings are articulated within discourses, and discourses are institutionally grounded, inter-articulated, sets of propositions which organize and constitute domains of knowledge and experience. These discourses *pre-exist* specific texts. In linguistic terms, we are talking about the domain of the *given*, the *taken for granted*, the *known*, the *presupposed*, the *axiomatic*. To offer up, for comprehension, an account which has been constructed within the terms of a specific discourse is to propose that discourse as the necessary or appropriate one for understanding its domain of knowledge. Now the project of comprehension is oriented not to the 'givens' of the discourse, but to the 'news' of the text. We customarily say that someone has 'understood' a message if they are capable of reproducing its overt propositional content. When they go beyond this, for example, by 'explaining' something they have seen on TV, they are producing a new text, but drawing (or so it seems) upon the same discourse (in this case, of national economic policy) which informs the text – as well as drawing directly upon the text itself:

> . . . He's doing it [taxing] because he's borrowing fifty billion next year, and to do that he's got to put tax on everybody, right? And it's how he's distributing the taxes basically, you know, to cover that fifty billion which he's borrowed, you know. At the end of the day, he's got to . . . spend, get enough taxes back to pay for that fifty billion he's going to borrow, you know? (Unemployed viewers)

This is from a discussion of some material which was originally broadcast earlier than the text we have been exploring here: our viewers also watched the coverage on two channels (BBC and ITN) of the 1993 Budget, in which the shock news was the proposal to raise a consumer tax on gas and electricity for the first time. The reference to 'fifty billion' here relates to the size of the official Budget Deficit (Public Sector Borrowing Requirement) as announced by the Chancellor in the Budget. This was registered on all sides as surprisingly (and unacceptably) high: previous predictions had set it much lower.

The Chancellor's rationale for this tax measure went on to become a much-repeated piece of information, throughout the period of ensuing parliamentary debate. It was still a very salient piece of information by the time of our screenings in early May 1993. It is not surprising that viewers, sympathetic and unsympathetic, are familiar with the basic ideas. What is more interesting is the modality of the sentences in our unemployed viewer's account. He is critical of government policy and yet he essentially accepts the economic *necessity* of tax raises to offset a high PSBR. There was very little coverage during that period which indicated that there might be other possibilities, and in our respondent groups there is evident *difficulty* in their attempts to think in terms of other possibilities:

> And the point about the borrowing I couldn't understand is why they couldn't actually borrow more than what they already did. That was very sort of ske . . . , badly outlined, cos America's got a huge budget deficit. I mean, where do they get their money from? Why can't Britain get as much money as they can? I mean it just seemed like it was basically explaining why the Government was doing that, and um not really showing alternative options where the City wouldn't be so heavily involved. Breaking away from the City. (Student viewers)

References to 'the City' in this context act as a shorthand for the financial institutions operating out of the London Stock Exchange. The modern visual imagery of financial trading is internationally recognizable. It is certainly true, as this viewer says, that the Budget programmes we screened do not entertain the thought that deficit financing might be viewed as a *satisfactory* national economic policy. We can go further: nowhere within mainstream media coverage had there been any support for such an idea. Of course a viewer who knows that America has a huge budget deficit might also be expected to know something about the problems which followed from that: but this viewer does not know, and is left with questions about the Government's economic policy options.

Buerk's script here embeds a more formal discourse of economics with a fairly light touch. The second sentence of the headline can be compared with the second sentence of the intro:

> The latest figures show the economy growing again for the first time in two and a half years.

> Official figures show the gross domestic product – that's the total value of goods and services produced after ruling out erratic oil production – rose by 0.6 per cent in the first three months of this year.

The second of these sentences is an expanded version of the first and one which moves more in the direction of economic and policy discourses, both in using the technical term 'gross domestic product' and in offering a parenthetic gloss on that term for uninitiated viewers. One viewer, from the student group, remembered this gesture and commented favourably upon it:

> I didn't think it was brilliantly done although they did try to explain what GDP was. That was quite good, the way they actually gave a definition almost.

Elsewhere in the item, however, the journalists' responsibility towards these official frames of reference is *not* discharged in this fashion. There is very little use of technical vocabulary as such, and there are no further examples of explicit explanatory statements such as the definition of GDP that Buerk provides here.

Instead there are a variety of linkages made through juxtapositions which indicate to the viewer in fairly non-technical terms the kinds of things that they ought to understand about the economy and economic reasoning. Buerk does this himself at the end of his introduction before handing over to the economics correspondent:

> During the recession, unemployment doubled and sixty thousand companies went bust.

This sentence, positioned as it is, serves to enhance dramatic values by telling or reminding viewers how bad the recession was. This is to read it as a scale-enhancing device, like those which rely upon emphasizing how long it has been since things were as bad as they became in the early 1990s. It can be read in other ways too. It can be read as a device for showing what a recession is. We have already learned, or previously knew, that a recession is about falling or static growth rates. This sentence reminds or tells us that it is also about job losses and company bankruptcies. It can also be read as a device of *justification*, as well as one of explanation. It justifies constructing recession as a Bad Thing by relating it to facts which are *obviously* bad. Any other evaluation of recession/negative growth would be perverse, at least in terms of the dominant public discourse on offer via the broadcast media, for it would entail a neutral or a positive assessment of job losses and bankruptcies. Of course, there are ways of thinking within which redundancies and bankruptcies can be welcomed. The discourse of 'downsizing' offers a way of constructing job losses positively, from within the perspective of those who have to implement them. From the perspective of national government, high unemployment keeps wage demands down, unions weak, and workers more compliant. Yet within the public discourse, these are not the officially sanctioned perspectives, and they are not usually the ones employed to organize news accounts.

The text also helps to reinforce the idea that the recovery hypothesis cannot be sustained on a single indicator: many signs are better than one. Buerk's introduction carries this thought initially when he reports:

> The Chancellor said there were now clear signs of recovery across a broad front.

Then, later, Lamont is actually seen to say:

> We have low inflation. We have the lowest interest rates in Europe. Productivity has been rising so that our exports are very competitively priced.

This thought, too, is one that we found our respondents readily able to reproduce, as this Labour viewer does:

> Well, I mean, after two years of talking about 'green shoots', you'd have thought that they'd have learnt to be a little bit cautious, a little bit qualified or guarded, about reporting growth and, you know, any . . . I mean all . . . admittedly now there are a lot of indicators that are beginning to show encouraging signs of recovery, but they're all . . . very small moves in the right direction. And it's still too early to show whether they're sustained, I believe.

7   Conclusions

In this chapter I have tried to demonstrate the value of coupling the analysis of media discourse with the analysis of reception of that discourse. Very little work of this kind has been done, in spite of the enormous growth of reception research within media studies. There are theoretical pay-offs from undertaking such work: it pushes us into analysing more clearly how 'comprehension' is produced and how it is put to use within the informational and evaluative frameworks which viewers possess. Likewise, there are substantive pay-offs. In the present case, the research would not be of value unless it produced greater understanding regarding the kinds and levels of understanding of 'the economy' which underlie the communication between television news and its audience.

One of the lessons of this research concerns the possibility of approaching respondent data as 'text', which requires as much analytic attention as the 'primary texts' to which it responds. Transcripts of interviews with respondents are a different kind of data from broadcast news programmes: the interviews are conducted face-to-face; the primary medium is that of speech; group dynamics and power relations play a part in determining who says what and whether or not 'consensus' is displayed; there is scope for views to change (and be changed) as discussion progresses, and so on. But if it is important in analysing media texts to attend to unspoken but implied or assumed meanings as well as explicit ones, so too is it important to do this in analysing the texts which result from the viewing experience and the invitation to discuss it. The most successful reception analyses will be those which can insightfully map between the different framings of knowledge – those offered by the broadcasters and those offered by the respondents. In doing this, however, it will always be necessary to recognize the complex character of the discursive relations involved. The broadcasters' text interprets reality, and so does that of the respondents. But the text of the latter is also an interpretation of a *text* – that of the broadcasters. It is the custom of audience research to regard it *primarily* in this character, and only secondarily as an alternative account of reality. This 'double discourse' can result in such characteristics as judgements about the veracity of the broadcasters' account in the light of the viewers' independent sources of information.

It must be acknowledged that the research setting is a favourable site for eliciting *critical* responses to TV material: perhaps more critical than is the case under 'normal' viewing conditions. Even if this is true, it is not without value to show what viewers are capable of under these more artificial conditions. The conditions are not especially testing for the participants: it is by no means unnatural for them to produce critical TV talk about programmes of this type, even if it is not normal for them to do so all the time in the domestic situation.

The approach adopted for the present study could certainly be extended to other kinds of media discourse, though any reception analysis which does take seriously the goal of relating textual form/meaning to audience response is committed to 'intensive' forms of analysis impossible to reconcile with survey requirements desirable in certain kinds of social science research. Only a very limited amount of quantification of broadcast or audience data is possible when the methods of analysis are as intensive as the ones recommended here, and as in all research, there are opportunity costs. What is gained in analytic depth is lost in generalizability. Nevertheless, argument-by-example and case-study models are not unfamiliar in the social sciences either, and have much to recommend them as contributions to a field of study in which different methodologies are seen to complement one another.

NOTES

1   Previous relevant work includes: Glasgow University Media Group, 1976; Morley, 1980, which contains work on Budget coverage; Emmison, 1983, which considers various media depictions (Emmison, 1985 is also relevant); Jensen, 1986, which looks at economic news and 'political ritual'; Rae and Drury, 1993, which uses discourse analysis to examine the construction of 'recession' in the print media.

2   For the benefit of readers unfamiliar with the now extensive literature in reception studies, the best place to begin is chapter 3 of Morley's (1992) book *Television, Audiences and Cultural Studies*, which is an edited version of Morley's influential 1980 publication *The 'Nationwide' Audience*. Tracing Morley's ideas 'backwards' leads to Stuart Hall's encoding–decoding paper of 1973 (see also Hall, 1994a and 1994b) and, in sociology, to Parkin (1971). Subsequently the field can be divided into work concerned principally with questions of taste, pleasure and domestic leisure (e.g. Ang, 1985), or with questions of public knowledge (e.g. Jensen, 1986). The collected articles in Seiter et al. (1989)

provide a useful set of examples of the 'state of the art' in the mid- to late 1980s. Corner (1991) is a critical overview of developments in reception studies, and Morley (1992) responds to these and other points in his introduction. Recent book-length works in this field besides Morley's own include Ang (1991), Lewis (1991), Moores (1993), Cruz and Lewis (1994).

Chapter 9

Media – Language – World

Paddy Scannell

What is the question to ask in respect of the media *and* language? Is it about language *in* the media? Or the language *of* the media? And in either case, what is the point of the question? Is it to discover something about language or media or both? Simple though these questions may seem, they are seldom asked. Our aim here is to pose those questions that tend to be presumed in most studies of something that might be called 'media language'. In order to do so, we will try to reconstruct the *attitudes* to media and language as we find them in various approaches to these themes. A broad distinction can be made between two prevailing ways of approaching media and language: the ideological and the pragmatic. We will review the gross implications of these two approaches before finally comparing them with our own approach, which is phenomenological.

1 Ideology and Media

'The concept of ideology stands like a colossus over the field of media studies', writes Masterman (1985: 123) in a textbook for teaching this emerging academic subject. It was erected as such in the UK, in the 1970s, at the Centre for Contemporary Cultural Studies at Birmingham University when Stuart Hall was Director of Studies there. For Hall, the question of ideology was central to the analysis of the impact of the media – the press and broadcasting – on modern societies. The concept was derived from Marx and given a particular inflection in relation to the Centre's object of study, namely contemporary popular culture. As a critique of contemporary culture, it differed from the earlier critique of mass culture elaborated by the members of the 'Frankfurt School' in the 1930s and 1940s.

For Adorno and Horkheimer (1985), the key issue was the commodification of culture; the penetration, into the sphere of culture, of the rationale and techniques of the capitalist mode of production. Mass-produced goods, characterized by standardization and uniformity, pointed to the liquidation of difference and individuality. As such, they were part of the logic of domination whereby the daily life of individuals was colonized by increasingly centralized social forces: economic (monopoly capitalism), political (the authoritarian state) and cultural (the 'culture industry', epitomized by Hollywood).

This critique no longer 'fitted' the conditions of the 1960s and 1970s, the period in which Hall developed a new synthesis for the study of contemporary culture (cf. Allan, this volume). On the one hand the study of contemporary 'popular' culture needed rescuing from the condescensions of 'high culture' (and the Frankfurt School's position now seemed 'pessimistic' and 'elitist'). At the same time, it was necessary to avoid an uncritical populism, a simple cultural pluralism. Hall's work attempted to repoliticize the question of culture (the Frankfurt School by then seemed guilty of political quietism) by returning to class struggle not in the workplace but on the terrain of contemporary culture. And lastly, in this return to Marx, it was necessary to rescue the cultural from economic determinism – that tendency of 'vulgar' Marxism to interpret the political and the cultural as mere superstructural indicators of economic forces. 'The relative autonomy' of the cultural was a key to the New Left readings of contemporary culture that began to develop in the 1970s. The media – the press, broadcasting and cinema – became primary sites for the analysis of contemporary popular culture and the mediating critical concept for this analysis was that of 'the dominant ideology'.

Whereas the Frankfurt School's cultural-critical reading of Marx focused on his analysis of commodity fetishism in *Capital*, Hall's reading of Marx focused on *The German Ideology* and in particular Marx and Engel's formulation about the class-based nature of 'ruling ideas' at any one time (Hall, 1977). Those who control the means of material production tend to control the means of mental production as well. The 'dominant ideology' thesis, elaborated around this proposition, regarded beliefs, attitudes and values as they were expressed at any time as universalizing the interests of dominant social forces. This process was not a simple one whereby values were simply imposed on subordinate social groups. Meanings and values were always understood historically (as 'in process') and as the site and source of struggles over the control and definitions of meanings. The media were seen as a prime site in which the contestation of meanings was played out in contemporary society.

Hall set out a highly influential model for the analysis of this process in his 'encoding/decoding' article (1980), which attempted to account for the social relations of cultural production in respect of television (cf. Allan's and Richardson's chapters in this volume). The object of analysis was the relationship between the processes of production, the products (programmes) and the processes of reception. The key argument was that there was no necessary correspondence between the moments of encoding (production) and decoding (reception). Although programmes might encode a 'preferred meaning' that supported, say, official definitions of controversial issues in broadcast news, it was not to be supposed that in any simple way such meanings would be 'bought' by viewers. How they themselves interpreted what they saw and heard depended in part on their social position, on such factors as class, ethnicity and gender. Hall proposed three types of possible decoding of 'the television message': dominant, negotiated and oppositional.

Media products were considered as texts to be subjected to critical readings of their ideological effectivity. To this end, an updated version of semiotics (a mix of Saussure, Volosinov and Barthes) was applied to the signifying practices of the press and television (Hall, 1982). The kind of analysis that developed was a mix of semiotic theory, marxist aesthetics and literary criticism. What it lacked was any specific linguistic input. That was supplied by a group of linguists – notably Kress, Fowler and Fairclough – who attempted to formulate a *critical linguistics* that focused particularly on the question of ideology as a feature of language (Fowler et al., 1979; Kress and Hodge, 1979; Fairclough, 1989). The ideological was 'shown' in language in various ways: by the analysis of specific lexicons that contained negative evaluations of that to which they referred (race and gender, most obviously); by the analysis of aspects of grammar (pronouns of power, for instance) and more ambitiously by the attempt to demonstrate that certain syntactical structures (agency deletion and passivization, for example) were devices that effectively rendered invisible the operations of power in language and society (Fowler, 1991).

It is not our purpose here to review the considerable contribution to the development of ideology critique made by these and other writers (notably, van Dijk) who can broadly be described as critical discourse analysts. Their work is well represented in this collection. Rather it is a question of seeing not only 'where they are coming from' but also where they think they are going. What is their 'take' on language and on media, and why and how is it focused in and through the concept of ideology? Rather than attempt yet again to pin down this notoriously elusive term, we will try a different tack and consider it as both articulating and legitimating a particular attitude towards language and world.

2   Suspicion: Depth Theories

There are, broadly speaking, two possible attitudes towards 'reality' (the reality of world and language): either to take it at face value or not. The former accepts and recognizes, in the first instance, reality as it is. The latter regards this reality with a principled suspicion. At the least, it wishes to put in question what appears as unquestionable from the former stance. Each attitude embodies a particular way of interpreting reality. We will call them the hermeneutics of trust and of suspicion, a distinction first suggested by Ricoeur (1974). Ideology critique is a hermeneutics of suspicion. This is particularly evident, as we will show, in its attitude to common sense and everyday life (cf. Allan, this volume).

Ideology critique is an instance of Depth Theory, a way of thinking that regards the appearance of things as potentially unreliable and deceptive. To get beneath the superficial 'naturalism' of phenomena is the task of Theory. It must find the hidden structural, structuring causes that produce things as they are. Much modern theorizing is, in this way, a *structuralism* of one kind or another (Hall, 1986). It hypothesizes an underlying structure that, when found, will serve to explain the form and content of things as they ordinarily appear to us.

Two other Depth Theories that are highly relevant to ideology critique, and which inform its analysis, are Freudian psychoanalysis and Saussurian linguistics. Freud's momentous discovery of the *unconscious* claimed that it structured conscious psychic life 'behind the back' of the individual. The unconscious manifests itself indirectly; ordinarily it 'speaks' in dreams and in the small psychopathologies of everyday life (momentary forgettings, slips of the tongue etc.). In cases of severe psychic disorder, the unconscious reveals itself as a full-blown neurosis (hysteria was the classic instance analysed by Freud). Freud always insisted on the determinacy of the unconscious which made its presence felt in hidden ways, in ways that individuals were themselves entirely unaware of and which it was the task of the analyst patiently to interpret for the patient.

Saussurian linguistics as a Depth Theory shows most obviously in the famous distinction between *parole* and *langue*. *Parole* as utterance (language in use) is discarded as incapable (unworthy) of analysis. To understand language, it must be thought of as *langue*, an abstract system of signification. *Langue* is pure structure. It is a system of difference whose differences allow for various possible combinations that are actualized in and as lexical, grammatical and syntactic structures. *Langue* is shown to be arbitrary in the first instance and conventional in the second instance. This is demonstrated in respect of the sign, and the nature of the relationship between signifier and signified. The effect of this approach is to denaturalize language, to reveal it as a social construct. It is not a given, natural thing, and to treat it as if it were is to misrecognize it.

These three Depth Theories or Structuralisms, here briefly sketched in – marxism, psychoanalysis and linguistics – converge in ideology critique. Ideology can be understood in two ways. As a neutral term it refers to any articulate system of values and beliefs (Catholicism, marxism, Thatcherism etc.). As a critical term it refers to distorted value systems, beliefs which – the theory supposes – 'in reality' work against the interests of the majority. Ideology critique identifies a process whereby the interests of some (property owners; men; whites) are universalized as the interests of all (the propertyless; women; non-whites). Particular ideologies (class, sexism, racism) *work* by concealing their real (exploitative) nature. But how do they do this? How is it that the exploited fail to see the real nature of their conditions of life? Ideology critique presupposes that rational self-interest (that great principle of the Enlightenment) would stir the exploited to overcome their exploitation, if only they understood it properly. The aim of ideology critique is to make that understanding available as a basis for political action to overcome oppression. Its task is to expose the ways in which ideologies render themselves invisible in such ways as to escape notice. In so doing, it demystifies experience, freeing it up for conscious, critical, political praxis.

This entails a critique of everyday life as 'lived experience' or the terrain of common sense. Everyday practices rest upon taken-for-granted attitudes, deeply ingrained habits of doing and thinking. As such, they do not put themselves in question and hence are unreflexive and uncritical. The language of everyday usage and the everyday practices of the media are part of this unthinking (unwitting, unconscious) process whereby the world reproduces itself as it is (Hall, 1982). This means, in effect, that it reproduces unquestioningly (without putting in question) a distorted dominant reality that mystifies social inequalities. The media and language are both systems of representation that, in ordinary practice and use, misrepresent the reality which they re-present. Hall insists that the primary function of media is ideological: Bennett (1982) has called language 'the home of all ideology'.

Neither language nor media are, in this analysis, to be trusted. Both should be regarded with caution. The aim of media studies as ideology critique is to teach students that both media and language should not be thought of as natural phenomena but as social constructions of reality. Ideology critique takes a *constructivist* view of media and language. Both are conventional systems of representation which unreflectingly misrepresent the social reality (world) that they construct. The educative task of media studies is to deconstruct media and language; to alert students to their dangers, their slipperiness, their deceptiveness. In all these ways ideology critique mobilizes a hermeneutics of suspicion against media and language.

3   Trust: Reception Studies and Conversation Analysis

Let us now, by way of contrast, turn to approaches to media and language that accept them as naturally occurring social phenomena and regard them – without preconceptions – as things that simply, routinely and ordinarily *work* (whether for or against human interests is not, *in the first instance*, at issue). Such 'pragmatic' approaches presuppose, we will try to show, a hermeneutics of trust. 'Pragmatics' is used here in a fairly broad (non-linguistic) sense as referring to any kind of study of broadcasting and the press that considers both the institutions and their output (programmes, newspapers) in the contexts in which and for which they exist. Pragmatics is always context-sensitive: it attends to the specificities of things in respect of their where and when and the way that they occur. Two established lines of pragmatic enquiry into media discourses are reception studies and conversation analysis.

Reception studies makes a cardinal distinction between 'the act of reading and the text as read' (Radway, 1984). That is, it treats the contexts of reception – the actual spaces within which television is watched, radio is listened to, etc. – as significant in themselves. Radway's seminal study of *Reading the Romance* emphasized the ways in which the women she studied created a space for themselves, within their daily routines, in which they allowed themselves the pleasure of 'escaping' into the fictional world of the romance. Morley's study of the ways in which families watch television showed, amongst other things, the small tensions and power-plays between family members over who decided, for example, what channel to watch. This seemed to depend on who had the TV-remote, and that usually turned out to be the dominant male (Morley, 1986). This kind of work indicated the 'relative autonomy' of the moment of decoding, by emphasizing the active nature of media reception or, more exactly, the ways in which media were used as everyday resources in everyday contexts of use.

However, there was a tendency for this kind of work, and the closely related field of 'qualitative' audience studies (for a review of both, see Moores, 1993), to uncouple the moment of decoding from that which was to be decoded (the 'text') and the manner of its encoding. Thus what began to be lost sight of was the great virtue of Hall's model – the effort to think of the social relations of cultural production *as a whole* (production–products–audiences). At worst, audience/reception studies of (mainly) television ended up in a celebration of active viewers (a reaction against earlier notions of the 'passive viewer') and their freedom to interpret what they saw more or less as they liked. Richardson's contribution to this collection indicates a welcome return to linking texts to their 'readers'. She emphasizes the relative determinacy of the text – the ways in which (in her example) the discourses of television news affect the ways in which it is understood. A key instance is the presence (or not) of source attribution ('The government claims . . .') which is both attended to by viewers in discussion and interpreted variously according to different social positions and attitudes. Thus what Richardson and others are beginning to develop is a fuller understanding of the moment of decoding, in which text and the situation of the 'decoder' are taken together (cf. Corner, 1996).

Conversation analysis (CA) came to the study of media, if not accidentally, at least tangentially. What is CA's object of study? It is not language, but social interaction. Sacks more or less stumbled across ordinary talk as an object of study because the tape-recorder seemed to make it available as a naturally occurring social phenomenon. For Sacks, talk instantiates social interaction in a very pervasive and universal way. The production of talk is understood as a jointly managed co-operative enterprise between two or more participants who collaborate in the task of initiating, sustaining and disengaging from it as a primary kind of human, social (sociable) activity. It was part of Sacks' genius to see this, and to show the fine-grained detail of the intelligibility of talk-in-its-unfolding. The detailed studies of such things as an adolescent telling of a dirty joke, of a depressive's suicidal remark ('you do it to see if anybody cares') or, perhaps most famously, a small child's story ('The baby cried. The mommy picked it up') are astonishingly brilliant. In each case, starting from the smallest details, Sacks' investigations open up much wider issues about the nature of social life and what it is to be human.

CA points up the cardinal importance of attention to even the smallest of social phenomena. Its study of talk opens up entirely new perspectives on language and particularly the fundamental question of how understanding in language is routinely accomplished. CA does this by showing how participants in talk show each other – from moment to moment – how they are (or are not) *with* each other: 'with' in the sense of understanding (*uhuh* [I'm with you. Go on]); 'with' in the sense of involvement (displayed by response tokens: *mmm, uhuh, oh, really*, etc.); 'with' in the sense of a focused attentiveness to all aspects of the matter to hand (displayed by noticings and remarkings of the smallest aspects of what is being said and how, including what is not said; CA shows the meaningfulness of small silences and momentary hesitations). In all its work CA has attended to what has simply been ignored and overlooked by classical linguistics and ordinary language philosophy, which have failed to recognize the meaningfulness of talk in all its particularities as the proper locus for the study of language – if, that is, it is properly to be thought of as a human, social activity. CA is concerned to show how people go about the utterly mundane task of *being* in conversation by attending to how they do it. In so doing, it illuminates from within the involvement-structures of talk. It is parsimonious in respect of Theory, preferring to go about its task without preconceptions other than the firm conviction that the procedural regularities of talk are there to be found by those with eyes to see and ears to hear.

Whereas Sacks focused mainly on 'ordinary, plain talk' as it occurred in various everyday settings, those who have followed him have begun to contrast it with talk in institutional settings in order to display the differences and continuities between them. An essential difference is that, in institutional contexts, turns at talk are pre-allocated according to established distributions of performative roles. Thus, in the classroom, courtroom or broadcasting studio the distribution of communicative entitlements (who is entitled to speak and when) are pre-allocated in such ways as to contribute to establishing the nature of the institutional occasion in each case.

The work of Heritage and his colleagues, Greatbatch and Clayman, has focused on a particular instance of broadcast talk – the political news interview (e.g. Greatbatch, this volume; Heritage, Clayman and Greatbatch, forthcoming). It points to the ways in which the political interview requires the collaboration of the participants in this kind of talk for it to appear as such, not just or only for the participants in the interview but, crucially, for absent listeners or viewers. They show that the design features of the news interview indicate that it is meant for reception by absent audiences. And this, in turn, establishes the intrinsically public nature of broadcast talk. Talk-in-public, especially political talk, is 'on the record' and this has consequences for what can and cannot be said and for ways of saying or not saying. The close study of the news interview establishes how, within its frame, interviewers and interviewees struggle for control and definition of the topic. When the struggle becomes too fierce the interview goes beyond its boundaries and becomes something else: a confrontation.

In his celebrated 'breaching experiments', Garfinkel (1984) demonstrated the extent to which ordinary social members – routinely and 'as a matter of fact' – take for granted the normality of the situation (whatever it may be) as that which is always already shared and between themselves and others. Indeed this must be so: for a lecture to be a lecture, a joke to be a joke, or TV news to be TV news – for the world to be that which in fact it is – depends upon a hermeneutics of trust; an always already given and taken-for-granted mutual and shared anticipation of whatever it is as that which it is and is meant to be. The very possibility of the appearance of things as what they are normally (and normatively) taken to be depends upon them being always already anticipated as such. Garfinkel's experiments demonstrated the extent to which a faith in the normality of the situation was, from moment to moment, a taken-for-granted moral basis for ordinary, everyday contexts of social interaction. Trust in the ordinary meaningfulness of talk in everyday contexts sustains trust in the meaningfulness of the everyday world as such.

4   Phenomenology and the Media

We have contrasted two broad approaches to the study of language and media in terms of two different hermeneutics: one of suspicion, the other of trust. Let us now attempt an ontological interpretation of them both. Ontology's question is: 'What is being?' What, then, is the being of these two hermeneutics? Let us turn them around a little by describing a hermeneutics of suspicion as being-in-doubt, and a hermeneutics of trust as the undoubtedness of being. What is the relationship between these two ontologies? Consider Wittgenstein's argument for the necessarily public character of language. He points out that a radically private (a purely subjective) language is impossible. For it to be such, it would have to be a language that was in principle and practice intelligible only to the one and only begetter of that (thus essentially) private language. But this is not possible. For such a language could have no rules (i.e. recognizable procedural regularities) and if it did, then it would be – of course – intrinsically public (open to being understood by others). Private language is thus impossible because it would always be unintelligible. The necessary intelligibility of language indicates the necessary intelligibility of the world as a matter we can, in the first instance, take on trust.

A hermeneutics of distrust must always already presuppose, as the condition of its possibility, a taken-for-granted trust in the world in which it operates. Suppose we try to imagine a world which operated on the principle 'Shoot first and ask questions later'. Such a world, if it adhered strictly to this as its first principle, would rapidly depopulate itself. Or again, counter-factually, imagine a world in which every morning one could never be sure that things today would be as they had been yesterday. Such a nightmarish world of uncertainty is, of course, by and large impossible (except for those suffering from such distressing neurological disorders as described by Oliver Sacks). Trust in the given facticity of language and world is a necessary condition for the very possibility of each and both.

This points to the question of where each ontology is located. Being in suspicion is in the head, while the undoubtedness of being is (undoubtedly) in the world. Being-in-the-head knows itself (variously) as the philosophy of consciousness, the Cartesian *cogito* or the Western episteme. It is this ontology that is vigorously attacked by Heidegger for privileging consciousness at the expense of being, the *cogito* at the expense of the *sum* and knowledge at the expense of truth (Heidegger, 1962). But how is being as consciousness being in distrust? In a principled way, Descartes' 'method' was to doubt everything in principle in order to discover that of which, in fact, one could be certain. A radical scepticism – a principled suspension of 'faith' – underpins the whole modern search for that which can be known beyond doubt. Enlightenment thinking is cast in this mould, as is ideology critique.

In a well-known passage, Heidegger quotes Kant's remark that the scandal of philosophy is that it can give no sure and certain proof of an external reality (a world outside consciousness). To this, Heidegger retorts that the real scandal is that such proofs are demanded *over and over again* (Heidegger, 1962: 249). The critique of the philosophy of consciousness, so devastatingly developed in *Being and Time*, is that it has lost sight of where it is coming from. It has engaged with the *cogito* to the exclusion of the *sum*; the fundamental claim that human beings, in each case, make is: 'I am.' This assertion of being is earlier than any claims of consciousness. Consciousness (being-in-the head) is a derived possibility of being in the world, and *not* the other way round. It is not that I *think* I am in the world, or that I *choose* to be in it, or that I am in it now and then. Overwhelmingly being-in-the-world indicates the facticity of being as that which I (or anyone) am *in* and have to be. Being is, first and last, not a matter of choice, reason or consciousness, all of which indicate various ways of detached (abstracted, abstract) being in which I-or-anyone momentarily stand outside my self and the world. The philosophy of consciousness starts from a worldless, self-doubting subject struggling to insert itself into a world external to its self, yet of which it cannot be certain. It has forgotten the world from which it has abstracted its self.

Modern views of language encourage a view of an external reality that is outside the subject and outside language, because language is thought in ways that remove it from the world. The effect is to establish language as an object of knowledge only by uncoupling it from praxis and being. But whatever theoretical abstractions we may make of language (as 'the symbolic', 'representation', 'signification', 'difference' and so on), and despite 'proving' that Language is a social construct (arbitrary, conventional etc.), we must surely admit that we are *closer* to language than this. Human being is being-in-language, which is another way of saying that language *worlds*. The world in which we dwell includes language. *Our* world *languages*. It speaks us and we speak it. This is its nearness to us. It is what we live in. Although CA has refrained on the whole from reflecting on what its work shows about language, this indeed is a primary thing that it discloses through its careful attention to the matter to hand: namely that in initiating, sustaining and disengaging from talk human beings are in the business (the busyness, the concern, the care) of talking into being that of which they speak in the ways in which they speak of the matter(s) to hand, whatever they may be. This is how language worlds. It brings into being the common world that is *between* the participants in the interaction. This world may be one that is literally talked into being (e.g. the news interview), or it may be that the talk produced is *of* a particular world (an event, a person, a place).

This last point indicates the limits we encounter in attempting to think 'the media and language'. Although language is at the heart of the social, sociable, communicative practices of the press and broadcasting, it does not fully encompass what they are about. Language points beyond its sociable self. Intrinsically *in* the world, it constantly speaks about and of the world. A purely social view of language does not get to engage with this. CA, in its recent formal modalities, for instance does not think its object beyond the 'merely' social (though Sacks always did). If language is world-disclosing, we must attend to the world and worlds that it discloses. A mediatized world is not a hyper-reality or indicative of an 'external reality' (external to what or whom, we may ask?). It is a historically specific, specifically historical way of being for those who live in such a world. A phenomenology of media language would have as its task the job of investigating the connections between media, language and world (e.g. Scannell, 1997).

Phenomenology indicates the temporality of being: not being in time, but the time of being. Dasein's temporality is indicated in two ways: in its finitude (its being-towards-death) and in its being caught up in the time of its being. The time of being is the phenomenal now, the 'that which is', the *da* of dasein (Heidegger's neutral term for human being) as being *in* concern. The liveness of radio and television indicates in all its ways the phenomenal now of being in the world. It is this that shows in all its practices. Through its being-there (its da-sein), broadcasting creates new ways of being in the world – of being in two places at once, two times at once.

Marriott's (1996) scrupulous linguistic analysis of the temporality of instant replays on live TV sports programmes shows how time is doubled in such moments. The 'then' (the moment just past) has re-entered the 'now', creating a now-and-then. Bell's examination of the chronologic of news stories, in this collection, indicates that the moment for which they are written to be read is the phenomenal now, the now of concern, the how it matters *now* for me-or-anyone. The newness, the newsiness, of news indicates that central characteristic of human being as being in concern, that what matters is what matters *here* and *now* for me-or-anyone. All news practices point to that moment (the now that matters: the what matters now) and that is why news stories take it as their point of departure.

This concern to show the liveness of everyday media as indicating the aliveness of being is not some kind of Panglossian celebration of the best of all possible worlds. To the contrary, its concern is with the world as it is – as it shows itself and is found to be. If in the first instance what is to be shown is the facticity of world (how it is that which it is) such investigations will certainly point to ways in which this 'how it is' serves to cover over the truth of the world. Such uncovering is a proper critical task for the study of media, language and world. Nevertheless, such uncovering only makes sense – can only be undertaken – from a prior assumption of truth (which rests on an understanding of the manifest, manifold nature of things). Critical Theory could never ground its point of critique. If it saw its task as that of exposing falsehood, lies and deception, that task always already presumed the truth as its point of departure. But what that truth was could not be named by Critical Theory. Its lame appeals to 'marxism', 'autonomy', 'happiness' or some such thing were always unpersuasive. If it sought to mobilize people in the name of justice, freedom etc., it could only see these as future, utopian possibilities in a kind of world as yet not existing.

But whatever truth there is, whatever truth there is to be pursued, is always already there to be found by those who seek it. It is not to be found in some imagined future world, but in the manifold manifest world in which we dwell.

The central critical concept of Critical Theory is reification. This, as synthesized by Lukács, drew on Marx's analysis of commodity fetishism (brilliantly anticipating the then unpublished early writings on alienation) and on Weber's critique of instrumental (bureaucratic) rationality. In Lukács's synthesis, it is consciousness as such that is reified (Lukács, 1971). The world-in-thought (the world as thought) is thingified as a dead Thing. This insight is shared by Heidegger and is basic to the whole project of Division One of *Being and Time*. His concern is to get behind modernity's ontology (abstract consciousness) and recover that which it has covered over; namely the primacy of the facticity of world. This world – this everyday world in which I or anyone have my being – is not the abstract world of consciousness, theory, etc.; it is the world in its immediacy and aliveness, the pre-Theoretical world of praxis, of being-in and being-with as active and engaged agency. It is care and concern. It is what matters and how, here and now, for me or anyone.

In rediscovering the lost ontology of being as being in the world, Heidegger restored what Critical Theory mourned as its lost Object of Desire: namely the wholeness of being and the wholeness of world. Modernity could no longer think the world as a whole, for it had lost any sense of the wholeness of being. Marcuse expressed this cryptically at the end of a short essay on 'The Dialectic': 'The whole is the truth. But the whole is false' (Marcuse, 1978). What had been falsified, by the commodification of the world, was substantive (ends-oriented) reason. Modernity had perfected a technical, formal, means-oriented rationality. The technical-scientific calculation of means really worked. It enormously valorized human control of Nature. But to what ends? The private accumulation of wealth by the few to the deprivation of the many and the degradation of Nature itself. Modernity was thus characterized by a rationality of the parts and the irrationality of the whole. If it increasingly experienced the world as meaningless, this was because it had, in fact, made it so. The mark of this loss of meaning was reification: the specific pathology of modernity. Heidegger reunited the torn halves of a lost understanding: being and world. In returning one to the other, he restored the meaningfulness of both. He showed that being-in-the-head is, in fact, a specific found possibility that derives from the lost and prior ontology of the immediacy of being. The differences between these two ontologies can be expressed in various ways – one is between Theory (being-in-the-head) and Praxis (being-in-the-world). But the vital difference is between an inert, reified view of things as Things, as *Nature morte* (and hence as mere 'stuff' to be mastered, exploited, manipulated etc.), and a returning sense of the aliveness of the world in all its manifold, manifest truth of being. This world is, and always has been, magical.

Magical language bears witness, now as ever, to the magic of world and of being in it. It is caught in poetry and song – this sense of the ecstasy of being. Love poetry expresses the Being of being-in-love, of Being caught up in an enchanted now that cannot fade. Song (which knows no reason) every day everywhere bears witness to the everyday joys and sorrows of being in the world. The ordinary magic of language shows in voice as the expressive register of being. Being angry or sad, being funny or serious, being sincere or insincere, being seductive . . . all such and other ways of being are marked in ways of saying. Ways of saying are always noticed and attended to (including 'pointed ignorings' etc.). And all these things can be shown in the ordinary talk on radio and television.

Voice especially shows in radio, that beautiful medium so largely overlooked by current preoccupations with television. In radio, attention is necessarily focused on voice, since it is the only manifestation of the embodied presence of the speaker(s) at the microphone. To attend to voice means that you must listen. In listening you are hearing the self of speaker and the self of language: language itself. The ontological moment of language is not in speaking but in hearing what is said in speaking. Listening *before* speaking, for listening is a necessary precondition for anything to be said at all. To listen, then, is to *hear* what speaks in saying: the being of the speaker in his or her way of saying (Scannell, 1996). Listening is understanding and, as such, has a fundamentally anticipatory character; for understanding is futural, a structural indication of human being as being-ahead-of-itself (Heidegger, 1962: 236ff).

5   Conclusion

The structure of this chapter might seem to suggest that it seeks to privilege an ontology of being-in-the-world at the expense of being-in-the-head, and to privilege being and praxis at the expense of theory and consciousness. But to do so would be to replace one absurdity (the denial of world) by another (the denial of self-reflecting reason). It seeks rather to draw attention to the existence of these two ontologies, or ways of being, and to explore their differences in respect of the study of media and language. Their differences are real and incommensurate. The aim of epistemology is knowledge of Things, whereas that of ontology is understanding of Being. Knowledge is what is always already not yet known, whereas understanding always already is. The outcome of knowledge is power. The outcome of understanding is truth. Modernity has degraded truth by regarding it as the sum of knowledge and power. But truth is the fruit of a different tree.

The relationship between media, language and world can be thought along the axis of power/knowledge *and* that of understanding/truth. These two ontologies, each with their particular hermeneutic (distrust/trust), should not be thought in an either/or fashion. To privilege one at the expense or exclusion of the other is to distort the manifold reality of the world that we are in. To clarify their differences is to restore that manifold reality. Language and media can be thought in various ways, but to think them truly will be to return them to the common world that each and both, in their different ways, reveal as the world that we and they (language and media) are in.

References

Adorno, Theodore and Max Horkheimer, 1985. *Dialectic of Enlightenment*. London: Verso.

Allan, Stuart, 1994. 'When discourse is torn from reality': Bakhtin and the principle of chronotopicity. *Time and Society*, 3, 193–218.

Allan, Stuart, 1995. News, truth and postmodernity: unravelling the will to facticity. In Barbara Adam and Stuart Allan (eds), *Theorizing Culture: An Interdisciplinary Critique After Postmodernism*. London: UCL Press; New York: NYU Press, 129–44.

Allan, Stuart, 1997a. News and the public sphere: towards a history of objectivity and impartiality. In M. Bromley and Tom O'Malley (eds), *The Journalism Reader*. London: Routledge, 296–329.

Allan, Stuart, 1997b. Raymond Williams and the culture of televisual flow. In J. Wallace, S. Nield and R. Jones (eds), *Raymond Williams Now: Knowledge, Limits and the Future*. London: Macmillan, 115–44.

Allen, Robert (ed.), 1992. *Channels of Discourse, Reassembled: Television and Contemporary Criticism*. 2nd edn. London: Routledge.

Anderson, Benedict, 1991. *Imagined Communities: Reflections on the Origins and Spread of Nationalism*. 2nd edn. London: Verso.

Ang, Ien, 1985. *Watching 'Dallas'*. London: Methuen.

Ang, Ien, 1991. *Desperately Seeking the Audience*. London: Routledge.

Ang, Ien, 1996. *Living Room Wars: Rethinking Audiences for a Postmodern World*. London: Routledge.

Antaki, Charles (ed.), 1988. *Analysing Everyday Explanation: A Casebook of Methods*. London: Sage.

Arnheim, Rudolf, 1982. *The Power of the Centre*. Berkeley: University of California Press.

Atkinson, J. Maxwell and John Heritage, 1984. *Structures of Social Action: Studies in Conversation Analysis*. Cambridge: Cambridge University Press.

Bakhtin, Mikhail, 1981. *The Dialogic Imagination*. Austin: University of Texas Press.

Barthes, Roland, 1967. *Elements of Semiology*. London: Jonathan Cape.

Barthes, Roland, 1973. *Mythologies*. London: Paladin.

Beck, Ulrich, 1994. The reinvention of politics: towards a theory of reflexive modernization. In Ulrich Beck, Anthony Giddens and Scott Lash (eds), *Reflexive Modernization: Politics, Tradition and Aesthetics*. Cambridge: Polity Press, 1–55.

Bell, Allan, 1983. Telling it like it isn't: inaccuracy in editing international news. *Gazette*, 31, 185–203.

Bell, Allan, 1984. Good copy – bad news: the syntax and semantics of news editing. In Peter Trudgill (ed.), *Applied Sociolinguistics*. London: Academic Press, 73–116.

Bell, Allan, 1991. *The Language of News Media*. Oxford: Blackwell.

Bell, Allan, 1994. Climate of opinion: public and media discourse on the global environment. *Discourse and Society*, 5, 33–63.

Bell, Allan, 1995a. Language and the media. *Annual Review of Applied Linguistics*, 15, 23–41.

Bell, Allan, 1995b. News Time. *Time and Society*, 4, 305–28.

Bell, Allan, 1996. Text, time and technology in news English. In Sharon Goodman and David Graddol (eds), *Redesigning English: New Texts, New Identities* (*The English Language, Past, Present and Future*, Book 4). London: Routledge. Milton Keynes: Open University, 3–26.

Bennett, Tony, 1982. Theories of the media, theories of society. In Michael Gurevitch, Tony Bennett, James Curran and Janet Woollacott (eds), *Culture, Society and the Media*. London: Routledge.

Bernstein, Basil, 1990. *The Structuring of Pedagogical Discourse*. London: Routledge.

Billig, Michael, 1988. The notion of 'prejudice': some rhetorical and ideological aspects. *Text*, 8, 91–110.

Blundell, Valda, John Shepherd and Ian Taylor (eds), 1993. *Relocating Cultural Studies*. London: Routledge.

Boden, Deirdre and Don H. Zimmerman (eds), 1992. *Talk and Social Structure: Studies in Ethnomethodology and Conversation Analysis*. Cambridge: Polity Press.

Bourdieu, Pierre, 1984. *Distinction: A Social Critique of the Judgement of Taste*. Trans. Richard Nice. London: Routledge.

Bourdieu, Pierre, 1991. *Language and Symbolic Power*. Cambridge: Polity Press.

Boyd-Barrett, Oliver, 1994. Language and media: a question of convergence. In David Graddol and Oliver Boyd-Barrett (eds), *Media Texts: Authors and Readers*. Clevedon: Multilingual Matters and The Open University, 22–39.

Brantlinger, Patrick, 1990. *Crusoe's Footprints: Cultural Studies in Britain and America*. London: Routledge.

Brewer, William F., 1985. The story schema: universal and culture-specific properties. In David R. Olson, Nancy Torrance and Angela Hildyard (eds), *Literacy, Language, and Learning: The Nature and Consequences of Reading and Writing*. Cambridge: Cambridge University Press, 167–94.

Bull, Peter, 1994. On identifying questions, replies and non-replies in political interviews. *Journal of Language and Social Psychology*, 13, 115–31.

Burns, Tom, 1977. *The BBC: Public Institution and Private World*. London: Macmillan.

Button, Graham and John Lee (eds), 1986. *Talk and Social Organisation*. Clevedon: Multilingual Matters.

Caldas-Coulthard, Carmen Rosa and Malcolm Coulthard (eds), 1996. *Texts and Practices: Readings in Critical Discourse Analysis*. London: Routledge.

Carey, James W., 1987. Why and how: the dark continent of American journalism. In Robert Karl Manoff and Michael Schudson (eds), *Reading the News*. New York: Pantheon, 146–96.

Centre for Contemporary Cultural Studies, 1978. *On Ideology*. London: Hutchinson.

Cheshire, Jenny and Lise-Marie Moser, 1994. English as a cultural symbol: the case of advertisements in French-speaking Switzerland. *Journal of Multilingual and Multicultural Development*, 15, 451–69.

Chibnall, Steve, 1977. *Law-and-Order News: An Analysis of Crime Reporting in the British Press*. London: Tavistock Publications.

Chomsky, Noam, 1987. *Pirates and Emperors: International Terrorism in the Real World*. Montreal: Black Rose Books.

Clayman, Steven, 1988. Displaying neutrality in television news interviews. *Social Problems*, 35, 474–92.

Clayman, Steven, 1989. The production of punctuality: social interaction, temporal organization and social structure. *American Journal of Sociology*, 95, 659–91.

Clayman, Steven, 1991. News interview openings: aspects of sequential organisation. In Paddy Scannell (ed.), *Broadcast Talk*. Newbury Park, CA: Sage, 48–75.

Clayman, Steven, 1992. Footing in the achievement of neutrality: the case of news interview discourse. In Paul Drew and John Heritage (eds), *Talk at Work: Interaction in Institutional Settings*. Cambridge: Cambridge University Press, 163–98.

Clayman, Steven, 1993. Reformulating the question: a device for answering/not answering questions in news interviews and press conferences. *Text*, 13, 159–88.

Clayman, Steven and Jack Whalen, 1988/1989. When the medium becomes the message: the case of the Rather/Bush encounter. *Research on Language and Social Interaction*, 22, 241–72.

Cohen, Stanley and Jock Young (eds), 1981. *The Manufacture of News: Social Problems, Deviance and the Mass Media*. London: Constable.

Connell, Ian, 1980. Television news and the social contract. In Stuart Hall, Dorothy Hobson, Andrew Lowe and Paul Willis (eds), *Culture, Media, Language*. London: Hutchinson, 139–56.

Cook, Guy, 1992. *The Discourse of Advertising*. London: Routledge.

Corner, John, 1980. Codes and cultural analysis. *Media, Culture and Society*, 2, 73–86.

Corner, John, 1991. Meaning, genre and context: the problematics of 'public knowledge' in the new audience studies. In James Curran and Michael Gurevitch (eds), *Mass Media and Society*. London: Edward Arnold, 267–84.

Corner, John, 1995. *Television Form and Public Address*. London: Edward Arnold.

Corner, John, 1996. Reappraising reception: aims, concepts and methods. In James Curran and Michael Gurevitch (eds), *Mass Media and Society*. 2nd edn. London: Edward Arnold.

Corner, John, Kay Richardson and Natalie Fenton, 1990. *Nuclear Reactions: Formal Response in Public Issue Television*. London: John Libbey.

Coupland, Justine, 1996. Dating advertisements: discourses of the commodified self. *Discourse and Society*, 7, 187–207.

Coupland, Nikolas, 1985. 'Hark, hark the lark': social motivations for phonological style shifting. *Language and Communication*, 5, 153–71.

Crow, Brian, 1986. Conversational pragmatics in television talk: the discourse of good sex. *Media, Culture and Society*, 8, 457–84.

Cruz, Jon and Justin Lewis (eds), 1994. *Viewing, Reading, Listening: Audiences and Cultural Reception*. Oxford: Westview Press.

Curran, James, 1990. Culturalist perspectives of news organizations: a reappraisal and a case study. In Marjorie Ferguson (ed.), *Public Communication: The New Imperatives*. London: Sage, 114–34.

Curran, James, Michael Gurevitch and Janet Woollacott (eds), 1977. *Mass Communication and Society*. London: Edward Arnold.

Dahlgren, Peter and Colin Sparks (eds), 1992. *Journalism and Popular Culture*. London: Sage.

Davies, Ioan, 1995. *Cultural Studies and Beyond*. London: Routledge.

Doane, Mary Ann, 1990. Information, crisis, catastrophe. In Patricia Mellencamp (ed.), *Logics of Television: Essays in Cultural Criticism*. London: British Film Institute, 222–39.

Drew, Paul and John Heritage (eds), 1992. *Talk at Work: Interaction in Institutional Settings*. Cambridge: Cambridge University Press.

Duszak, Anna, 1991. Schematic and topical categories in news story reconstruction. *Text*, 11, 503–22.

Eagleton, Terry, 1991. *Ideology: An Introduction*. London: Verso.

Eagly, Alice H. and Shelley Chaiken, 1993. *The Psychology of Attitudes*. Orlando: Harcourt Brace Jovanovich.

Elliott, Philip, 1972. *The Making of a Television Series: A Case Study in the Sociology of Culture*. London: Constable.

Ellis, John, 1992. *Visible Fictions: Cinema, Television, Video*. Revised edn. London: Routledge.

Emmison, Michael, 1983. 'The economy': its emergence in media discourse. In Howard Davis and Paul Walton (eds), *Language, Image, Media*. Oxford: Blackwell, 139–55.

Emmison, Michael, 1985. Class images of the 'economy': opposition and ideological incorporation within working class consciousness. *Sociology*, 19, 19–38.

Ericson, Richard, Patricia Baranek and Janet Chan, 1987. *Visualising Deviance: A Study of News Organisations*. Toronto: University of Toronto Press.

Ericson, Richard, Patricia Baranek and Janet Chan, 1989. *Negotiating Control: A Study of News Sources*. Toronto: University of Toronto Press.

Ericson, Richard, Patricia Baranek and Janet Chan, 1991. *Representing Order: Crime, Law, and Justice in the News Media*. Toronto: University of Toronto Press.

Fairclough, Norman, 1989. *Language and Power*. London: Longman.

Fairclough, Norman, 1992. *Discourse and Social Change*. Cambridge: Polity Press.

Fairclough, Norman, 1993. Critical discourse analysis and the marketization of public discourse: the universities. *Discourse and Society*, 2, 133–68.

Fairclough, Norman, 1994. Conversationalization of public discourse and the authority of the consumer. In Russell Keat, Nigel Whiteley and Nicholas Abercrombie (eds), *The Authority of the Consumer*. London: Routledge, 253–68.

Fairclough, Norman, 1995a. *Media Discourse*. London: Edward Arnold.

Fairclough, Norman, 1995b. *Critical Discourse Analysis*. London: Longman.

Fairclough, Norman, 1996. A reply to Henry Widdowson's 'Discourse analysis: a critical view'. *Language and Literature*, 5, 49–56.

Fenby, Jonathan, 1986. *The International News Services*. New York: Schocken Books.

Feuer, Jane, 1986. Narrative form in American network television. In Colin MacCabe (ed.), *High Theory/Low Culture: Analysing Popular Television and Film*. New York: St Martin's Press, 101–14.

Fishman, Mark, 1980. *Manufacturing the News*. Austin: University of Texas Press.

Fiske, John, 1987. *Television Culture*. London: Methuen.

Fiske, Susan T. and Shelley E. Taylor, 1991. *Social Cognition*. 2nd edn. New York: McGraw-Hill.

Foucault, Michel, 1984. The order of discourse. In Michael Shapiro (ed.), *Language and Politics*. Oxford: Blackwell, 108–38.

Fowler, Roger, 1991. *Language in the News. Discourse and Ideology in the Press*. London: Routledge.

Fowler, Roger, Bob Hodge, Gunther Kress and Tony Trew, 1979. *Language and Control*. London: Routledge and Kegan Paul.

Galtung, Johan and Mari Holmboe Ruge, 1965. The structure of foreign news. *Journal of Peace Research*, 2, 64–91.

Gans, Herbert, 1979. *Deciding What's News*. New York: Vintage.

Garfinkel, Harold, 1967. *Studies in Ethnomethodology*. Englewood Cliffs, NJ: Prentice Hall.

Garfinkel, Harold, 1984. Studies of the routine grounds of everyday activities. In *Studies in Ethnomethodology*. Cambridge: Polity Press, 35–75.

Genette, Gerard, 1980. *Narrative Discourse: An Essay in Method*. Ithaca, NY: Cornell University Press.

Gillespie, Marie, 1995. *Television, Ethnicity and Cultural Change*. London: Routledge.

Gitlin, Todd, 1980. *The Whole World is Watching: Mass Media in the Making and Unmaking of the New Left*. Berkeley: University of California Press.

Glasgow University Media Group, 1976. *Bad News*. London: Routledge.

Glasgow University Media Group, 1980. *More Bad News*. London: Routledge.

Goodwin, Charles, 1981. *Conversational Organization: Interaction between Speakers and Hearers*. New York: Academic Press.

Goodwin, Charles and John Heritage, 1990. Conversation analysis. *Annual Review of Anthropology*, 19, 283–307.

Graddol, David, 1994a. Three models of language description. In David Graddol and Oliver Boyd-Barrett (eds), *Media Texts: Authors and Readers*. Clevedon: Multilingual Matters and The Open University, 1–21.

Graddol, David, 1994b. What is a text? In David Graddol and Oliver Boyd-Barrett (eds), *Media Texts: Authors and Readers*. Clevedon: Multilingual Matters and The Open University, 40–50.

Graddol, David and Oliver Boyd-Barrett (eds), 1994. *Media Texts: Authors and Readers*. Clevedon: Multilingual Matters and The Open University.

Graddol, David, Jenny Cheshire and Joan Swann, 1994. *Describing Language*. 2nd edn. Buckingham: Open University Press.

Gramsci, Antonio, 1971. *Selections from the Prison Notebooks*. New York: International.

Gray, Ann, 1992. *Video Playtime: The Gendering of a Leisure Technology*. London: Routledge.

Greatbatch, David, 1986. Aspects of topical organisation in news interviews: the use of agenda shifting procedures by interviewees. *Media, Culture and Society*, 8, 441–55.

Greatbatch, David, 1988. A turn taking system for British news interviews. *Language in Society*, 17, 401–30.

Greatbatch, David, 1992. On the management of disagreement between news interviewees. In Paul Drew and John Heritage (eds), *Talk at Work: Interaction in Institutional Settings*. Cambridge: Cambridge University Press, 268–301.

Greatbatch, David and Robert Dingwall, forthcoming. Argumentative talk in divorce mediation sessions. *American Sociological Review*.

Greatbatch, David, Christian Heath, Paul Luff and Peter Campion, 1995. Conversation analysis: human computer interaction and the general practice consultation. In Andrew Monk and Nigel G. Gilbert (eds), *Perspectives on HCI: Diverse Approaches*. London: Academic Press, 175–98.

Grossberg, Larry, Cary Nelson and Paula Treichler (eds), 1992. *Cultural Studies*. London: Routledge.

Gurevitch, Michael, Tony Bennett, James Curran and Janet Woollacott (eds), 1982. *Culture, Society and the Media*. London: Routledge.

Haarmann, Harald, 1984. The role of ethnocultural stereotypes and foreign languages in Japanese commercials. *International Journal of the Sociology of Language*, 50, 101–21.

Hall, Stuart, 1973a. Encoding and decoding in the television discourse. Birmingham: Centre for Contemporary Cultural Studies, Stencilled Paper No. 7 (revised as Hall, 1980; also republished as Hall, 1994a).

Hall, Stuart, 1973b. A World at One with itself. In Stanley Cohen and Jock Young (eds), *The Manufacture of News*. London: Constable, 85–94.

Hall, Stuart, 1977. Culture, the media and the 'ideological effect'. In James Curran, Michael Gurevitch and Janet Woollacott (eds), *Mass Communication and Society*. London: Edward Arnold.

Hall, Stuart, 1980. Encoding/decoding. In Stuart Hall, Dorothy Hobson, Andrew Lowe and Paul Willis (eds), *Culture, Media, Language*. London: Hutchinson, 128–38.

Hall, Stuart, 1982. The rediscovery of 'ideology': return of the repressed in media studies. In Michael Gurevitch, Tony Bennett, James Curran and Janet Woollacott (eds), *Culture, Society and the Media*. London: Routledge, 56–89.

Hall, Stuart, 1986. Cultural studies: two paradigms. In Richard Collins et al. (eds), *Media, Culture and Society: A Critical Reader*. London: Sage, 33–48.

Hall, Stuart, 1994a. Encoding/decoding. In David Graddol and Oliver Boyd-Barrett (eds), *Media Texts: Authors and Readers*. Clevedon: Multilingual Matters and The Open University, 200–11.

Hall, Stuart, 1994b. Reflections upon the encoding/decoding model: an interview with Stuart Hall. In Jon Cruz and Justin Lewis (eds), *Viewing, Reading, Listening: Audiences and Cultural Reception*. Oxford: Westview Press, 145–60.

Hall, Stuart, Ian Connell and Lidia Curti, 1976. The 'unity' of current affairs television. Working Papers in Cultural Studies. Birmingham: Centre for Contemporary Cultural Studies (Spring).

Hall, Stuart, Chas Critcher, Tony Jefferson, John Clarke and Brian Roberts, 1978. *Policing the Crisis: Mugging, the State, and Law and Order*. London: Macmillan.

Hall, Stuart, Dorothy Hobson, Andrew Lowe and Paul Willis (eds), 1980. *Culture, Media, Language*. London: Hutchinson.

Halliday, M. A. K., 1985. *Introduction to Functional Grammar*. London: Edward Arnold.

Halloran, James D., Phillip Elliott and Graham Murdock, 1970. *Demonstrations and Communication: A Case Study*. Harmondsworth: Penguin.

Hammersley, Martin, 1996. On the foundations of critical discourse analysis. Paper presented at the Cardiff Language Seminar, 24 January 1996.

Harris, Sandra, 1991. Evasive action: how politicians respond to questions in political interviews. In Paddy Scannell (ed.), *Broadcast Talk*. Newbury Park, CA: Sage, 76–99.

Hartley, John, 1996. *Popular Reality*. London: Arnold.

Hartley, John and Martin Montgomery, 1985. Representations and relations: ideology and power in press and TV news. In Teun A. van Dijk (ed.), *Discourse and Communication*. New York: Walter de Gruyter, 233–69.

Heath, Christian, 1986. *Body Movement and Speech in Medical Interaction*. Cambridge: Cambridge University Press.

Heath, Christian and Paul Luff, 1993. Explicating face to face interaction. In Nigel Gilbert (ed.), *Researching Social Life*. London: Sage, 306–26.

Heidegger, Martin, 1962. *Being and Time*. Oxford: Blackwell.

Held, David, 1987. *Models of Democracy*. Cambridge: Polity Press.

Heritage, John, 1985. Analyzing news interviews: aspects of the production of talk for an 'overhearing' audience. In Teun van Dijk (ed.), *Handbook of Discourse Analysis*, vol. 3: *Discourse and Dialogue*. London: Academic Press, 95–119.

Heritage, John, 1989. Current developments in Conversation Analysis. In Derek Roger and Peter Bull (eds), *Conversation: An Interdisciplinary Approach*. Clevedon: Multilingual Matters, 21–47.

Heritage, John, Steven Clayman and David Greatbatch, forthcoming. *The Political News Interview*. London: Sage.

Heritage, John, Steven Clayman and Don Zimmerman, 1988. Discourse and message analysis: the micro-structure of mass media messages. In Robert P. Hawkins, John M. Wieman and Suzanne Pingree (eds), *Advancing Communication Science: Merging Mass and Interpersonal Processes*. Newbury Park, CA: Sage, 77–109.

Heritage, John and David Greatbatch, 1991. On the institutional character of institutional talk: the case of news interviews. In Deirdre Boden and Don H. Zimmerman (eds), *Talk and Social Structure*. Cambridge: Polity Press, 93–137.

Heritage, John and Andrew Roth, 1995. Grammar and institution: questions and questioning in the broadcast news interview. *Research on Language and Social Interaction*, 28, 1–60.

Herman, Edward S., 1992. *Beyond Hypocrisy: Decoding the News in an Age of Propaganda, Including a Doublespeak Dictionary for the 1990s* (illustrations by Matt Wuerker). Boston: South End Press.

Herman, Edward S. and Noam Chomsky, 1988. *Manufacturing Consent: The Political Economy of the Mass Media*. New York: Pantheon Books.

Hjarvard, Stig, 1994. TV news: from discrete items to continuous narrative? The social meaning of changing temporal structures. *Cultural Studies*, 8, 306–20.

Hobson, Dorothy, 1980. Housewives and the mass media. In Stuart Hall, Dorothy Hobson, Andrew Lowe and Paul Willis (eds), *Culture, Media, Language*. London: Hutchinson, 105–14.

Hoijer, Birgitte, 1993. Reception reconsidered from comprehension perspectives. Paper delivered at the 11th Nordic Conference for Mass Communication Research, Trondheim.

Holland, Patricia, 1987. When a woman reads the news. In Helen Baehr and Gillian Dyer (eds), *Boxed In: Women and Television*. London: Pandora, 133–50.

Hutchby, Ian, 1991. The organisation of talk on radio. In Paddy Scannell (ed.), *Broadcast Talk*. London: Sage, 119–37.

Inglis, K. S., 1983. *This is the ABC – The Australian Broadcasting Commission 1932–1983*. Melbourne: Melbourne University Press.

Jacobs, Ronald, 1996. Producing the news, producing the crisis: narrativity, television and news work. *Media, Culture and Society*, 18, 373–97.

Jaspars, Jos, Frank D. Fincham and Miles Hewstone (eds), 1983. *Attribution Theory and Research: Conceptual, Developmental and Social Dimensions*. London: Academic Press.

Jensen, Klaus Bruhn, 1986. *Making Sense of the News: Towards a Theory and an Empirical Model of Reception for the Study of Mass Communication*. Aarhus: Aarhus University Press.

Jensen, Klaus Bruhn, 1990. The politics of polysemy: television news, everyday consciousness and political action. *Media, Culture and Society*, 12, 57–77.

Jensen, Klaus Bruhn, 1994. Reception as flow: the 'new television viewer' revisited. *Cultural Studies*, 8, 293–305.

Jucker, Andreas, 1986. *News Interviews: A Pragmalinguistic Analysis*. Philadelphia: John Benjamins.

Kornblith, Hilary (ed.), 1994. *Naturalizing Epistemology*. 2nd edn. Cambridge, MA: MIT Press.

Kress, Gunther, 1994. Text and discourse as explanation. In Ulrike Meinhof and Kay Richardson (eds), *Text, Discourse and Context: Representations of Poverty in Britain*. London: Longman, 24–46.

Kress, Gunther and Robert Hodge, 1979. *Language as Ideology*. London: Routledge and Kegan Paul.

Kress, Gunther and Theo van Leeuwen, 1990. *Reading Images*. Geelong: Deakin University Press.

Kress, Gunther and Theo van Leeuwen, 1996. *Reading Images: The Grammar of Visual Design*. London: Routledge.

Labov, William, 1972. The transformation of experience in narrative syntax. In William Labov, *Language in the Inner City*. Philadelphia: University of Pennsylvania Press, 354–96.

Labov, William and Joshua Waletzky, 1967. Narrative analysis: oral versions of personal experience. In June Helm (ed.), *Essays on the Verbal and Visual Arts (Proceedings of the 1966 Annual Spring Meeting of the American Ethnological Society)*. Seattle: University of Washington Press, 12–44.

Larrain, Jorge, 1979. *The Concept of Ideology*. London: Hutchinson.

Lau, Richard R. and David Sears (eds), 1986. *Political Cognition*. Hillsdale, NJ: Lawrence Erlbaum Associates.

278 References

Lazarsfeld, Paul F., 1948. The role of criticism in the management of mass media. *Journalism Quarterly*, 25, 115–26.

Lehrer, Keith, 1990. *Theory of Knowledge*. London: Routledge.

Lewis, Justin, 1991. *The Ideological Octopus*. London: Routledge.

Livingstone, Sonia and Peter Lunt, 1994. *Talk on Television: Audience Participation and Public Debate*. London: Routledge.

Lukács, Gyorgy, 1971. *History and Class Consciousness*. London: Merlin Press.

Lutz, Benedikt and Ruth Wodak, 1987. *Information für Informierte: Linguistische Studien zu Verständlichkeit und Verstehen von Hörfunknachrichten*. Vienna: Verlag der Österreichischen Akademie der Wissenschaften.

Manoff, Robert Karl and Michael Schudson (eds), 1987. *Reading the News*. New York: Pantheon.

Marcuse, Herbert, 1978. A note on the dialectic. In Andrew Arato and Eike Gebhardt (eds), *The Essential Frankfurt School Reader*. Oxford: Blackwell, 444–51.

Marriott, Stephanie, 1995. Intersubjectivity and temporal reference in television commentary. *Time and Society*, 4, 345–64.

Marriott, Stephanie, 1996. Time and time again: 'live' television commentary and the construction of replay talk. *Media, Culture and Society*, 18, 69–86.

Masterman, Len, 1985. *Teaching the Media*. London: Comedia.

McGuigan, Jim, 1992. *Cultural Populism*. London: Routledge.

Meinhof, Ulrike H., 1994. Double talk in news broadcasts: a cross-cultural comparison of pictures and texts in television news. In David Graddol and Oliver Boyd-Barrett (eds), *Media Texts: Authors and Readers*. Clevedon: Multilingual Matters and The Open University, 212–23.

Montgomery, Martin and Stuart Allan, 1992. Ideology, discourse and cultural studies: the contribution of Michel Pêcheux. *Canadian Journal of Communication*, 17, 191–219.

Moores, Shaun, 1993. *Interpreting Audiences: The Ethnography of Media Consumption*. London: Sage.

Morley, David, 1980. *The 'Nationwide' Audience*. London: British Film Institute.

Morley, David, 1986. *Family Television: Cultural Power and Domestic Leisure*. London: Comedia.

Morley, David, 1992. *Television, Audiences and Cultural Studies*. London: Routledge.

Morley, David and Kuan-Hsing Chen (eds), 1996. *Stuart Hall: Critical Dialogues in Cultural Studies*. London: Routledge.

Morse, Margaret, 1986. The television news personality and credibility: reflections on the news in transition. In Tania Modleski (ed.), *Studies in Entertainment: Critical Approaches to Mass Culture*. Bloomington and Indianapolis: Indiana University Press, 55–79.

Nightingale, Virginia, 1996. *Studying Audiences: The Shock of the Real*. London: Routledge.

Ohtsuka, Keisuke and William F. Brewer, 1992. Discourse organization in the comprehension of temporal order in narrative texts. *Discourse Processes*, 15, 317–36.

Parkin, Frank, 1971. *Class Inequality and Political Order*. London: Paladin.

Paterson, Richard, 1990. A suitable schedule for the family. In Andrew Goodwin and Garry Whannel (eds), *Understanding Television*. London: Routledge, 30–41.

Pêcheux, Michel, 1982. *Language, Semantics and Ideology*. New York: St Martin's Press.

Pedelty, Mark, 1995. *War Stories: The Culture of Foreign Correspondents*. London: Routledge.

Radway, Janice, 1984. *Reading the Romance: Women, Patriarchy and Popular Literature*. Chapel Hill, NC: University of North Carolina Press.

Rae, John and John Drury, 1993. Reification and evidence in rhetoric on economic recession: some methods used in the UK press, final quarter 1990. *Discourse and Society*, 4, 329–56.

Reeves, Jimmie L. and Richard Campbell, 1994. *Cracked Coverage: Television News, the Anti-Cocaine Crusade, and the Reagan Legacy*. Durham, NC: Duke University Press.

Richardson, Kay and John Corner, 1986. Reading reception: mediation and transparency in viewers' accounts of a TV programme. *Media, Culture and Society*, 8, 485–508.

Ricoeur, Paul, 1974. *The Conflict of Interpretations: Essays in Hermeneutics*. Evanston, IL: Northwestern University Press.

Robinson, James D. and Tom Skill, 1995. Media usage patterns and portrayals of the elderly. In John Nussbaum and Justine Coupland (eds), *Handbook of Communication and Aging Research*. Mahwah, NJ: Lawrence Erlbaum Associates, 359–91.

Rumelhart, David E., 1975. Notes on a schema for stories. In Daniel G. Bobrow and Allan Collins (eds), *Representation and Understanding*. New York: Academic Press, 211–36.

Scannell, Paddy (ed.), 1991. *Broadcast Talk*. London: Sage.

Scannell, Paddy, 1996. *Radio, Television and Modern Life*. Oxford: Blackwell.

Scannell, Paddy, 1997. Saying and showing: a pragmatic and phenomenological study of a television documentary. To appear in *Text*.

Schegloff, Emanuel, 1988/1989. From interview to confrontation: observations on the Bush/Rather encounter. *Research on Language and Social Interaction*, 22, 215–40.

Schegloff, Emanuel and Harvey Sacks, 1974. Opening up closings. In Roy Turner (ed.), *Ethnomethodology*. Harmondsworth: Penguin, 233–64.

Schlesinger, Philip, 1980. Between sociology and journalism. In Harry Christian (ed.), *The Sociology of Journalism and the Press* (Sociological Review Monograph 29). Keele: University of Keele, 341–69.

Schlesinger, Philip, 1987. *Putting 'Reality' Together: BBC News*. 2nd edn. London: Methuen.

Schlesinger, Philip, 1990. Rethinking the sociology of journalism: source strategies and the limits of media-centrism. In Marjorie Ferguson (ed.), *Public Communication: The New Imperatives*. London: Sage, 61–83.

Schlesinger, Philip, Graham Murdock and Peter Elliot, 1983. *Televising Terrorism: Political Violence in Popular Culture*. London: Comedia.

Schudson, Michael, 1982. The politics of narrative form: the emergence of news conventions in print and television. *Daedalus*, 111, 97–112.

Schudson, Michael, 1989. The sociology of news production. *Media, Culture and Society*, 11, 263–82.

Seiter, Ellen, Hans Borchers, Gabriele Kreutzner and Eve-Maria Warth, 1989. *Television Audiences and Cultural Power*. London: Routledge.

Silverstone, Roger, 1994. *Television and Everyday Life*. London: Routledge.

Stam, Robert, 1983. Television news and its spectator. In E. Ann Kaplan (ed.), *Regarding Television*. Los Angeles: University Publications of America, 23–43.

Storey, John, 1996. *What is Cultural Studies?* London: Arnold.

Talbot, Mary, 1992. The construction of gender in a teenage magazine. In Norman Fairclough (ed.), *Critical Language Awareness*. London: Longman.

Tedeschi, James T. (ed.), 1981. *Impression Management Theory and Social Psychological Research*. New York: Academic Press.

Thompson, John B., 1984. *Studies in the Theory of Ideology*. Berkeley: University of California Press.

Thompson, John B., 1990. *Ideology and Modern Culture: Critical Social Theory in the Era of Mass Communication*. Stanford, CA: Stanford University Press.

Thompson, John B., 1991. *Ideology and Modern Culture*. Cambridge: Polity Press.

Toolan, Michael J., 1988. *Narrative: A Critical Linguistic Introduction*. London and New York: Routledge.

Tuchman, Gaye, 1978. *Making News: A Study in the Construction of Reality*. New York: The Free Press.

van Dijk, Teun A., 1977. *Text and Context. Explorations in the Semantics and Pragmatics of Discourse*. London: Longman.

van Dijk, Teun A., 1984. *Prejudice in Discourse*. Amsterdam: Benjamins.

van Dijk, Teun A., 1985. Semantic discourse analysis. In Teun van Dijk (ed.), *Handbook of Discourse Analysis*, vol. 2. London: Academic Press, 103–36.

van Dijk, Teun A., 1987a. *Communicating Racism: Ethnic Prejudice in Thought and Talk*. Newbury Park, CA: Sage.

van Dijk, Teun A., 1987b. Episodic models in discourse processing. In Rosalind Horowitz and S. Jay Samuels (eds), *Comprehending Oral and Written Language*. San Diego, CA: Academic Press, 161–96.

van Dijk, Teun A., 1988a. *News Analysis. Case Studies of International and National News in the Press*. Hillsdale, NJ: Lawrence Erlbaum Associates.

van Dijk, Teun A., 1988b. *News as Discourse*. Hillsdale, NJ: Lawrence Erlbaum Associates.

van Dijk, Teun A., 1991. *Racism and the Press*. London: Routledge.

van Dijk, Teun A., 1993. *Elite Discourse and Racism*. Newbury Park, CA: Sage.

van Dijk, Teun A., 1995. Discourse semantics and ideology. *Discourse and Society*, 6, 243–89.

van Dijk, Teun A. and Walter Kintsch, 1983. *Strategies of Discourse Comprehension*. New York: Academic Press.

Van Zoonen, Liesbet, 1991. A tyranny of intimacy? Women, femininity and television news. In Peter Dahlgren and Colin Sparks (eds), *Communication and Citizenship*. London: Routledge, 217–35.

Volosinov, V. N., 1973. *Marxism and the Philosophy of Language*. Cambridge, MA: Harvard University Press.

Widdowson, Henry G., 1995. Discourse analysis: a critical view. *Language and Literature*, 4, 157–72.

Widdowson, Henry G., 1996. Reply to Fairclough: discourse and interpretation: conjectures and refutations. *Language and Literature*, 5, 57–69.

Williams, Raymond, 1961. *The Long Revolution*. London: Chatto and Windus.

Williams, Raymond, 1974. *Television: Technology and Cultural Form*. London: Fontana.

Williams, Raymond, 1977. *Marxism and Literature*. Oxford: Oxford University Press.

Williams, Raymond, 1986. An interview with Raymond Williams, with Stephen Heath and Gillian Skirrow. In Tania Modleski (ed.), *Studies in Entertainment: Critical Approaches to Mass Culture*. Bloomington and Indianapolis: Indiana University Press, 3–17.

Wilson, Tony, 1993. *Watching Television: Hermeneutics, Reception and Popular Culture*. Cambridge: Polity Press.

Wodak, Ruth, 1987. 'And where is the Lebanon?' A socio-psycholinguistic investigation of comprehension and intelligibility of news. *Text*, 7, 377–410.

Wren-Lewis, Justin, 1983. The encoding/decoding model: criticisms and redevelopments for research on decoding. *Media, Culture and Society*, 5, 179–97.

Zimmerman, Don, 1988. On conversation: the conversation analytic perspective. In James A. Anderson (ed.), *Communication Yearbook 11*. Newbury Park, CA: Sage, 406–32.

Index